The
BALKAN
COOKBOOK

To BARBARA,
in and out of the kitchen

The
BALKAN
COOKBOOK

VLADIMIR MIRODAN

Pelican Publishing Company
Gretna 1989

First published by Lennard Publishing in the United Kingdom, 1987

Published by arrangement with Lennard Publishing by Pelican Publishing Company, Inc., 1989

First Pelican edition, 1989

Library of Congress Cataloging-in-Publication Data

Mirodan, Vladimir, 1951-
    The Balkan cookbook/Vladimir Mirodan. — 1st Pelican ed.
      p.   cm.
    "First published by Lennard Publishing in the United Kingdom,
1987"—Tp. verso.
    Includes index.
    ISBN 0-88289-738-1
    1. Cookery, Balkan. I. Title. II. Title: Balkan cook book.
TX723.5.B3M57 1989
641.59496—dc20   89-35639
                                                  CIP

The publishers are grateful to Editura Meridiane for permission to reproduce material from Paul Petrescu: *Creatia Plastica Taraneasca* (Bucuresti, 1976)

The drawings in the main text are from *Two Vagabonds In the Balkans* by J. and C. Gordon.

Manufactured in the United States of America
Published by Pelican Publishing Company, Inc.
1101 Monroe Street, Gretna, Louisiana 70053

CONTENTS

INTRODUCTION

"The Balkans?" cried my friend the writer over the noise of someone's birthday party in Hampstead – "The Balkans never cooked up anything but wars!" I laughed with him at the time, but now, looking back over the two hundred recipes in this book and the many more I might have added, I cannot help feeling he did not get it right. There have been no end of wars in the Balkan countries, placed as they were at the hub of Europe, only a step away from a Levant that was at once threatening and beckoning, while they were fiercely determined to keep their European identity. There has also been some remarkable high living for hundreds of years, that has produced a unique cuisine which deserves to be widely known, and enjoyed.

A mixture of southern Slav tribes (Yugo-Slav means just that: the Slavs of the south) settled at the fall of the Roman Empire on the southern banks of the Danube, then spread south towards Greece and west to the edges of the German territories, and to Italy itself. On the northern bank, however, in the Roman province of Dacia, now abandoned by the legions, the local population, speaking a strange mixture of Scythian dialects and vulgar Latin, stayed put. Thus arose Romania, an enclave of Latin indulgence in a sea of Slav earthiness. Standing for centuries in the way of marauding Tartars and conquering Turks, the countries either side of the lower Danube managed to evolve strikingly specific cultures, sometimes in spite of the troubles and sometimes because of them. This extraordinary talent for making their own the various influences radiating from the major cultures around (Russian to the north, Austro-Hungarian to the west, Greek and Turkish to the south) makes these cultures, and in particular the cooking of Bulgaria, Romania and Yugoslavia, most unusual European phenomena. The Levant is still felt at its strongest in Bulgaria and the southern provinces of Yugoslavia (Bosnia, Hertzekovina and Kosovo), due to their centuries of life under direct Turkish rule. Northern Yugoslav provinces are strongly under Hungarian and German influence, while Romanian cooking seems to have absorbed from the surrounding countries every conceivable culinary influence and then recreated them in its own specific form, indistinguishably blended with its own peasant traditions. While spreading aromatic clouds of Turkish tobacco over the remnants of a bottle of *Odobesti* wine in a Moldavian restaurant the hero of a now almost forgotten novel of the inter-wars years declares, half in earnest and half with his tongue in a cheek already half filled by the tip of his pipe, "look at our cooking and wonder at how well we have understood our national destiny. Our amazing instinct for self-preservation shows itself at its best in the way in which we have been able to transplant the dishes of our neighbours and give them full residential rights here. We are an eclectic people and the wisdom to be so open has come to us through our refined cooking. It has taught us that it is one thing to wage war on the Hungarians, the Russians, the Poles or the Turks and a better thing altogether to appropriate their best dishes without a blow struck in anger. Hungarian paprika, Serbian *djuvec,* Polish dishes in butter and soured cream, Russian borsht, caviar and marinades, Turkish moussakas and stuffed aubergines (imambaialdi) – we looted all these without any battles, we annexed them without peace treaties and we perfected them until we could call them our very own national treasures"* (Cezar Petrescu, *La Hotel Paradis*)*

Behind the general description of Balkan states lies a mosaic of disparate provinces, sometimes with their own languages and distinct cultures, like the republics of Yugoslavia; sometimes united by a common language, like the three Romanian provinces, but separated by centuries of independent political development. The present-day Romanian state is only

* *I am indebted to the excellent* Album Literar Gastronomic *published by the monthly* Viata Romaneasca *(Bucuresti 1982) for pointing me in the direction of this and several of the following quotes and references.*

some 70 years old, yet its cultural unity comes not so much from a common political past as through the age-old mingling of peoples forced to live together by the constants of a shared landscape. Nowhere is this hotch-potch of cultures more apparent than in Transylvania, the magic 'land beyond the forest'. Cluj, the capital, seems to the native eye perhaps the most Central European of all Balkan cities, yet it appears to the Western traveller as a city of contrast, 'always surrounded by the turmoil of the battles which took place here, and containing the clash of nationalities which gives to the whole province its characteristic appearance. Here are Hungarians, Romanians, Saxons, Szekels, Jews and Gypsies, all of them conscious of their individual qualities, but living at peace. . .' (Walter Starkie, *Raggle-Taggle; Adventures with a Fiddle in Hungary and Romania,* 1929).

The raggle-taggle has however a distinctive quality which should not be mistaken either for the Oriental bazaar to the south, or for the orderly markets to the west. This cultural unity is shaped by the landscape: the Danube, which crosses and separates the three countries, the long Black Sea coast of Romania and Bulgaria, the combination of mountainous terrain (Carpathians in Romania, The Balkans themselves in Bulgaria and the various ranges of Yugoslavia) with the huge expanses of the Danubian plains, essentially the same regardless of whether they are called the Slovenian Plains in Yugoslavia, the puszta in Hungary or the enormous (and immensely rich in food) Baragan in Romania. These plains used to be the granaries of Europe until the First World War and the advent of cheaper American and Australian grain, but they are still producing massive quantities of wheat and of maize, the staple crop of the region and the main ingredient of the porridge (polenta) which forms the basis of the peasant diet from Slovenia to the Danube Delta. Traditional peasant food is, like anywhere else in the world, based on the produce easily culled from the surroundings, but as these surroundings are so varied the food of the region includes a surprising variety of 'old', peasant dishes. From the mountains comes game, which included in older days bear, boar and a wild bull similar to the bison, as well as red deer and large wild goats. Fishing, mainly in the fresh waters of the Danube and the Transylvanian lakes, yields pike, perch, bream, sterlet and three superb varieties of sturgeon, caught in the Danube Delta, with its excellent caviar. The extensive Danubian plains are great producers of cereals as well as ideal shooting grounds for quail, partridge and woodcock.

The peasant population, of whatever nationality, once settled in a particular place tended to stay put, tied to the land by centuries of serfdom (Romanian serfs were only freed towards the middle of the nineteenth century) and by the deep-seated affections of the hereditary grower of food, leaving it to the Jews and the Gypsies to wander about the land in search of trade. It is no chance, therefore, that the first professional cooks were Gypsies. The peasant and his family were needed to work the land, while the Gypsies (bound to the 'boyar' by a kind of slavery which went far beyond the servitude of the labourers, and allowed the master to hire out, sell or lose whole Gypsy families at a game of 'besique') formed the natural recruitment basis for the squire's household staff. Gypsies became skilled first at making and lining copper pots, then at making the wooden spoons still widely used in the kitchens of the region, and so it was only natural for Gypsies to expand their kitchen-related skills into the realm of cooking as soon as the master called for a modicum of sophistication at his table. The Gypsies brought into the kitchen some of the skills and tastes of their nomadic life, and to this day there is nothing Romanians love more than good quality meat grilled over a charcoal grill, preferably kindled with dried vine branches and placed outside under the proverbial walnut tree.

The early Gypsy cooking in the households of the country noblemen was matched only by the cooking done in the kitchens of the monasteries. Most of the Balkan countries fell under the jurisdiction of the Byzantine Orthodox church and the Greek influence pervaded anything to do with religion, from the high church services to the organization of the monastic kitchen. Much of the church's hierarchy was originally Greek and most of the local monks were sent for their education to the Greek-speaking seminaries at Mount Athos. There they acquired not only fancy Kirie Eleisons, but also the taste for Greek food and cooking. Returned to their monasteries, they became skilled in adapting local produce and methods of cooking to their newly acquired tastes, as well as importing into the northern Balkans Greek ingredients like olive oil, lemons and figs. Furthermore, the monks devised creative ways of overcoming the numerous, and strictly respected, Orthodox days of abstinence by creating the rudiments of an imaginative vegetarian cuisine. This cuisine has been preserved to this day, mainly in Bulgaria where vegetarian dishes abound, reflecting the country's 'market garden' agriculture.

Wine and spirit making, a monastic preoccupation all over Europe, has an even clearer link to the monasteries in the Balkans than elsewhere. In Romania spirits were originally made from either wheat or barley. By the seventeenth century, however, the Romanian Principalities had became the granaries of the Ottoman Empire and the use of cereals for alcohol making was severely restricted in order to ensure that the quotas set by the Turks could be fulfilled. Here the monasteries came into their own. Alcohol began to be made from fruit and the monasteries, wine growers from time immemorial, soon had some of the best orchards as well as the finest vineyards. They first distilled their wine surplus into a rough form of brandy and then they took over Western technology, imported by Polish Jews and Germans, which enabled them to distil rum from fruit. Rum is still a great favourite in Romania, but it is used nowadays mainly for lacing tea or for making a particularly potent version of rum coffee called Marghiloman. Rum was soon superseded, however, by alcohol distilled from plums, a fruit easily grown in the region and therefore cheaper. Plum brandy comes under a variety of regional variations, the best of which are the Romanian *tzuika* and the Yugoslav *slivovitz,* especially the one made from the excellent Bosnian plums. Plum brandies soon spread far beyond the walls of the monasteries and by the late nineteenth century they had mostly abandoned independent production, although some spirit making remains the province of a particular order, like the Slovenian monks who make the *viljamovka,* an excellent pear brandy.

The spread of cooking and distilling techniques was facilitated by a great Balkan institution: the ambulant food seller. Any popular food or drink which needed even the smallest degree of technique in its preparation soon became the province of a particular group of travelling sellers, usually specializing along ethnic lines. The Bulgarians took on the selling of soft drinks, starting with their greatest invention, yoghurt, and continuing with a whole gamut of traditional drinks like real iced lemonade, sweet cold *braga* and savoury *salep* – a nourishing, soup-like hot drink often taken as a dawn breakfast by the workers making their way to work through the dark, snow bound streets of old Bucharest or Belgrade. The Gypsies tended to appear in the autumn, selling chickens and corn on the cob, boiled in milk. They were usually followed by Transylvanian or Moldavian shepherds who came to the big cities to sell their sweet, white cheeses and curds (sweet *kash* and *urda* still retaining an aftertaste of fresh milk, or *telemea,* the Romanian version of fetta cheese). The Greek street sellers brought north their olive oil, lemons and dried fruit while the Oltenians (from the south west region of Romania) specialized in fresh herbs and the 'bouquet garnis' which forms the basis for all Romanian *chorbe* (tangy soups). The Armenians were sought after above all else, because they brought to the streets a variety of sweet and savoury pies, bagels and doughnuts. They carried their wares on huge trays balanced on top of their heads and they became the focus of interest for the whole neighbourhood as soon as the tray was lowered, slowly, ritually, onto the pavement. Sometimes the enterprising seller of *braga*, Turkish delight and other delicacies, would attach to his container a sort of small 'wheel of fortune'. "The customer could spin it around until the wing marked with an arrow stopped against one of the delights on sale: lemonade, sweet sherbet dipped in iced water or sesame halva. The customer had the double satisfaction of mixing the pleasures of the gourmet with the thrills of the gambler." (C. Kiritzescu: *A life, a world . . .*).

These early restaurants on two feet both satisfied and encouraged the Balkan taste for eating al-fresco whenever possible. I think more eating in the streets is done in the Balkans than anywhere else in Europe. The long, hot summers of Eastern Europe encouraged the development of the 'garden restaurant' as a national institution. Around the turn of the century, the major restaurants in the capitals of the Balkans started having two locations: a winter one in the centre of town and a summer garden usually situated on the outskirts, where land was cheap and the old trees, essential if you wanted to eat away from the mid-day sun, had not yet been cut to make room for houses. In time, a whole area of the city was taken over by these gardens, like the 'chaussee' in Bucharest, creating a Balkan equivalent to the Viennese Grinzing. As we shall see, this tradition is still very much alive.

The dominant feature of these restaurants is the outdoor charcoal grill. Romanians in particular are great meat eaters and the beef and lamb coming from the sub-Carpathian grazing fields is of good enough quality to be eaten without being disguised with sauces. The Romanians have developed a national passion for grilled steaks, smothered with garlic and sprinkled with fresh thyme, as well as for rather more unusual cuts like brains, udders and above all *momitze, maduvioare* and *fudulii* – in other words bull's testicles. The squeamish Westerner may well shudder, but in the Balkans these are considered tasty morsels and with good reason.

In more affluent times and in richer parts of the town, some of the street vendors settled down to become increasingly sophisticated grocers. Helped by the strength of the Romanian economy at the turn of the century, when Romanian agricultural produce was feeding most of Europe and when the Romanian treasury could mint its own gold coins, the increasingly affluent middle classes developed expensive tastes for the best of local produce, like sturgeon caviar, smoked loin of pork and fresh game, as well as for imported lobster or wines. The groceries in the centre of town often incorporated an improvised drinking parlour, somewhat like a rural pub-and-shop in Ireland. The grandest of them all, 'Dragomir's' in the Calea Victoriei – the central artery of Bucharest's culinary and social life – was able to stun its customers with displays of whole boars and deer hanging on both sides of the entrance, or with pyramids of hares and partridges flanked by large jars of caviar. In the drinking section of the shop a long table would be laden with a variety of cold dishes, of the 'piquant', sharp or salty kind, essential to accompany the Balkan man's early evening aperitif. These aperitifs of *tzuika* were usually taken at around six and seven o'clock in the evening, standing around high round tables in the front room of a 'bacanie' (grocery) and accompanied by a selection of small caviar canapés, fried cheese croquettes and a variety of pickles. But the main attraction was provided by the smells of the groceries next door, smells of fish soused in brine, of freshly ground coffee, of smoked pork loin and black oily olives, of roast hams and oranges. By now, however, the rustic simplicity of the street vendor had been supplanted by a truly sophisticated native cuisine, which had even had the time, in somewhat less than a full century, to develop two divergent traditions.

Towards the beginning of the eighteenth century the Turks were getting fed up with a succession of rebellious Romanian princes, but remained fearful of the consequences of imposing direct Muslim rule (as they had already done in their Bulgarian and Yugoslav possessions) on the fiercely Orthodox and Latin populace. They decided the solution lay in the appointment of tame princes, drawn not from the native nobility but chosen among the inhabitants of the Fanar, a Greek suburb of Istanbul. These rulers, known as the Fanariots, took root with relative ease in a country already full of Byzantine mores, and they brought to the Romanian principalities a period of unprecedented political decadence. In spite of the political softening, or perhaps because of it, the pursuit of leisure and above all the arts of the kitchen flourished as never before. Building on the Greek traditions kept in the monasteries, these new rulers and their extended families brought to Romania their tastes and expected the local nobility to follow them or perish, politically and sometimes even physically. Stories are told of minor nobles elevated to high Court office for providing the right meals to their Princes, while others were just as easily brought down for refusing to follow the new fashions. The Fanariots expanded the Romanian taste for cold, piquant starters by bringing in from the Levant a variety of favoured dishes and adapting them to the local produce. A meal would always start with a display of cold starters to accompany the aperitif of native plum brandies, as well as anisette from Kos, or *mastika* from Corinth. This display might include marinaded small fish, like sardines or a kind of whitebait fished in the Black Sea; small saucers full of sturgeon caviar; smoked fish; sardines fried and dipped in Greek olive oil and lemon juice; sweet olives from Thessaloniki; figs from Santorini and sweet sesame halva brought all the way from Adrianopolis. These starters with Mediterranean flavour soon gave way to absolutely Romanian *chorbe* (soured soups) like pike boiled in cabbage brine, followed by another round of dishes mixing the native and the Levantine: *iahnii* (white beans in a tomato sauce); *plachii* (usually fish cooked in a tomato sauce, but occasionally a vegetable, like green beans); carp stuffed with sultanas, and finally, a whole turkey stuffed with chestnuts, and a suckling pig or lamb roasted whole on a spit slowly rotating over a grill, with dried vine branches burning among the charcoal.

The dishes made their way rapidly from the court of the Prince into the local boyar's household and thence into a variety of cafes and small taverns modelled on the eating houses of the bazaar. These first proper city restaurants became so widespread during the next century that as late as the 1870s there was still only one Western cafe in the whole of Bucharest ('Cazes', run by a Frenchman on Parisian lines and sporting no less than seven billiard tables), while all the rest were still in the Greek style, with small wicker stools on which the customers squatted while sipping Turkish coffee and puffing at elaborated hookah pipes.

A few generations later, however, a revolution took place in Balkan tastes, following the Russo-Turkish war of 1877 which brought in its wake the independence of Bulgaria, Romania (without Transylvania) and Serbia. One can measure the extent of this landslide by the fact that less than 50 years later there were almost no oriental cafes left in any of the major cities. The habits of that lost world, however, passed to some extent into the new, westernized brasseries. A typical half and half establishment of this type was the famous Cafe Fialkovski in Bucharest known equally for its Parisian chocolates and its back room, frequented by (mainly Liberal) politicians. Here the important customers could still play backgammon with traditional bons-mots and risqué jokes, safely away from the refined business of tea drinking and cake eating better left to the ladies in the front room. Here the western veneer of reputable pillars of the society could slip off to reveal their true byzantine spirit.

The war between the two styles, new and old, West and East, had begun almost as soon as the way to the West was opened by a more affluent, more tolerant Europe following the

French Revolution. By the 1840s it was customary for noble families to send their heirs to Vienna or Paris to learn manners and discrimination. The radical changes in taste these young men and women brought back did not take place without pain. Upstairs, ancestral beards had to be shaven off and large stomachs used to loose caftans had to be squeezed into tight breeches. Downstairs, the cooks had to learn new dishes with strange names. Vasile Alecsandri, a Moldavian writer of the period and himself one of the bright young sparks, tells the story of his father's cook, a master at rabbit stews and stuffed cabbage, but undergoing the tortures of hell over the fashionable blancmanges which more often than not came out tasting of soap. The long suffering chef, already humiliated, had then to endure the supreme punishment: he was ordered to eat the entire soapy mess himself.

To make up for this deficiency in native cooking talent, as it was perceived by the modernizers, the top restaurants began importing Western chefs. 'Hugues', the best restaurant in Bucharest in the 1880s, brought to its kitchens in around 1882 the great Trompette, the most famous chef in Paris. He had been head chef to Leon Gambetta, the Liberal politician, but had been forced to look for new challenges when his master fell from power, and he seems to have found them in the Balkans.

Western culinary tastes were helped above all by their image: they were identified with the new, the progressive and the free-thinking, and were thus enthusiastically welcomed by the intelligentsia. In the Balkans, where intellectual is not a dirty word, the professional and artistic classes tend to play an unusually large role in shaping the tastes of the nation. Western cooking had finally won its battle when some of the leading personalities of the day espoused its cause. Thus in 1841 the first professional cookery book was published at Iassi, the capital of Moldavia, not by a cook but by two leaders of the Romanian Enlightenment: Costache Negruzzi and Mihail Kogalniceanu. Their book contained some 200 recipes, mostly collected during the authors' extended visits to the West and stressing the values of *cuisine bourgeoise*. The book displays, however, a typical Romanian bias towards sweet things – there are a great number of recipes for sweet steamed puddings, probably collected from the nuns of Lunéville convent in France and adapted to take into account the best Romanian produce: wild strawberries, Morello cherries, pistacho nuts, coffee, and so on. Alongside the sweets we get some rather complicated recipes for a crushed soup made with spring chicken meat ground in a mortar; for crayfish (always a Romanian favourite and the local fresh water substitute for shrimps and lobster) as well as for a variety of dumplings filled with brains, crayfish, almonds and mushrooms. Game is well featured, (both authors came from landed families, with large shooting grounds), in particular roast wild duck and haunch of venison. Through this book Romanian cooks gained direct access for the first time to the spirit, if not the letter of Brillat-Savarin and Berchoux and the two learned authors could hope, perhaps somewhat facetiously, to be remembered chiefly as, the founders of the culinary arts in Moldavia, (G. Calinescu, *Cronica Gastronomica*).

Mixing literature with cooking became almost an epidemic towards the end of the century, spurred by the fact that most writers found it impossible to earn a living with their pens alone. Prominent among these literary cooks was the great Romanian playwright I.L. Caragiale, who owned a series of beer halls in Bucharest, including the aptly named 'Academia Bene Bibenti'. From the other end of the literary spectrum came the critic Dobrogeanu-Gherea who tried to supplement the meagre income he derived from writing by holding the franchise of the station buffet in the small town of Ploiesti.

But even in those heady days, the victory of Western cooking over the oriental traditions was never absolute. During the twentieth century the two traditions blended to the point where the origins of most modern dishes became unrecognizable. This blend brought about a specifically Balkan cuisine which found its high priests in the best restaurant chefs and its apostles around many of the region's dinner tables. Perhaps the most remarkable of these local chefs was the maestru Andrei Cernea, the head chef of the Continental Hotel and Restaurant in Bucharest during the 1930s. The Continental had been built on the site of a *belle-epoque* hotel called 'Broft' made famous by two illustrious guests: Plon-Plon, otherwise known as Prince Napoleon, the Emperor's nephew, come on an official mission to King Carol of Romania; and Osman Pasha, the Turkish commander taken prisoner during the Russo-Turkish war and kept in luxury prisoner-of-war camp in Bucharest, before being taken to Russia. A couple of generations later the Continental hotel had been superseded by more modern establishments, (notably the grand, and rather Edwardian 'Athenee Palace' situated opposite the Royal Palace) but had acquired a deserved reputation for serving the best Romanian food in Bucharest, including traditional dishes like *chorba cu perisoare* (sour soup with meat balls), *sarmale* (cabbage, vine leaves or spinach leaves stuffed with mince and rice) and a selection of *tocanitze* (stews cooked with paprika and dumplings) and *ostropeluri* (rabbit or hare in a rich tomato sauce). At the other end of the culinary spectrum loomed large the trinity of hotel, cafe and restaurant known under the name of Capsha's. Here the cooking was mainly derived from France, but many of the dishes which survived until the 1970s, like *batog* (smoked sturgeon) salad or chicken breasts in a soured cream and dill sauce, had an unmistakable Balkanic air about them. Above all, Capsha's was famous for its café and for the cream cakes and chocolates served there. It was founded in the 1850s by two enterprising brothers who strove first and foremost to create a distinctive style for their luxury establishment, worthy of the collection of local nabobs and international personalities, like Sarah Bernhardt, who frequented it. The brothers decorated it in the highest Victorian style, full of gilt mirrors and red velvet curtains and they proceeded to import almost everything from Paris, from the chef patissier to absinthe and from fresh pineapples to the boxes in which they sold their exquisite chocolates.

By the 1920s and 1930s the cafe at Capsha's had become the haunt of the literary boheme, as well as a favourite watering-hole for the political journalists from the newspapers across the road in Sarindar, the Fleet Street of Bucharest. The great Romanian poet Tudor Arghezi could write in 1925: 'Capsha's is the meeting of all roads and all roads lead to Capsha's. . . at least once a day. Here one can live in perpetual ecstasy among the yellow chantilly, the strudels and the cream cakes. . .'. This glorious tradition of quality cooking and service lived on until as late as the 1970s, when it started to decline following the retirement of the great Papa Costea, the last of the old style managers.

Capsha's was the pinnacle of a pyramid of great coffee-and-cake houses which served and developed the extensive, discerning Romanian sweet tooth. There must be more cake shops in Bucharest than anywhere else in the world, one at almost every corner. Yet the beginnings of the Romanian sweet industry can be pinpointed with precision to the 1840s when Signor Felix Barla, an Italian pastry chef, settled in Iassi and became the doyen of the ice cream and biscuit corps, as M. Kogalniceanu described him. He introduced the Romanians, already used to rich preserves and Turkish delight, to the world of biscuits, boiled sweets, pralines, marzipan and ice creams. 'In short' writes Kogalniceanu 'Signor Felix introduced the whole literature of sugar to Moldavia'. After him a whole range of cake shops and coffee shops developed around the manufacture of sweets and chocolates culminating in the glories of Capsha's and the Café Fialkovsky.

All these restaurants, cafés, cooks and pastry chefs as well as a host of other lesser people and places dedicated to the pleasures of eating were by now the representatives of a truly original Balkan cuisine of some inspiration and originality. This cuisine reflected less of its origins and more of the landscape, the colours, the smells of the Balkans themselves.

The traveller crossing the Balkan plains in late summer, at harvest time, would be struck by two dominant colours: the mellow yellow of the wheat and maize, forming an undulating background for the intense white of the native peasant dress or of the fat oxen who until recently were still widely used for pulling carts. These two all-Romanian colours are reflected in some of the traditional dishes of the region: the golden *mamaliga* (a thick maize porridge) topped with lashings of sparkling white curd cheese and soured cream; the *alivanca,* a Moldavian pie made from the same ingredients; the small cheese pies folded 'with their skirts up' – a golden puffed crust on the outside revealing when opened the white of the sheep's cheese used for the filling; and even the yellow *coliva,* a ritual sweet dish with pagan origins, presented to the mourners at Romanian wakes. Further south, in Yugoslavia and Bulgaria, the landscape darkens in subtle shades of ochre and the dominant dishes turn with it towards the purple of olives and aubergines. At Yugoslav weddings the guests are presented with *drazgose* and *skofja loka:* hard baked biscuits, shaped either by hand or in special moulds to look like hearts, stars, fishes, etc., and decorated by hand with extravagantly complicated designs in rich, earth-like browns and umbers. These ritual offerings, still associated with pre-Christian fertility rites, echo in their decorations the geometric and floral designs carved into the doors and verandahs of the white-washed peasant houses, painted on the local pottery and embroidered in an infinity of variations on tablecloths and napkins. The colours and shapes of these folk decorations for the table are said to date from pre-Roman times and are found all over the Danube region. In addition, the country folk, like all the peoples who have to live through long winters year after year, are very keen to preserve something of the green of early summer into the dark months. The entire Balkan region is blessed with an abundance of water melons, sometimes striped with graded shades of green like those grown in the Dobrudja, by the Black Sea, but mostly of an intense dark green, displayed in pyramids by the side of the road like huge emeralds. Choosing and preserving water melons through the winter is a great Balkanic art. My grandfather made a special point of passing on his art to me, like his parents had done in the days before the war when they would buy a whole cartload of water melons at a time and store them in the cellar – the huge, 30 lb. ones to be eaten soon, the smaller ones to be sliced and pickled in brine for eating with grilled meats in winter. The memory of that striking combination of red and green came back on a recent visit to Ljubliana where the central market was flooded in October with huge bags of red, yellow and green peppers ready for preserving in brine or vinegar, flavoured with an amazing array of spices. The spices themselves were displayed on a long trestle table in small, immaculate white linen bags, adding sweeter shades to the dazzling colours of the market: yellow from the camomile, orange from the saffron and green from the mint.

Traditional food also endeavours to capture the fresh scents of the landscape. The Carpathians are entirely covered in fir-trees and pines, with their heady smell of resin. The Romanian shepherd captures this scent in his fresh white cheeses *(kash, urda, telemea)* while Romanian cooks, especially in Transylvania, are particularly fond of a sauce made with thin soured cream *(smetana)* and dill, reproducing the effect of pine needles in the snow. Finally, the Balkans have always cooked with that ultimate nouvelle cuisine ingredient: flowers. Their scent is captured in dishes like water-lily sherbet, rose petal preserve and pancakes with a filling made of sweet acacia flowers. Not everything smells of roses in the Balkans, of course, and the traveller venturing into the poorer parts of the city will soon be assaulted by a typical mixture of East and West: 'Stale fish, ground coffee, spices, garlic, the petrol of taxis, roast corn cobs and a pervading scent of human sweat' welcomed Walter Starkie on his first descent into the slums of pre-war Bucharest. Nowadays, a lot of the exotic has been expunged from Balkan eating, of course. The uniformity of modern convenience food saw to that. There are, however, enough unusual features left and there is enough love for good food to keep eating as central a preoccupation for the peoples of the Balkans as it is for their French or Italian counterparts.

People get up early in Eastern Europe, as the working day usually starts at around 7 o'clock. Breakfast is thus on the light side these days, from a glass of cultured buttermilk with sweetened bread rolls for the Bulgarian *zakuska*, to a simple selection of fetta cheese, olives and lemon tea at the Romanian *mic dejun* and up to the more elaborate Yugoslav *dorucak* where coffee would be accompanied by a selection of cold meats, butter and (especially in Slovenia) honey and jam.

The regional variations come into their own at lunchtime. In Bulgaria, lunch *(obed)* usually starts with a selection of whole tomatoes, cucumbers and green peppers sprinkled with a spicy combination called *chubritza* made of thyme, paprika, salt and black pepper. The raw vegetables are usually eaten as a starter together with a large white roll called *pitka*. The main specialities are warm vegetable stews, similar to small ratatouilles but bearing oriental names like *iahnia, plakia, djuvec, moussaka*. Although they do not on the whole use meat or fish, usually associated with these names in Greek or Turkish cooking, the methods are the same. The quality of fresh vegetables is very high in Bulgaria and most of the vegetarian dishes of the region come from there. Haricot or butter beans are a staple ingredient at a Bulgarian meal, almost always cooked in tomato juice and served with a selection of pickles.

In Romania and Yugoslavia, lunch *(prinz/rucak)* traditionally starts with an aperitif of plum brandy *(tzuika/slivovitz)* encouraged down by a slice of cheddar-type cheese *(cashcaval)* and a selection of marinaded peppers, mushrooms and so on. The most striking feature of Yugoslav cooking is the use of *kajmak,* a kind of very thick cream, slightly soured. It is used either as a basis for sauces or as a dressing for soups. Romanians use a lot of soured cream as well *(smintina)* but it tends to be thinner and sharper and it sometimes requires the addition of a little flour when used in thick sauces. The greatest of Romanian loves, however, are the tangy, soured meat soups *(chorbe)* usually served with a dressing of soured cream beaten into egg yolks. This could be followed by a stuffed vegetable, like cabbage, marrow or vine leaves served with the ubiquitous polenta and a delicate vegetable like baby marrows in a soured cream and tomato sauce.

In the three countries a good supper *(cina/vecera/vecereia)* would be preferably eaten al-fresco and would include a selection of meats and small spicy sausages *(mititei/cevapcici)* grilled over charcoal and cooled down with generous gulps of *spritz* – a mixture of ¾ wine with ¼ soda water. No table in one of the outdoor garden restaurants is complete without its syphon and its ice bucket for the wine, drunk chilled whether white or red. The indispensible feature of the garden is the Gypsy folk band *(taraf)* – there is a saying that you can make a peasant drunk on a glass of water and a gypsy violin. There is also a constant flow of street vendors, a remnant of older, more patriarchal days when the vendors were allowed to pester the diners with impunity. To this day, flower sellers are accepted as a necessary evil and as recently as the 1940s the Gypsy girls selling flowers with insistence and slightly risqué 'bons-mots' would be accompanied by 'men in white robes and wearing the red fez of the Turk (probably Bulgarians or Albanians) come in to sell penknives, photographs of naked women, brooches, Turkish carpets and embroideries' (W. Starkie). In the suburbs the garden restaurant used to take on the functions of social club as well, when a marquee was installed on Sundays and the local youth danced on the beaten earth covered with well watered sand. But the gardens really come into their own in the autumn, at wine-making time. Romanians adore drinking the grape juice ('must') before it has fermented fully into wine and while it is still sweet, only slightly alcoholic and full of the scent of grapes. The 'gardens' are decorated with coloured lights and rough garlands made of vegetables and reeds and an endless stream of earthenware jugs full of 'must' are drunk accompanied by grilled meats and pickles.

The regional variations have not affected some of the deepest rooted oriental habits, formed over centuries. The 'siesta' is obligatory all over the Balkans and it has hardly been disturbed by the social and political changes of the last fifty years. Equally respected is the ritual drinking of Turkish coffee with (rather than after) the sweet dish at the end of every meal, even if today it is no longer accompanied by the hookah pipe of older days. The art of making good Turkish coffee is preserved religiously: the best coffee beans come from Aden or Ethiopia (I find Old Java a suitable substitute in this country). They are roasted very lightly and ground to a very fine powder. The coffee is then made in individual thin copper pots containing two heaped teaspoons of coffee flavoured with a pinch of ground cardamom for every cup of water. Contrary to the common Western prejudice, Turkish coffee does not have to be terribly sweet. I allow ½ a teaspoon of sugar per person. The coffee should be brought to the boil extremely slowly, preferably over a tray of fine sand placed on top of the flame and it should under no circumstance be allowed to bubble. The legend has it that good coffee has to 'rise' and the foam be allowed to subside seven times before the right concentration has been achieved. Whether you have the patience for this or not, serve the coffee very hot, poured into small cups with the light brown froth (the 'cream') risen to the surface. In the eighteenth century, Turkish coffee was served as a starter and was often drunk with cream. This latter habit would be anathema in Romania today, where Turkish coffee is taken black and bitter, but is still kept in Bosnia where the coffee is occasionally served with *kajmak*.

Expert coffee making, like most other specialized skills, has become, since the war, the almost exclusive province of the home cook. The radical political changes which have swept Eastern Europe since the war have brought in their wake the stagnation and decline of the restaurant industry. With a few exceptions, the best of Balkan cooking is done today at home, by amateurs whose main concern is to preserve the old traditions rather than to innovate. While a decade ago this state of affairs might have been deplored by the innovative Western cook, in these post nouvelle cuisine days a region where the traditional values of country and bourgeois cooking are still very much to the fore should be widely welcomed. The recipes in this book reflect this traditional approach to cooking, especially in their use of foodstuffs associated with a non-industrial system of agriculture such as wild berries, dock leaves, nettles, flowers, and so on. On the other hand, there are 'city' recipes reflecting the status of Bucharest as the 'little Paris' of the years between the wars: recipes at once exotic and acceptable to Western tastes. I have also adapted some of the recipes to make them suit English palates better and to enable English cooks to attempt them with the foodstuffs available in this country. The last 'white patch' on the European culinary map, the cuisine of the Balkans is well worth discovering. Happy exploration!

London, July 1987.

17

PRACTICALITIES

If you are looking for ideas for a meal, without knowing precisely what you are going to cook – simply browse through the various chapters: see CONTENTS. Most recipes have suggestions of accompanying dishes at the end, to help you create a complete Balkan meal.

If you are looking for a specific recipe and you can remember its name – look in the alphabetical INDEX OF RECIPES BY TITLE (page 205).

If you are looking for ideas for making use of particular raw materials, whether because they are in season or because they are appropriate to a specific occasion – look in the INDEX OF RECIPES BY MAIN INGREDIENT (page 202). You will find recipes using combinations of main raw materials at several places in this Index, as I have tried to make it easier to locate a recipe even if the memory of what it contained is only vague (thus, you will find THREE MEAT BOSNIAN HOTPOT mentioned under Lamb, Beef and Pork as it contains equal quantities of each).

If you are wondering where to get an exotic sounding ingredient: it will be marked in the body of the recipe with an * – a sign that you will find it in WHERE TO GET BALKAN FOODS (page 189).

If you are looking for Balkan wines and spirits to serve with dishes from this book – look at BALKAN WINES AND SPIRITS (page 193).

All quantities and measurements in the book are given first in Imperial then in Metric sizes.

Oven temperatures are given in this order: Gas Regulo (British Standard)/Degrees Celsius/Degrees Fahrenheit. Oven temperatures are always given at the BEGINNING of a recipe, to indicate at a glance that an oven is required. Choose the exact time for preheating your oven according to the stages of the recipe and the heating time of your particular oven.

COLD
STARTERS

MARINADED PEPPERS

SERVES 4

Choose peppers as smooth and as unblemished as possible. Place the peppers on a tray under a hot grill, about 3"/9 cm. away from the flame, for 15-20 minutes, depending on their size. Turn on all sides, until skin has black areas and bubbles away from the flesh. Make sure the flesh of the pepper itself does not get burned. Dip your fingers in cold water and peel the skin off the peppers, making sure no blackened or tough patches are left. Most of the skin will come off easily, but you may

---

4 red or green peppers
½ fluid oz./15 ml. olive oil
2 fluid oz./60 ml. white wine vinegar
¼ tsp. salt
¼ tsp. fresh chopped dill or coriander or thyme (optional)

---

need to use a small knife to prise off some of the more awkward patches at the bottom and around the stalk. Take care not to pierce or damage the flesh. Leave the stalk attached. Place the peppers in a

shallow dish and pour over them the marinade made of oil, vinegar, salt and one of the herbs. (My favourite one is thyme, but dill or coriander will each give individual and flavourful results.)
Allow to cool, then place in the fridge for a few hours. You will still see these peppers served as a side salad with meat or fish all over the Balkans, or used to decorate AUBERGINE CAVIAR. See also PEPPERS STUFFED WITH AUBERGINE CAVIAR.

TOMATOES FILLED WITH PEPPERS

SERVES 4

Cut a lid off each tomato and scoop out ¾ of the flesh with a grapefruit knife. Sprinkle them with salt and pepper. Put a few drops of vinegar in each tomato and turn upside down to drain while you are preparing the filling.
Boil the rice until soft. Chop baked red peppers (see MARINADED PEPPERS) into

---

8 medium tomatoes
2 red baked peppers (see MARINADED PEPPERS)
3 oz./90 gr. rice
1 fluid oz./30 ml. vinegar
½ tsp. salt
¼ tsp. pepper
2 tblsp. home-made mayonnaise (preferably made with whole grain mustard)
or 3 tblsp. soured cream
1 tsp. chopped fresh dill (optional)
1 tsp. chopped parsley or lettuce leaves (for decoration)

---

small pieces. Mix together rice, peppers and mayonnaise or soured cream. Taste for seasoning and add salt, pepper and the chopped dill or parsley if desired.
Fill tomatoes with the mixture and replace the lids. Serve on a bed of lettuce, sprinkled with chopped parsley.

PICKLED STUFFED PEPPERS

Cut a lid around the stalks of the peppers and remove seeds. Drain, hole downwards, while you prepare the stuffing.
Shred finely the cabbage, carrots, celery (including leaves) and parsley root or parsnips. Add 1 tsp. salt for each 4 oz./125 gr. shredded vegetables and mix lightly. Allow to stand for 1 hour, until softened.
Pack the peppers fairly

Each 2 oz./60 gr. green pepper will take 2 oz./60 gr. stuffing.

Stuffing:
cabbage, carrots, parsley root or parsnips, celery (including leaves), salt.
Mix a pickling liquid according to the following proportions:
for 1 pt./600 ml. water – 4 flat tsp. salt and 3 fluid oz./90 ml. vinegar

tightly with the vegetable mixture.
Boil the water with the salt and vinegar. Wrap a glass jar in a wet towel, place filled peppers inside and pour the boiling liquid over them. Tie the mouth of the jar with greaseproof paper and keep in a cool, dark place for up to six months. They can be eaten after about 1 month.

PEPPERS FILLED WITH AUBERGINE 'CAVIAR'
SERVES 4

Preheat the oven to G5/ 190C/380F.

Cut a lid around the stalks of the peppers and discard stalks and seeds. Wash peppers well and place them hole downwards on a rack to drain.

Prepare aubergines as shown as AUBERGINE CAVIAR. Soak a crustless slice of bread in the milk and squeeze out as much of the liquid as you can by hand. Mix the soaked bread with the aubergines. Add the finely chopped onion, then add egg, 1 tsp. salt, pepper and fennel. Fill the peppers with the

8 green or red peppers
2 medium aubergines
1 fluid oz./30 ml. milk
1 slice white bread
1 onion
1 egg
2 tsps. salt
1 tsp. pepper
1 tsp. fennel seeds or 1 tblsp. fresh chopped fennel
2 oz./60 gr. butter
1 lb./500 gr. tomatoes
1 stick celery, with leaves
1 tsp. sugar
1 tsp. cumin seeds

aubergine mixture, roll them in a little flour, shake off

excess coating and fry them in heated butter until slightly brown on the outside.

To make the sauce: Blanch tomatoes in boiling water and peel them. Sieve them or blend in a food processor to obtain a thin tomato sauce. Add the celery stick, chopped, the remaining salt, sugar and cumin seeds. Place the peppers in a baking tray or similar container, pour the sauce around them and braise in a preheated oven for 45-50 minutes, or until soft.

AUBERGINE 'CAVIAR'
SERVES 4 - 6

Prick the aubergines slightly with a fork and place under a very hot grill about 3"/9 cm. away from the flame. (Use a barbecue grill, if you have one, for superb results). Turn them constantly until the skin has turned black on all sides and they are soft to the touch. (20-25 minutes, depending on how thick they are). Cut their stalks off and slit them open, scraping the flesh and seeds out. Discard the charred skin. You need not discard the seeds unless they are unusually large, but do throw away any hard bits left inside. Always use

4 medium ripe aubergines (about 2 lb./1 kg.) will make about 1 lb. 6 oz./650 gr. of Aubergine Caviar)
1 oz./30 gr. onion, finely chopped
⅓ tsp. salt
1 fluid oz./30 ml. vegetable oil
2 fluid oz./60 ml. vinegar

wooden or plastic utensils as metal will cause the aubergine flesh to turn black.

Press the flesh down with your hand to eliminate as much of the inner water as possible. The flesh will look stringy, but it will easily chop into a grey-green mass.

Chop it thoroughly and place it into a bowl. (Do not be tempted to use a food processor – the 'caviar' should not be too finely chopped). Add the oil slowly, mixing vigorously. Add the vinegar, salt and chopped onion at the very end.

Place in a fairly thin layer on an oval serving dish and serve surrounded by tomato quarters and decorated in the middle with black olives and strips of raw or marinaded red peppers (see MARINADED PEPPERS)

November 1999

S	M	T	W	T	F	S
	1	2	3	4	5	6
7	8	9	10	11	12	13
14	15	16	17	18	19	20
21	22	23	24	25	26	27
28	29	30				

"Women have served all these centuries as looking-glasses possessing the magic and delicious power of reflecting the figure of man at twice its natural size."

VIRGINIA WOOLF
A Room of One's Own, 1929

friday

MEMO

BARTLETT'S *Quote-A-Day*

① 273 –

②

③

④ Butter –

⑤

CUCUMBERS IN BUTTERMILK DRESSING

SERVES 4 - 6

Peel the cucumbers and dice into ½"/2 cm. cubes. If you are using set yoghurt, thin it with 2-3 fluid oz./60-90 ml. water and mix gently with the cucumbers. Buttermilk does not need diluting. Crush the garlic, chop the dill finely and add them to

A Bulgarian recipe, typical in its use of a combination of walnuts, garlic and buttermilk as a dressing for salads.

1 lb./500 gr. cucumbers
1 pt./600 ml. buttermilk or thin
  live hoghurt
2 oz./60 gr. walnuts
2 tblsp. olive oil
1 tblsp. fresh chopped dill
2 cloves garlic
1 tsp. salt

the salad.
Add the olive oil. Mix well and set aside for ½ hour. Grate the walnuts on the fine teeth of a grater or in a food processor to pinhead size. Sprinkle on top of the salad, do NOT mix again and serve chilled.

MARINADED MUSHROOMS

SERVES 4

Trim and wash the mushrooms. Cover them with salted water and boil for 10 minutes. Drain well and allow to cool.
Bring the vinegar to the boil with a pinch of salt. Allow to cool, then whisk in mustard.
Place the mushrooms in a jar

Fills a 1 lb./500 gr. jar

1 lb./500 gr. mushrooms
  (preferably small button
  mushrooms)
6 fluid oz./180 ml. vinegar
1 tsp. whole grain mustard
20 peppercorns
2 bay leaves
olive oil
pinch of salt

with the peppercorns and bay leaves. Pour marinade over them. Add about 1 finger of oil on top. Tie the mouth of the jar well with muslin or greaseproof paper and allow to marinate for at least 1 week in a cool place. Ideal as an accompaniment to iced, neat vodka!

EGGS FILLED WITH CHICKEN LIVERS

SERVES 6

Boil the eggs until hard. Shell them and cut in two, lengthwise. Remove the yolks and reserve. Boil the chicken livers until brown inside. Sieve or blend together with the egg yolks to obtain a paste, then blend

6 eggs
4 oz./125 gr. chicken livers
1 oz./30 gr. butter
¼ tsp. salt
¼ tsp. pepper
⅓ tblsp. chopped dill
lettuce leaves for decoration

in the butter. Add salt, chopped dill and pepper. Fill the scooped-out egg 'boats', place on a bed of crisp lettuce and serve sprinkled with chopped dill or parsley.

EGGS FILLED WITH CRAYFISH

SERVES 6

Boil the eggs until hard, shell them and cut in two, across. Cut a little of the white at one end, to stand eggs upright.

Remove yolks and grate or mash with a fork. Reserve 1 tblsp. grated egg yolk for later.

Mix the rest of the yolks with mustard, 1 raw egg yolk, salt and lemon juice. Add oil slowly, to make a

6 eggs
1 egg yolk
1 tsp. whole grain mustard
1 tsp. lemon
3 fluid oz./90 ml. oil
4 oz./125 gr. crayfish or boiled
**   white fish or prawns**
½ tsp. salt

thick mayonnaise. Mix in the crayfish, prawns or boiled fish cut in pieces. Fill the

egg whites with the mixture. Re-form the eggs, remove any extra filling with a knife (boil and fill more egg whites if you have too much mixture left), and sprinkle with reserved grated egg yolk.

Decorate with a crayfish placed on top of each egg. Serve on a bed of lettuce, surrounded if you wish by fresh diced aspic.

CARP ROE SALAD

Something of an acquired taste, but if you enjoy Greek taramasalata (originally made from the roe of red mullet, now more often than not made of cod roe) you will probably like this home-made carp roe salad even better.
Extremely popular in Romania and Serbia, it is delicious with a green salad and brown bread. Carp roe is seldom sold on its own in this country, but you will find it inside a large carp if you are cooking one of the CARP recipes in this book, or ask your fishmonger to set some aside for you when he cleans carps, as most people will discard the roe when cleaning the fish. Make sure you place roe in the fridge immediately after buying it – it goes off easily (fresh roe is white, but it will turn grey when off).

Wash the roe and squeeze water out by pressing it down with the palm of your hand on a flat surface. Pick off and discard the tough, opaque skins. Salt the roe and place on a flat metal dish (a thin, upturned metal lid will do) on top of a saucepan with simmering water. Heat gently for about 15 minutes, until roe becomes a faint reddish-brown colour. Shift occasionally to prevent sticking.
In the meantime, remove the crust of 2 slices of white bread and soak the bread in water. Squeeze water out by

8 oz./250 gr. carp roe
2 slices of crustless white bread (about ⅔ oz./20 gr.)
2 fluid oz./60 ml. olive oil
¼ tsp. salt
1 tblsp. lemon juice
¼ onion (optional)
4-6 large black olives

hand and mix the bread with ½ tblsp. olive oil. Using a fork, crush the cooked roe and mix it with the bread. Continue mixing in a bowl, with a wooden spoon, adding the rest of the oil, little by little. Alternatively, place the mixture in a food processor and blend well, pouring the oil in a steady trickle. You should get a white paste resembling mayonnaise.
Add lemon juice to taste, making sure the roe paste does not thin too much. Allow to stand for at least ½ hour in the fridge, then mix again, re-adjusting the lemon dressing. Mix in finely chopped onion at the last moment.
Serve on a bed of lettuce, surrounded by black olives. You can also use the carp roe mixture to fill 4 scooped and drained tomatoes or 2 avocado pears.

GOOSE OR CHICKEN TERRINE IN GARLIC ASPIC

Chop the onions roughly and boil in 4 pt./2 l. water until soft. Drain them and reserve the liquor. Sieve onion or puree in a food processor.

Bring the reserved liquid back to the boil and add carrot, bay leaf and peppercorns, then add the chicken or goose feet and heads. Boil for 10 minutes, then add the breasts and legs slowly and one by one so as not to disturb the stock too much. Simmer over a moderate flame for about 30 minutes, or until meat is soft but does not come off the bones by itself. Skim off any scum rising to the surface and wipe the edges of the saucepan with a wet cloth. Add salt. Remove breasts and legs with a slotted spoon and set aside. Strain the liquid into another saucepan. Reserve bay leaf and carrot and discard the other boiling ingredients. Bring liquid back to the boil and test it for the concentration of gelatine shed by the chicken legs and feet: a drop taken between forefinger and thumb should

---

1 lb./500 gr. chicken or goose heads and feet (ask your butcher to keep you some — he probably throws them away normally)
2 lb./1 kg. chicken or goose breasts and legs
5 cloves garlic
1 carrot
2 onions
1 bay leaf
10 peppercorns
1 tsp. salt
1 tsp. mild paprika

---

feel sticky and a few drops dripped onto a saucer and placed in the fridge should set quickly. If liquid is not ready, boil fast for another 10-15 minutes.*

Remove the white breast meat and dark thigh meat from the bones. Cut the meat into long strips, about /1 cm. thick, and place in alternating rows of dark and light strips, either on individual plates or in a loaf tin. Decorate the top of the plates or the BOTTOM of the tin with carrot rounds and the bay leaf.

Crush finely the cloves of garlic, in a mortar or garlic

⅓"crusher.

When the liquid is concentrated enough, remove from flame and cool in the saucepan for about 5 minutes, so that any residue will fall to the bottom. Pour it carefully over the puréed onions without disturbing the residue at the bottom of the saucepan, and mix in the crushed garlic, salt and paprika.

Pour the seasoned liquid over the slivers of meat on the plates or in the tin. Place in the fridge for a few hours until aspic has set well. If you have used a loaf tin, dip its bottom in a basin of hot water for 30 seconds and unmould it, revealing the carrot and bay leaf decoration. Cut into slices and serve as a starter with buttered bread and boiled new potatoes. You can use turkey leftovers in the same way.

If the liquid does not contain enough natural gelatine and is reducing too much, you can add a sachet of gelatine mixed in 1 cup of the hot liquid. Do not bring liquid to the boil after adding the gelatine.

CHICKEN LIVER PÂTÉ WITH GREEN HERBS

SERVES 2-4

Fry the chicken livers, with the chopped onion, in a little butter. Grate the cooked chicken livers on the medium teeth of a manual grater or in a food processor. Mix well with a wooden spoon, the grated liver, the hard boiled eggs, 1 oz./30 gr. butter, mustard and herbs. Season to taste. Set in an earthenware dish or in individual ramekins and serve decorated with

4 oz./125 gr. chicken livers
½ small onion, chopped
2 hard boiled eggs
1 oz./30 gr. butter
2 heaped tsp. whole grain mustard
¼ tsp. salt
½ tsp. pepper
2 tsp. each of chopped fresh herbs: dill, parsley, coriander
4 black olives

black olives and thin lemon slices to contrast with the green, coarse pate. Serve with fresh brown toast. Although it is usually served cold, I like to serve it still slightly warm, with the herb flavouring at its strongest. If chilled for 24 hours, however, the flavours will blend and mellow considerably and the herbs will become less overpowering.

CRAB WITH WALNUT DRESSING

SERVES 4

Pass the walnuts through a fine mincer or grate to paste consistency in a food processor. Remove the crusts from the bread and soak it in milk until liquid is fully absorbed. Squeeze out as much liquid as you can by hand. Crush the garlic cloves and mix with the soaked bread and 2 tsp. lemon juice until you obtain a smooth paste. Add walnuts and continue mixing, by hand or in a food processor, adding

8 oz./250 gr. crab meat (both white and brown) or crayfish or langoustines
4 oz./125 gr. walnuts
2 fluid oz./60 ml. walnut oil
2½ fluid oz./75 ml. lemon juice
2-3 cloves garlic
⅓ tsp. freshly ground black pepper
1 slice white bread
2 tblsp. milk

oil very slowly. Add pepper and the rest of the lemon juice and mix well. The final consistency of the dressing should be like a mayonnaise. It will set even more if placed in the fridge for a few hours.
Place dressing in the middle of a serving plate and arrange crab meat, crayfish or langoustines around it. Sprinkle with lemon juice and chopped coriander and serve cool.

BEAN AND POTATO PASTE

SERVES 4

Soak the beans overnight. Drain and place in a pot over a low flame, covered with cold water. Bring slowly to the boil. Once the water has started to bubble, drain again and replace beans over the flame, covering the beans well with hot water. Add the wine, and simmer over a medium flame for 1 hour, skimming. Add more water if necessary.

In the meantime, peel the potatoes, boil them and mash well. Chop the onion finely. Slice the belly of pork into small pieces and fry both in oil until onion begins to brown. Add the

All over the Balkans, traditional starters are made out of puréed haricot beans, mixed with fried onion and garlic. Here is a Yugoslav variation, which demonstrates the method while lightening the result by the addition of potatoes and olives.

8 oz./250 gr. haricot or white
    butter beans
8 oz./250 gr. potatoes
4 fluid oz./120 ml. red wine
2 oz./60 gr. belly of pork
    (preferably smoked) or
    smoked streaky bacon
½ small onion
1 clove garlic
½ tsp. salt
1 tsp. mild paprika (add a pinch
    of hot paprika if desired)
1 tsp. chopped parsley
1 tsp. oil
8-12 black olives

crushed garlic, salt and pepper towards the end. Reserve 4 olives for decoration and cut the rest in half. Remove their stones. Blanch the olive halves in boiling water for 5 minutes and drain. Blend or sieve the softened beans, olives and potatoes. Place in a bowl and mix well with the contents of the frying pan. If the paste is too thick, add a little of the bean cooking liquid.

Pipe or spoon the paste in a ring around small individual plates and place cold meats in the middle. Decorate with reserved black olives and sprinkle with parsley.

CHICORY LEAVES
FILLED WITH NUTS

SERVES 4-6

Trim the stalks off chicory heads and prise 16 leaves off, without tearing.

Chop or grate the nuts to pinhead size on the fine teeth of a grater or in a food processor. Squeeze the juice from 2 oranges. Squeeze the juice of ½ a lemon. Mix alternating teaspoonfuls of orange and lemon juice into

2-3 heads chicory (you need 16-24 nice leaves)
8 oz./250 gr. walnuts or hazelnuts
2 oranges
½ lemon

the nuts, tasting every time to balance the sweet and the tangy. The final result

should be moist, light and refreshing, with very little trace of the oiliness of the nuts, but with a little crunch left.

Fill each chicory leaf with the mixture, chill slightly and serve as a light, summery starter or as part of a buffet table at a party.

SOURED CREAM
AND DILL SAUCE

SERVES 4

Melt butter in a small saucepan and mix with the flour to make a roux. Pour milk over the roux and mix well to avoid lumps. Add thick soured cream, chopped dill, salt and lemon juice or rind. Lower the flame to a minimum and heat gently

You are likely to come across either dill or soured cream in some form or other in almost any Balkan recipe. They come together in this sauce which can be used both cold — as a dressing for salads and cold white meats — and warm, with roast meats, fish, savoury dumplings, etc.

until sauce bubbles up 2-3 times (do not increase the flame at any point as the soured cream might curdle). Serve immediately over boiled breasts of chicken, or omit the flour and serve cold over peeled diced cucumbers or green peppers and lettuce.

4 fluid oz./120 ml. soured cream
3 fluid oz./90 ml. milk
1 oz./30 gr. butter
1 tblsp. fresh chopped dill
¼ tsp. salt
1 tsp. lemon juice or grated lemon rind
1 tblsp. flour

HOT
STARTERS

FIELD MUSHROOMS WITH POLENTA CAKES

Wash and peel the mushrooms. Cover with water and boil, adding a little salt and the pepper, for 3-5 minutes, until almost soft. Drain well and cut in thin slices if necessary. Crush the garlic in a mortar. Add ½ tsp. salt and beef stock or vinegar diluted in 1 fluid oz./30 ml. water. Stir well with a wooden spoon, to get a thin paste.

1 lb./500 gr. chanterelles or field mushrooms
3 large cloves garlic
¼ tsp. salt
1 fluid oz./30 ml. vinegar or 2 fluid oz./60 ml. beef stock
1 tblsp. chopped parsley
⅛ tsp. pepper
8 polenta cakes (see POLENTA CAKES)
1 oz./30 gr. butter

Pour over the mushrooms and mix well to coat mushroom slices. Sprinkle with chopped parsley. Allow to cool.
Fry polenta cakes lightly in the butter and place on a serving dish or individual plates. Put the cold mushroom salad on top or around the sizzling polenta cakes and serve immediately.

MUSHROOMS FILLED WITH HERBS

Wash the mushrooms. Remove their stalks carefully and set aside. Put a pinch of salt and a minute sliver of butter inside each mushroom cup and sweat over a gentle flame until fairly soft. Chop the mushroom stalks very finely. In a small saucepan, sweat them in a little butter with salt and the black pepper. Allow to cool.

8 oz./250 gr. button mushrooms
½ tblsp. finely chopped dill
½ tblsp. finely chopped parsley or coriander
½ tsp. freshly ground black pepper
1½ oz./45 gr. butter
½ tsp. salt

Chop the herbs very finely and mix with the cooled mushroom stalks. Fill the mushroom cups with the herb mixture.
This is traditionally a cold starter, but if you, like me, prefer it hot, sprinkle 1 tblsp. grated parmesan cheese over the stuffed mushrooms and brown under a hot grill for 2-3 minutes.

MUSHROOMS FILLED WITH FETTA CHEESE

SERVES 4-6

Wash and trim the mushrooms. Remove their stalks carefully, so as not to damage the mushroom cups. Place the tiniest sliver of butter and a minute pinch of salt in each cup and sauté in 2 oz./60 gr. of the butter until almost soft. Sprinkle with freshly ground black pepper as they fry. Remove them with a slotted spoon, making sure the melted butter in each cup does not spill out. Chop the stalks finely and

A lovely starter, in which the salty fetta cheese contrasts deliciously with the buttery, juicy mushrooms.

1 lb./500 gr. nicely shaped mushrooms
8 oz./250 gr. fetta cheese or Romanian 'telemea'*
3 oz./90 gr. butter
¼ tsp. pepper
1 tblsp. grated parmesan
3 tblsp. finely chopped dill

sweat separately in a saucepan with ½ oz./15 gr.

butter. Sieve or blend the cheese to obtain a smooth paste, then mix this paste with the sweated stalks and the finely chopped dill. Fill each mushroom cup with the paste, then sprinkle them with grated parmesan and add a small sliver of butter on top. Place mushrooms in a heat-proof dish and grill under a hot grill for about 5 minutes or until brown on top and sizzling. Serve **very** hot.

SHEEP'S CHEESE SOUFFLÉ

SERVES 6

Preheat the oven to G5/ 190C/380F.
Melt the butter and make a white sauce base by mixing it with the flour and milk. Whisk well to eliminate any lumps. Cool a little and mix in 3 egg yolks. Mix in the fetta cheese cubed in ½"/1.5 cm. cubes. Add pepper. Beat 6 egg whites with salt and cream of tartar until very

This is a Bulgarian recipe making sophisticated use of the famous Bulgarian white sheep cheeses. Use fetta cheese instead if you cannot get a white, salty, highly flavoured sheep's cheese.

8 oz./250 gr. fetta cheese or white sheep's cheese*
6 eggs
4 oz./125 gr. butter
3 oz./90 gr. flour
1 oz./30 gr. breadcrumbs
10 fluid oz./300 ml. milk
pinch salt
pinch cream of tartar
2 oz./60 gr. grated parmesan cheese
⅛ tsp. black pepper

stiff and standing on the whisk held upright. Fold whites into soufflé base. Butter a soufflé dish well and sprinkle with breadcrumbs. Pour the mixture in and sprinkle with grated parmesan on top. Bake in the middle of the preheated oven for 20 minutes or until fully risen and brown on top.

BREADED CASHCAVAL CHEESE
SERVES 4

Cashcaval* is the Romanian version of cheddar. A strongly flavoured, slightly salty cheese, it grates well and makes a perfect topping for gratin dishes. As a cooked snack on its own, it has spawned two lovely dishes: the breaded version below and the chewy, deliciously messy FRIED CASHCAVAL ('Cascaval la capac' – literally: on a lid). Both are simple but unusual alternatives to the ubiquitous fried camembert at your local wine bar.

8 oz./250 gr. cashcaval* cheese or mature cheddar
2 oz./60 gr. flour
2 eggs
6 oz./180 gr. fine brown breadcrumbs
2 oz./60 gr. butter
2 tsp. rose petal jam (see ROSE PETAL PRERSERVE) or rose petal jelly* or quince jelly

Cut the cashcaval cheese into thick triangles or thin slices (triangles will give you a juicier, stringier result; slices will be slightly drier, but will require less cooking time – handy for a party). Beat the eggs in a bowl and get flour and breadcrumbs ready on two separate plates. Pass the cheese pieces first through flour, then through beaten egg and finally through breadcrumbs. Pass them a second time through egg and breadcrumbs and shake off superfluous coating.

Heat the butter in a frying pan, lower the heat to moderate and fry the cheese pieces on all sides until golden-brown all over. Serve hot, on a bed of crisp lettuce with ½ tsp. pungent fruit jelly on the side.

FRIED CASHCAVAL*
SERVES 4

You will need 4 flame-resistant individual dishes for this snack.

4 oz./125 gr. cashcaval* or swiss cheese
2 oz./60 gr. butter
¼ tsp. paprika
1 oz./30 gr. whole or flaked almonds (optional)

Put 1 tsp. butter in each dish and place a thin slice of cheese on top. Place each dish over a lively flame until the cheese has melted. Put the almonds over the cheese, sprinkle with paprika and serve in the cooking dish. The cheese should be stringy and chewy, but not browned. Serve it on its own with thin slices of toast or with a hot BULGARIAN 'SHOPSKA' SALAD.

CUMIN AND CHEESE BOUCHÉES

Preheat the oven to G4/ 180C/355F.
Bring the milk to the boil and melt the butter in it. Remove from the heat and stir the flour in slowly, mixing vigorously, to avoid lumps. While the mixture is still hot, mix in the grated cheese until fully melted and the mixture is homogeneous. Allow to cool then add 3 eggs, stirring continuously.

---

5 fluid oz./150 ml. milk
3 oz./90 gr. butter
5 oz./150 gr. grated cheddar
   cheese
2 tblsp. cumin seeds (or
   caraway if you prefer)

Dip you hand in flour and form bouchées, taking a desert spoon of the mixture at a time. They should be the size of a large walnut.

Place them on a greated baking tray, about 2"/6 cm. apart, to allow room for expansion.
Brush them with egg yolk and sprinkle with cumin or caraway seed. Bake in a moderate oven until golden all over (about 45 minutes). Serve as a starter, at parties or with a delicate dish like BAKED BRAINS WITH MUSHROOMS.

RICOTTA CHEESE FLAN
SERVES 4 as main course or 8 as a starter

Preheat the oven to G6/ 200C/400F.
Separate the eggs. Beat the whites. Mix together the cheese, egg yolks, butter, semolina, flour and chopped dill to obtain a smooth paste. Gently fold the egg

---

1 lb./500 gr. ricotta cheese or ½
   ricotta and ½ cream cheese
2 oz./60 gr. butter
1 flat tblsp. semolina
1½ tblsp. flour
3 tblsp. dill, finely chopped
3 eggs
½ tsp. salt
5 fluid oz./150 ml. soured cream

---

whites in. Place the mixture in a buttered flan dish. Bake it in the preheated oven for 25 minutes. Cool for a few minutes – it will cut easily into slices. Serve warm with soured cream on the side.

ATHENEE PALACE MEAT BALLS

Boil the onion, parsnip, carrot and celeriac for about 10 minutes. Drain while vegetables are still crunchy. Blend to a paste in a food processor or pass through a sieve.

Mince meats finely. Add minced meats to the vegetables. Add crushed garlic, dill, parsley, pepper, paprika. Grate red pepper

The Athenee Palace is the most famous hotel in Bucharest, the centre of much social and political intrigue between the wars. Built in grand Edwardian style directly opposite the Royal Palace, it saw some celebrated parties in the affluent Bucharest of the 1920s and 30s. These minute, light, party meat balls come from that tradition.

8 oz./250 gr. pork
8 oz./250 gr. beef
1 carrot
1 large parsnip or parsley root
1 celeriac
1 onion
1 large red pepper
2 cloves garlic
1 tblsp. chopped fresh parsley
1 tblsp. chopped dill
1 tsp. black pepper
1 tsp. hot paprika
1 egg
3 tblsp. breadcrumbs
3 fluid oz./90 ml. oil

finely and add to the mixture. Add the egg. Mix well until smooth.

Form minute meat balls by rolling 1 tsp. of the mixture at a time between your palms. Roll balls in breadcrumbs and fry in oil until golden on all sides. Serve sprinkled with chopped parsley.

SALADS

CUCUMBER AND DILL SALAD

Peel the cucumber and slice into extremely thin slices (they should be almost transparent) with a sharp knife or using the fine slicer in a food processor. If you have used a food processor, separate the slices. Salt them, and place in a collander to drain for at least ½ hour. Make the dressing by mixing

Cucumbers and dill are familiar, of course, in their pickled embodiment. You will find them, however, all over the Balkans, as a fresh salad, ideal to accompany the heavier meat or fish dishes in this book.

10 oz./300 gr. cucumber
¾ tsp. salt
⅛ tsp. freshly ground black pepper
2 tsp. finely chopped fresh dill
½ tblsp. oil (optional)
1 tblsp. white wine vinegar

vinegar, pepper and dill (and oil if you wish, although I find it unnecessary in this fresh, summery salad). Place the cucumber slices in a serving dish decorated with flowers and pour dressing over them. Chill for ½ hour and serve as a side salad.

BULGARIAN 'SHOPSKA' SALAD

Grill green peppers as shown at MARINADED PEPPERS. In the meantime, chop the cucumbers finely, with the chillies, tomatoes, onions and parsley.
When the peppers are soft,

4 green peppers
4 tomatoes
2 long green chillies (if this is too hot for you, use only 1)
2 cucumbers
2 onions
1½ tsp. salt
1 tblsp. fresh chopped parsley
5 fluid oz./150 ml. soured cream or smetana

skin them and discard their stalks and seeds. Chop them into thin strips. Mix together the ingredients, add salt and soured cream, and mix again. Serve chilled.

YUGOSLAV 'SHOPSKA' SALAD

SERVES 4

Cut the tomatoes into thin rounds, the peppers into long strips and the onions into quarter rings. Make a dressing by whisking the oil and vinegar with the salt, pepper and marjoram. Pour over the salad ingredients and mix well.

Grate the cheese on the course teeth of a grater, making sure cheese slivers do not turn into a paste.

Despite an identical name, this salad has neither the hot chillies nor the soured cream which give its Bulgarian counterpart its distinctive flavour. Here the peppers are not baked, and the fresh, natural taste of the vegetables is underlined through the addition of white Fetta-type cheese.

8 oz./250 gr. tomatoes
4 oz./125 gr. onions
4 oz./125 gr. green peppers
6 oz./180 gr. white salty
   cheese (Romanian
   'telemea'*; or Greek
   'Fetta' or 'Haloumi')
1 fluid oz./30 ml. olive oil
2 fluid oz./60 ml. vinegar
½ tsp. salt
1 tsp. pepper
2 tsp. sweet marjoram

Sprinkle the cheese over the salad, do not mix any more, and serve chilled.

If the 'telemea' or 'fetta' are too salty for your taste, soak the cheese in cold water for a few hours while still in one piece and it will shed most of its salt; 'Haloumi' cheese, however, is not very salty and it has a slightly minty aftertaste.

GREEN PEPPERS STUFFED WITH RED CABBAGE

Grate the cabbage very finely in a food processor or on the fine teeth of a manual grater. Add salt and caraway seeds and leave for 2-3 hours to soften. In the meantime, cut a lid off the peppers and remove stalks, seeds and inner flesh.

Add 1 tblsp. vinegar per 4 oz./125 gr. cabbage and mix well to allow cabbage to absorb it. Stuff the peppers with cabbage and put in rows in a large jar.

Bring the vinegar and water to the boil. Allow to cool slightly and pour over peppers. Add peppercorns. Tie mouth of jar well and keep for up to 6 months in a cool place.

Ingredients per 4 oz./125 gr. pepper:
4 oz./125 gr. red cabbage
1 tblsp. vinegar per 4 oz./125 gr. cabbage
5 fluid oz./150 ml. vinegar diluted in 5 fluid oz./150 ml. water
5 peppercorns
½ tsp. salt
¼ tsp. caraway seeds

OLIVE PURÉE SALAD
SERVES 6

Cut the olives in half and discard the stones. Remove crusts from the bread and soak it in milk. Squeeze out as much of the milk as you can by hand. Blend olives and bread in a food processor or pass them through a mincer. Mix in the oil: only a few drops at a time at first, then in a steady trickle, to obtain a smooth paste. Chop onion very finely and add it to the paste. Add lemon juice. Wash and trim finger-long leaves of lettuce, chicory and raddichio. Cut the cucumber into oval slices, without peeling. Spread a little of the mixture on each cucumber slice and place about 1 tsp. of the mixture on each salad leaf.

Serve on individual plates, alternating green and reddish leaves and cucumber slices.

**8 oz./250 gr. black olives
3 fluid oz./90 ml. milk
2 fluid oz./60 ml. lemon juice
3 slices white bread – about 5 oz./150 gr.
4 fluid oz./120 ml. olive oil
1 onion
6 small leaves of each: iceberg lettuce, chicory, raddichio
1 small cucumber**

RADISH AND CHEESE SALAD

Chop the stalks off the radishes and grate coarsely on the wide teeth of a manual grater. Grate the cheese as well, or chop it for a few seconds in a food processor, to obtain a white crumbly mass, but NOT a

Radishes are used a lot in Romania, especially the small young ones which flood the markets in spring (they bear the romantic name of 'moon radishes') and are often eaten on their own – dipped in a little coarse salt – for their crunchy, refreshing, sharp taste. In this recipe the salt comes from the fetta cheese.

1 lb./500 gr. young radishes
1 lb./500 gr. fetta cheese
3 fluid oz./90 ml. olive or
    walnut oil
½ tsp. black pepper
1 tblsp. chopped fresh dill

paste. Mix the radishes and cheese-crumbs, add pepper and oil and mix well but gently, until the oil has coated the salad. Sprinkle with dill, chopped very finely, and serve cool.

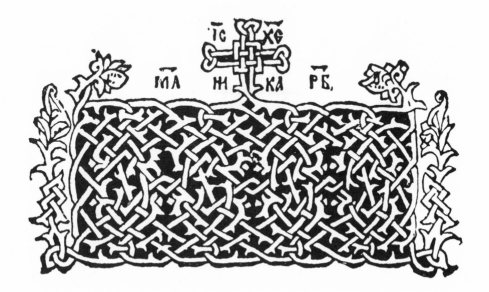

RED CABBAGE
AND APPLE SALAD
SERVES 4-6

Grate the cabbage finely in a food processor or on the fine teeth of a manual grater. Mix in ½ tsp. salt and leave for ½-1 hour. Take a fistful of cabbage at a time and squeeze out as much of the water as you can.

Dilute the vinegar in 1 fluid oz./30 ml. water and add ¼ tsp. salt. Bring to the boil

8 oz./250 gr. red cabbage
1 medium cooking apple (6 oz./180 gr.)
1 small horseradish root
1 tblsp. olive oil/walnut oil
2 fluid oz./60 ml. wine vinegar
¾ tsp. salt

and pour boiling dressing

over cabbage to absorb as much of the dressing as possible.

Grate the apple very finely. Mix with the cabbage until apple takes the red cabbage colour. Add oil. Mix well again. Chill for about 1 hour. Place salad in a serving dish and sprinkle grated horseradish all around it.

SPINACH SALAD
SERVES 4

Wash the spinach thoroughly in plenty of cold water. Discard ruthlessly any wilted leaves. Cut off as much of the tails as you can and discard all stringy bits. Plunge the spinach leaves for 30 seconds in plenty of salted boiling water.

Drain well, shaking the collander from side to side. Split the garlic clove in two and rub the sides of a glass or earthenware bowl with it (or crush half the clove into

1 lb./500 gr. very young fresh spinach
1 fluid oz. olive oil
2 fluid oz. vinegar
¼ tsp. French mustard
⅓ tsp. salt
¼ tsp. freshly ground black pepper or cayenne pepper
1 large clove garlic
2 boiled eggs

the bowl if you prefer a stronger garlic flavour). Put

the spinach into the bowl. Whisk together a dressing of oil, vinegar, mustard, salt and pepper. Pour over the spinach, stir well but gently, to coat the leaves with dressing, and serve surrounded by slices of hard boiled eggs.

The salad should be eaten within an hour of preparation as it will not keep its fresh appearance and taste.

WALNUT AND EGG SALAD
SERVES 4

Pound the walnuts finely to pinhead size. Chop the onions very finely, then heat the butter in a frying pan, and sweat the onion and walnuts over a low flame until onions have turned into a golden purée. Peel hard boiled eggs and mash them with a fork, or in a mortar. Add the contents of

4 oz./125 gr. walnuts
4 oz./125 gr. spring onions
2 hard boiled eggs
½ tsp. salt
¼ tsp. white pepper
1 tblsp. lemon juice
   (optional)
2 oz./60 gr. butter

the frying pan and mix well until smooth. Add salt, pepper and lemon juice if you wish. Serve still slightly warm, spread on thin cucumber slices, chicory leaves or crisp iceberg lettuce. It can also be served with very thin slices of toast or toasted TARRAGON YEAST CAKE.

BULGARIAN YOGHURT DRESSING

Legend has it the Bulgarians discovered yoghurt hundreds of years ago when a shepherd who was bringing sheeps' milk to market in leather saddle bags, saw the milk had turned slightly acid during the jerky journey down the mountain. Whatever the truth, yoghurt is undoubtedly the best known contribution brought by Bulgarians to the world of cooking and Bulgarian live yoghurt (and its relations further south in Greece and Turkey) remains the best in the world.

Place the flour, crushed garlic, sugar, mustard, vinegar and 5 fluid oz./150 ml. water in a saucepan and simmer over a very low flame, stirring continuously, for 5 minutes until you get a fairly thick sauce base. Simmer for a further 3 minutes and remove from heat.

Allow to cool for 3 minutes, then whisk in the egg yolks. Whisking constantly with one hand, pour in the olive

---

2 fluid oz./60 ml. live
   yoghurt
2 egg yolks
5 fluid oz./150 ml. olive oil
2 tblsp. tarragon vinegar
1 tblsp. flour
1 clove garlic
½ tsp. sugar
½ tsp. french mustard
3 tblsp. chopped dill or
   watercress

---

oil very slowly, first drop by drop, then in a steady trickle. Place in the fridge for 2-3 hours until thoroughly chilled.

Mix in the yoghurt and watercress. Whisk very fast for at least three minutes, until dressing has risen, gained in volume and is smooth and fluffy. Chill again for ½ hour and serve on its own with a summer green salad or with peeled and diced cucumbers mixed together.

RED CABBAGE RELISH

Grate the cabbage very finely in a food processor or on the fine teeth of a manual grater. Mix in ¾ tsp. salt and leave aside for ½ hour -1 hour. Squeeze as much water out of the cabbage as you can by hand.

Dilute the vinegar with 2 fluid oz./60 ml. of water and add ¼ tsp. salt.

Bring to the boil and pour this boiling dressing over

---
1 lb./500 gr. red cabbage
3 tblsp. walnut/olive oil
4 fluid oz. wine vinegar
1 tsp. salt
---

cabbage. Mix well for a few minutes with a wooden spoon, to allow cabbage to absorb as much of the dressing as possible. Chill for one hour at least. You can serve it

immediately, (in which case add the oil and mix lightly) or place it in a tightly closed jar and keep for several weeks in a cold place. Use as a garnish with boiled meats, game, and so on, or as a basis for RED CABBAGE AND APPLE SALAD or to stuff GREEN PEPPERS STUFFED WITH RED CABBAGE (see below). Always add oil just before serving.

ROMANIAN GARLIC DRESSING (MUJDEI)

Place the garlic in a wooden or stone mortar with the salt and crush it, rubbing against the walls of the mortar until you get a smooth paste. (If you are using a garlic crusher, pass the garlic through it several times, then mix it with salt to get

A simple, yet extremely pungent dressing widely used in Romania to spread over grilled and barbecued meat and fish.

For 1 whole fish or 4 steaks or similar:
6 cloves garlic
¼ tsp. salt
3 fluid oz./90 ml. beef stock or water
1 tblsp. wine vinegar
---

the paste). Pour stock or water and vinegar on top and mix again to obtain a thin but aromatic sauce. Use it to brush over BARBECUED CARP, SPICY ROMANIAN SAUSAGES, POLENTA CAKES, etc.

47

WALNUT DRESSING
(SCORDOLEA)
SERVES 4

Pass the walnuts through a fine mincer or grate in a food processor until they turn into a paste. Remove crusts from bread and soak in milk until the liquid is fully absorbed. Squeeze out as much of the liquid as you can by hand. Crush the garlic cloves and mix with the soaked bread and 2 tsps. lemon juice until you have obtained a smooth paste.

4 oz./125 gr. walnuts
2 fluid oz./60 ml. walnut oil
2 fluid oz./60 ml. lemon juice
2-3 cloves garlic
⅓ tsp. freshly ground pepper
1 slice white bread
2 tblsp. milk

Add walnuts and continue mixing, by hand or in a food processor, adding oil very slowly, as though making mayonnaise. Add pepper and the rest of the lemon juice and mix well again. The final consistency of the dressing should resemble a thick, set yoghurt. The dressing will set more if placed in the fridge for a few hours.

Serve chilled with boiled crayfish, cold chicken breasts or cucumber salad.

CABBAGE PICKLED IN BRINE

Pickled cabbage, whether in vinegar or brine, whole or shredded (sauerkraut), occupies just as important a place in Balkan cooking as in the better known neighbouring cuisines of Germany or Russia. The major difference is that Romanian cooking makes use of the flavoured brine liquid as well as of the actual pickled vegetable, mainly for souring 'CHORBE'. The leaves of cabbages which have been pickled whole are widely used for stuffing, for savoury puddings, etc.; while a bed of shredded pickled cabbage is often used to bring out the flavour of carp or duckling. Further on in this book you will find quite a few recipes using cabbage in one form or another – although they are all described using fresh cabbage, you will often get results closer to the Balkanic taste for the sour by using whole cabbages pickled in brine as described below. One can buy whole pickled cabbages out of huge oak vats in any decent market, anywhere from Zagreb to Sofia. In this country, however, while sauerkraut is widely available in the shops, you will probably need to pickle your own whole cabbages for stuffing or for soured soups, with much tastier results. The dedicated Romanian or Bulgarian cabbage eater will probably pickle a whole oak vat (filled with over 100 cabbages) every autumn, but for more restrained Western appetites, here are the proportions and quantities for a smaller barrel. You will still need a wooden container with a tap at the lower end and a certain amount of dedication and patience.

Scrub the barrel well and wash it out with boiling water. Allow it to dry in the fresh air. Place the barrel on a trestle table, or similar, in such a way as to be able to drain easily the cabbage juice accumulating at the bottom of the barrel during the pickling process. Remove all yellowed or stained outer leaves from the heads of cabbage, cut a cross into the stalks with a sharp knife, scoop out some of the hard stalk and put a little salt in its place. Set aside 3-4 cabbages and place the rest in tight rows in the barrel. Add the sweetcorn, chopped horseradish and the whole quince. Cover with water salted in the proportions shown and press cabbages down with a flat board or lid weighted down with brass weights or a large clean stone.

For 20 small (about 1 lb./500 gr. each) cabbages you will need:

1 oz./30 gr. sweetcorn, off the cob
1 small horseradish root
1 large quince
salted water in the proportion of 2 oz./60 gr. coarse salt to every 2 pt./1 l. water

---

Leave in a cool place (ideally a cellar) for 3 days. The cabbages will settle considerably and will begin to shed some of their juice. Remove lid and top up the cabbages with the heads you had set aside, making sure the container is full to the brim. Replace weighted lid and leave for 3 more days. Place a large saucepan under the tap of the barrel, fill it with pickling liquid and pour this liquid back into the barrel, from the top, removing the lid temporarily. This is done to aerate the brine and prevent the cabbages from softening or rotting. Repeat this operation every 2-3 days for a fortnight, until all the brine has been aerated. The pickling process will take about 5 weeks altogether. In order to keep the cabbage crisp, remove any mould forming on the top of the brine and wash the lid well every time you need to remove it. Pickled whole cabbage leaves are used for STUFFED CABBAGE (SARMALE); FILLED CABBAGE LEAVES 'STANIMASHK'; BAKED CARP or DUCKLING ON A BED OF CABBAGE; while the cabbage juice can be used for any of the soured soups ('CHORBE') described in this book and especially for SMOKED PORK CHORBA and CHORBA WITH MEAT BALLS.

VEGETABLE RELISH (PINDZUR)

Prick the aubergines with a fork in a few places. Place the aubergines, peppers and tomatoes under a hot grill, about 3″/9 cm. away from the flame and grill on all sides until the skins of the tomatoes and the peppers are crinkled and bubbling away from the flesh, and the aubergines turn black. The tomatoes will be done first (about 10 minutes), but take care not to allow the flesh of the peppers to burn or blacken. Place the grilled vegetables in a wooden or earthenware bowl, cover with a cloth and allow to cool until soft (about ½ hour–1 hour).

Peel the vegetables and

This is a fiery, garlicky Yugoslav version of the vegetable 'Zakuska'. I like it, either as a starter or as an accompaniment to grilled meats.

8 oz./250 gr. green peppers
8 oz./250 gr. aubergines
8 oz./250 gr. ripe tomatoes
2 oz./60 gr. garlic
1 tblsp. olive oil
1 fluid oz./30 ml. vinegar
1 small dried chilli pepper or 1
    long green chilli
½ tsp. salt

replace in the bowl (do not drain away the liquid they have left behind while cooling). Mash them coarsely with a wooden spoon (do not be tempted to use a blender, the mixture should be fairly chunky). Add the crushed or chopped garlic (it may seem a lot, but the recipe calls for a very garlicky flavour), oil, vinegar and salt. Mix well and check seasoning. Add finely chopped chilli, including the seeds (you can omit the chilli if you prefer it less hot).

Allow to mellow, covered, in a cool place (not in the fridge) for at least three hours. Serve cold as a starter with pitta bread to dip into it, or with brown bread and butter; or as an accompaniment to grilled or smoked meat and fish.

SOUPS
AND
'CHORBE'

The glory of Romanian cooking, and perhaps its most original feature, is the enormous body of "chorbe" (the word is of Turkish origin and means soured soups). In their search for natural substances suitable for souring meat or fish soups, the Romanian cooks have not contented themselves with the obvious, such as lemon juice or vinegar. A whole panoply of souring agents has been assembled, among them highly unusual ingredients like wax plums (myrobalan) or the juices derived from fermenting bran, called 'borsh,' having nothing but its name in common with the well known Northern European beetroot soup. These souring liquids are usually added to meat or fish stocks, flavoured in their turn with pungent herbs like lovage or with strong meats like tripe or poultry giblets.

BRAN 'BORSH'

Bran 'borsh' is the main souring agent used in Romanian cooking and it is of ancient Moldavian origin. The great historian Nicolae Iorga mentions a 'borsh woman' (i.e. a professional borsh maker) at Iassi as far back as 1760 and the trade is associated until today with small, home-based borsh sellers who advertise their wares by chalking proudly on the nearest garden wall 'We have fresh borsh'. Bran borsh is the colour of amber and it is supposed to be as clear as possible. When the decanted liquid is still too clouded, the old women 'scold' it with a green cherry branch, supposedly capable of purifying the liquid on the spot. It is obtained by fermenting the protein contained in the aleurone (outer) layer of the grain of wheat in small oak vats. Bran borsh forms the basis of any 'chorba' (soured soup) and it is used to sour dishes in the same way that in the West one would use vinegar or lemon juice. There is one major difference, however: while lemon juice or vinegar are intensely sour, and require diluting or careful rationing, bran borsh is only mildly acid and keeps all the natural flavour of the grain. It is therefore used both as souring agent and as boiling liquid for soups, etc. and is diluted only slightly, usually in the proportion of 1 part borsh to 1 of water. In Romania you can buy home-made borsh by the bottle in any neighbourhood, but in this country you will have to be adventurous and make your own. It is not difficult and the results are definitely worth it: you will discover an unusual, highly flavoured taste for soups and cooked vegetables.

You will need a 20 pts./8 l. oak vat or earthenware pot. Wash it well and clean with boiling water to eliminate any impurities. Fill it up to ¼ with natural bran mixed with polenta flour. Sprinkle about 2 pt./1 l. of cold water over the bran and mix well. Pour over them 12 pt./5 l. boiling water to fill the pot up to ¾ of its height. Mix well with a wooden rolling pin or stick and add 1 lb./500 gr. of soured bran left over from a previous lot

---
7 lb./3 kg. natural bran*
4 oz./125 gr. polenta* maize flour
1 lb./500 gr. soured bran (see below) or 5 fluid oz./150 ml. white wine vinegar

---

of 'borsh'. Alternatively, sprinkle bran with 2 pt./1 l. liquid 'borsh' instead of water at the start of the process or, failing this, with 15 fluid oz./450 ml. water mixed with 5 fluid oz./150ml. white wine vinegar.

Mix again well, cover with a clean linen cloth and place pot in a warm place (by the fire, radiator, or in the kitchen by the oven) for 24 hours. Strain borsh through a fine sieve to obtain a clear, pale yellow liquid which can be bottled and kept in a cool place for months. Remember to keep 1 lb./500 gr. soured bran for the next 'borsh' making and discard the rest. Good luck!

BEETROOT BORSH

Cut the meat into medium sized cubes. Bring the stock to the boil and simmer meat and marrow bone in it, covered and on a small flame, while you prepare the vegetables. Skim it occasionally. Add salt. Chop all the vegetables finely. Tie the herbs in a bundle so they stay together while cooking and can be removed easily at the end. Scrub potatoes and leave whole. Add vegetables to the stock in 2 lots: First add the chopped onions, carrots, parsnips, swede, bobby beans and tied herbs. Simmer for 30 minutes, covered, then add the second batch: diced beetroot, chopped cabbage, quartered tomatoes and whole potatoes. Add

2 lb./1 kg. lean beef
1 large marrow bone
1 lb./500 gr. raw beetroot
1 large onion
2 carrots
1 parsnip
½ small swede
4 oz./125 gr. bobby beans or
    green beans
8 oz./250 gr. white cabbage
4 small potatoes
3 tomatoes
1 small bunch of parsley
1 small bunch of dill
1 small bunch of lovage
4 tblsp. lemon juice or 1 pt./600
    ml. BRAN BORSH*
1 egg yolk
4 fluid oz./120 ml. soured cream
1 tsp. salt
4 pt./2 l. beef stock or water

lemon juice or bran borsh* (if you are using bran

borsh* start with only 3 pt./1.5 l. stock or water in the first place) and simmer for another 45 minutes or until potatoes are cooked through, but not crumbly, and the beetroot has shed all its red colour.
Remove the herbs and the marrow bone. Mix the egg yolk and soured cream in a tureen and then pour a ladle of soup over them. Mix well, then pour the rest of the soup into the tureen. Serve hot with a potato for each person. You can strain the soup if you wish and serve the meat (diced or in 1 piece) separately for the main course, dressed with a SOURED CREAM AND DILL SAUCE and accompanied by CABBAGE FILLED WITH MAIZE.

'CHORBA' WITH MEAT BALLS

Cut the vegetables into thin slices (including tomatoes, de-seeded if possible). Place the bones in a saucepan with 3 pt./1.5 l. water and bring to the boil. Add the vegetables and the herbs (kept in a bunch and tied at the tail end with an elastic band so that they stay together and can be easily removed). Simmer covered for 2 hours until you get a well flavoured stock. Skim occasionally.

In the meantime, soak the bread in 1 fluid oz./30 ml. water and squeeze out as much of the water as you can by hand. Mince through a fine mincer or in a food processor the meat, the soaked bread and the onion. Mix in the egg, salt, cayenne pepper. Boil the rice separately and mix it into the meat mixture when soft. Dipping your hand in cold water, take 2 tsp. at a time of the mixture and shape balls the size of a walnut by rolling them in between your palms.

When the stock has boiled

Of all Romanian 'chorbe' (tangy soups) this one is probably the best loved and certainly the one most often encountered in restaurants. It is basically a clear meat 'bouillon' highly flavoured with a souring agent and with the all-important lovage and served with small savoury meat balls. ('perisoare' – literally: 'little pears')

For the soup:
10 fluid oz./300 ml. BRAN BORSH or the juice from soured cabbage or 6 tblsp. lemon juice
4 fluid oz./120 ml. soured cream
1 lb./500 gr. marrow bones
1 carrot
1 parsnip
1 celery
1 celeriac
2 onions
2 tomatoes
1 bunch parsley or mixed parsley and dill
1 egg yolk
1 tsp. salt
3 tblsp. chopped lovage

For the meat balls:
1 lb./500 gr. lean beef
1 slice bread
2 tblsp. rice
1 onion
1 egg
1 tsp. salt
½ tsp. cayenne pepper

sufficiently, add the souring agent. I prefer the cabbage brine; it may be difficult to get (unless you make your own: see PICKLED CABBAGE) but you can use lemon juice if you want – the taste will be closer to that of Greek soups. If you are using cabbage pickling liquid, boil it separately FIRST and skim several times. If you are using bran 'borsh' also boil separately first and pass it through a fine sieve or muslin to eliminate any impurities.

Bring the broth to a fierce boil and plunge the meat balls into the broth. Boil for 15 minutes or until the meat inside the balls is fully cooked. Beat the egg yolk and mix it with the soured cream. Place mixture at the bottom of a tureen and pour a ladle of broth on top. Mix well then strain rest of the broth over it through a collander. Replace the meat balls in the broth and sprinkle generously with chopped lovage. Serve very hot.

'CHORBA'
WITH STUFFED COURGETTES

Chop the soup vegetables into small pieces. Bring the stock to the boil and simmer the soup vegetables and marrow bone (if any), covered, while you prepare the stuffed courgettes (use the full 3 pt./1.5 l. stock if you are using lemon juice for souring and 2 pt./1 l. if you are using bran borsh). Scrub the courgettes well and if their skins are too thick, scrape them with a knife. Cut the courgettes in half across the middle and scoop out with a grapefruit knife and teaspoon about ¾ of the inner flesh.
Make the stuffing:
Soak the crustless slice of bread in a little water for a few minutes.
Squeeze out as much of the water as you can by hand. Mince the meat in a fine mincer or in a food processor. Chop the onion finely and sweat in oil until soft but not brown. Add the courgette flesh and rice, fry for 3 minutes on a low heat and add 3 fluid oz./90 ml. water.

For the soup:
1 pt./600 ml. BRAN BORSH or 3 tblsp. lemon juice
2-3 pt./1-1.5 l. beef or veal stock
1 carrot
1 parsnip
1 onion
6 oz./180 gr. peas
1 marrow bone (optional)
1 egg yolk
4 fluid oz./120 ml. soured cream
1 tblsp. fresh chopped dill
1 tblsp. fresh chopped parsley, lovage or coriander
½ tblsp. chopped chives
1 tsp. salt

For the stuffed courgettes:
6 young courgettes or baby marrows
8 oz./250 gr. lean beef
1 slice bread
1 small onion
1 egg
4 oz./125 gr. rice
½ tsp. salt
¼ tsp. hot paprika
½ tblsp. chopped dill

Allow the rice to absorb the water, then mix together the minced meat, the contents of the frying pan, soaked

bread, egg, salt, paprika and chopped dill. If you have any mixture left, make it into small balls as shown at CHORBA WITH MEAT BALLS and add them to the soup as well. They will give you an easy indication of when the filling inside the courgettes is cooked.
Fill the courgettes with the mixture. Drop them into the soup and add lemon juice (if you are using bran borsh, boil separately first, skim thoroughly and add it now to the stock, having used only 2 pt./1 l. of stock in the first place). Add the green peas and simmer over a moderate flame for 30 minutes.
In the meantime, mix egg yolk and soured cream into a smooth paste at the bottom of a tureen. Add finely chopped herbs and chives and when soup is ready, strain it slowly into the tureen. Put back the filled courgettes and meat balls, and discard the other ingredients. Serve warm.

GIBLET 'CHORBA'
(CHORBE DE POTROACE)
SERVES 6-8

Like its soul-sister TRIPE 'CHORBA', this tangy soup made of poultry giblets and a flavoured meat stock, is part of the heavy drinker's repertory of means of recovery. The souring agent here is the brine left from pickling cabbage, but you can replace it, if you wish, with lemon juice or a delicate white wine vinegar (about 1 tblsp. of juice or vinegar to every 1 pt./600 ml. of soup).

If you are **not** using stock, boil the bones with half the cleaned and chopped vegetables for 2 hours on a low flame.

Bring stock to the boil and add poultry giblets. Boil on a moderate flame, covered, for 1 hour. In the meantime, chop the vegetables finely and add to the broth when giblets are soft. Add salt and boil for another ½ hour or until carrots and rice are soft.

---

3 pts./1.8 l. beef stock or water with 2 lb./1 kg. beef bones
2 lb./1 kg. turkey or goose giblets (neck, liver, kidneys, wings, feet, etc.)
4 oz./125 gr. carrots
5 oz./150 gr. onions
4 oz./125 gr. celery
4 oz./125 gr. parsnips
2 pts./1 l. cabbage pickling brine (see above)
3 oz./90 gr. rice
2 egg yolks
2 oz./60 gr. chopped lovage
1 tsp. salt
2 tsp. hot paprika
½ tblsp. chopped fresh dill
½ tblsp. chopped fresh parlsey

Bring the cabbage brine to the boil, skim well and add to the broth.

Add salt, paprika and lovage. Boil for 15 minutes, taste for seasoning and sourness (the broth should be fiery and fairly sour – it is meant to make you jump) and serve with the 2 egg yolks beaten and mixed in and sprinkled generously with chopped dill and parsley.

SMOKED PORK 'CHORBA'
SERVES 6

Soak the beans overnight in cold water.

Wash the pork well and boil, covered, in a saucepan with 3 pts./1.5 l. water together with the bay leaves and peppercorns, for about 1 hour.

Chop the pickled cabbage into long strips (you can use sauerkraut if you wish) and boil it in plenty of water (not with the pork) until soft.

Drain the beans and cover again with cold water. Bring

---

1 lb./500 gr. smoked belly of pork, preferably in 1 piece
8 oz./250 gr. haricot or broad beans
12 oz./360 gr. pickled cabbage
8 oz./250 gr. potatoes
2 oz./60 gr. lard or butter
1 oz./30 gr. flour
1 oz./30 gr. onions
3 cloves garlic
1 tsp. salt
6 peppercorns
2 bay leaves
5 fluid oz./150 ml. soured cream

---

to the boil and skim 2-3 times. Drain again and cover with warm, slightly salted water.

Simmer over a medium flame until a bean taken between forefinger and thumb crumbles with ease. Drain and sieve or blend in a food processor to obtain a thick paste.

Peel potatoes and boil them whole in slightly salted water.

When all the ingredients are boiled, reserve the meat

boiling liquid (with the peppercorns and bayleaves) and drain potatoes and cabbage.
Chop the meat and potatoes into 1"/3 cm. cubes.
Chop the onions finely and brown them in the melted fat, in a saucepan.
Add flour and make a roux by browning it for 3-4 minutes, stirring constantly.

Take a few tblsps. of the pork stock and pour it over the roux, again stirring constantly until flour has dissolved completely. Pour the rest of the pork stock into the saucepan with the roux, add potatoes, meat cubes, shredded soured cabbage and bean paste. Mix well and add the reserved bay leaves and peppercorns

and the crushed garlic. Bring the broth to the boil and allow it to simmer for 5 minutes.
Take a ladle of broth and mix it with the soured cream in a bowl. Add the diluted soured cream into the broth, away from the flame, give it a few stirs and serve immediately.

GRANDMOTHER'S 'CHORBA'

SERVES 6-8

Slice the bacon into thin strips. Chop onion finely. Chop the beans if they are too big, but leave bobby beans whole with only the stringy ends removed. Grate the carrots and parsnips. Chop the celeriac finely. Heat the oil well and sauté bacon slices until browning and sizzling. Lower heat and add grated carrots and onions. Sweat for 5 minutes until the onions are soft but not too yellow. Add the parsnips, celeriac and green beans. Sweat for 3 more minutes, mixing well. Transfer the contents of the

A tangy soup based on green beans, rather than the haricot beans normally associated with smoked bacon. The souring agent in this case is lemon juice, which gives the soup a delicate, summery flavour.

1 lb./500 gr. green beans or bobby beans
8 oz./250 gr. smoked bacon or smoked belly of pork
4 oz./125 gr. carrots
4 oz./125 gr. parsnips
4 oz./125 gr. onions
4 oz./125 gr. celeriac
2 oz./60 gr. rice
2 tblsp. lemon juice
2 fluid oz./60 ml. olive oil
1 tblsp. chopped fresh parsley
1 tblsp. chopped fresh dill
1 tsp. salt
¼ tsp. pepper
2 eggs

frying pan to a saucepan and add 4 pts./2 l. boiling salted water. Simmer on a moderate flame for 20 minutes or until the beans are soft. Add the rice, salt, peppercorns and lemon juice.
Simmer for 15 more minutes or until the rice is soft.
Beat the eggs well at the bottom of a tureen. Mix in 1 ladle of the soup and then pour rest of soup on top. Sprinkle with chopped herbs and adjust seasoning and lemon juice. Serve warm, but not too hot.

TRIPE 'CHORBA'
(CHORBA DE BURTA)

SERVES 4

This sour broth, like its sister made with poultry giblets (GIBLET 'CHORBA'), is associated in Romanian folk memory with long drinking nights and hungover dawns. It used to be a speciality of the pubs and popular restaurants around the main market in Bucharest before the war, catering at first for peasants arriving through the night with their produce and appropriated later by fashionable men about the town combining slumming with heavy all night drinking. By the 1930s the area had become the Balkans' answer to the Parisian *halles*, complete with a local substitute for a 'drinkers' soup', taken as ritually as the Soupe a l'oignon des noctambules was imbibed at the 'Pied de Cochon'. Tripe 'Chorba' was supposed to have miraculous properties for curing a hangover, presumably because of the reaction between the sour vinegar (acetic acid) it contains and the alcohol still in the stomach. Tripe was a specifically southern dish, where they prefer vinegar to bran borsh. In Moldavia giblet 'Chorba', especially made with turkey giblets, was considered the proper antidote to over indulgence.

The tripe you can buy at the butcher's these days is already cleaned and white. If you happen to get tripe which has not been cleaned already, rub it with coarse salt or coarse maize flour (POLENTA) and scrub it with a rough brush until completely white.

Put the tripe, pig's trotter, and the whole carrot, parsnip, quartered onions, peppercorns and bay leaf to boil in the stock or water. Cover and simmer on a medium flame for 2 hours. (If you are not using stock, add 1 lb./500 gr. beef bones and simmer for 3 hours.) Remove the tripe with a slotted spoon, allow it to cool a little and slice it into long strips about ⅓"/1 cm. wide (the size and length of

2 pts./1 l. beef stock or water
1 lb./500 gr. tripe
1 small pig's or veal's trotter
1 carrot
2 onions
1 parsnip
1 bay leaf
10 peppercorns
1 tblsp. white wine vinegar or
    the juice of ½ a lemon
1 egg yolk
1 tsp. salt
2 cloves garlic
1 small horseradish root
    (optional)
2 tblsp. chopped lovage
½ tsp. pepper

macaroni).
Strain the broth and discard vegetables, bones and trotter (you can pick the meat off the trotter and add it to the broth as well if you wish).

Replace the clear broth on the heat, put back strips of tripe in it and bring back to the boil. Let it bubble up for 2-3 minutes.
In the meantime, crush the garlic and make a paste with it and the vinegar or lemon juice. Beat the egg yolk and whisk in the garlic paste. Mix a ladle of broth with the paste at the bottom of a tureen, then pour the rest of the broth on top. Sprinkle generously with chopped lovage and grated horseradish if you like, adjust seasoning (add more vinegar or lemon juice if you like it sour or you have really been over indulging the old plum brandy) and eat warm, without reheating.

POTATO 'CHORBA' WITH WHEY

SERVES 6

Peel the vegetables (not the potatoes) and cut them into thin rounds or slices. Boil them in 1 pt./600 ml. water for 20 minutes or until they are soft.

In the meantime, peel potatoes and cube them into ½"/2 cm. cubes.

When the vegetables are soft add the cubed potatoes and whey or buttermilk (or live

Whey and/or soured milk are staple ingredients in the Romanian and Bulgarian shepherd's diet. Whether simply poured over a maize porridge or used in more complex recipes like this 'Chorba' (a Balkan version of vichyssoise), it provides an exotic yet slimming alternative to cream.

yoghurt thinned with 1 pt./600 ml. milk if you cannot get either of the above). Add salt and pepper. Simmer for another 20 minutes or until potatoes are soft but not mushy.

Cool, place in fridge for a couple of hours and serve chilled with the dill stirred in at the last minute.

10 oz./300 gr. potatoes
1 carrot
1 small head of celery
1 parsnip
1 parsley root
1 tblsp. finely chopped dill
2 pt./1 l. whey or soured
    buttermilk
1 tsp. freshly ground black
    pepper
1 tsp. salt

SUMMER SOUP WITH CUCUMBERS

SERVES 6

Clean and chop the spring onions, celeriac, carrots and parsnip. Bring the stock to the boil and drop the vegetables in it. Bring them back to the boil, simmer covered for 1 hour and set aside to cool. Place in the fridge for a few hours, until the fat has risen and formed a crust on top of the soup. Remove solidified fat carefully and thoroughly. Strain the soup carefully through a sieve or collander into an earthenware pot,

2 pt./1 l. well flavoured beef stock (or 1 lb./500 gr. lean beef and 1 lb./500 gr. beef bones boiled in 2 pt./1 l. water)
8 oz./250 gr. cucumber
4 oz./125 gr. spring onions or young leeks
2 carrots
1 celeriac
1 parsnip
½ tsp. pepper
1 tsp. salt
1 pt./600 ml. soured buttermilk or whey
10 fluid oz./300 ml. soured cream
1 tblsp. fresh chopped dill

taking care not to disturb the sediment at the bottom of the saucepan.
Discard the vegetables.
Mix the soured cream with buttermilk or whey and add to the soup.
Peel the cucumber and dice it into small (½"/2 cm.) cubes. Place the cucumbers cubes in the soup, chill again in the fridge for at least 1 hour and serve sprinkled generously with fresh chopped dill.

STYRIAN SOUR BROTH

SERVES 6-8

Get your butcher to chop the trotters into halves, lengthways. Chop the tails into 1"/3 cm. pieces. Wash them well and place them in a saucepan with 3-4 pts./1.8-2.5 l. water. Boil for about 1½ hours, covered, on a medium flame.
Chop the vegetables except the onion and add to the broth. Now chop the onion and the garlic and soften in the melted fat. Add flour to make a roux and fry stirring gently for 3-4 minutes. Pour

3 lbs./1.5 kg. pig's trotters and ox tails
2 lbs./1 kg. potatoes
1 onion
1 parsnip
2 sticks celery
1 large carrot
3 cloves garlic
2 oz./60 gr. lard or oil
1 tsp. coarsely ground black pepper
1 tsp. salt
1 tblsp. white wine vinegar or lemon juice for each 1 pt./600 ml. broth
2 tblsp. fresh chopped lovage

the roux with onion and garlic over meat. Bring to the boil, allow to bubble up 3-4 times and add salt and vinegar or lemon juice. Simmer over a low flame for another ½ hour or until potatoes are cooked. Add pepper.
Remove the trotters with a slotted spoon and shred the meat off the bones. Replace meat in the broth and serve hot, sprinkled with chopped lovage.

SPRING LAMB BROTH WITH DUMPLINGS

SERVES 6-8

Soups served with dumplings are popular in Transylvania and in the Vojvodina region of Yugoslavia, where dumplings are traditionally used in preference to rice or pasta.

Soup dumplings are usually small and made with flour, borrowed in both name ('galushka') and way of cooking from the Hungarians next door. 'Galushka' dumplings are bite-sized, very light and with a chewy texture, while the soup dumplings popular in southern Romania are usually made of semolina and are large and soft (see SEMOLINA DUMPLINGS).

Bring 2 pts./1 l. water to the boil. Add salt and the lamb meat and bone. Bring back to the boil, skim and add the chopped carrot, parsley root or parsnip and onion. Cover and simmer until the carrot has softened. In the meantime chop the ends off the bobby beans and add them to the broth, together with the lemon juice, lovage, chopped parsley and chopped spring onions. Simmer covered for 2 hours. Meanwhile mix 1 egg with the butter. Add flour slowly to create the consistency of a thick mayonnaise. Mix in the chopped parsley and salt.

2 lb./1 kg. neck of lamb
1 lamb bone (optional)
1 carrot
1 parsley root or parsnip
1 onion
4 oz./125 gr. bobby beans
2 tblsp. chopped fresh parsley
1 small bunch lovage
2 fluid oz./60 ml. lemon juice
1 tsp. salt
3 spring onions
1 egg yolk (optional)
2 tblsp. soured cream (optional)

For the dumplings:
1 egg
1 oz./30 gr. butter
1½ oz./45 gr. plain flour
¼ tsp. salt
1 tsp. chopped parsley

When the broth is almost ready, bring it to a fierce boil and drop dumpling mixture (a tsp. at a time – the mixture will expand when boiled) into the bubbling broth. Boil for another 15 minutes. Mix the soured cream with egg yolks to make a smooth paste. Place at the bottom of a soup tureen. Strain broth into the tureen, add dumplings and discard or re-use the meat and vegetables. Serve the clear, tangy broth steaming hot, with the dumplings floating on top.

SPRING CHICKEN BROTH

Bring 2 pts./1 l. water to the boil. Add salt and the chicken, including wings, neck and giblets. Bring back to the boil, skim well and add the carrot, parsley root or parsnip, onion, all chopped roughly. Cover and simmer until the carrot is soft. Add the chopped herbs, lovage, chopped onions, quartered tomatoes and lemon juice. Add rice, cover and simmer for 1½-2 hours.

Mix well, in a tureen, the egg yolk with the soured cream. Pour in 2 tblsp. of

1 spring chicken or 3 lb./1.5 kg. chicken, quartered
1 carrot
1 parsley root or parsnip
1 onion
2 tblsp. chopped fresh parsley or mixed parsley and dill
1 small bunch of lovage
1 tsp. salt
3 spring onions
2 tomatoes
3 tblsp. rice
1 egg yolk
2 tblsp. soured cream
2 fluid oz./60 ml. lemon juice

the soup and mix well. Remove the chicken meat and vegetables from the broth and reserve. (Use boiled chicken for CHICKEN TERRINE IN GARLIC ASPIC for example).

Pour the broth, including rice and herbs, into the tureen. Serve warm, but not too hot.

You can replace rice with either flour or semolina dumplings, in which case see SPRING LAMB BROTH WITH DUMPLINGS or SEMOLINA DUMPLINGS.

CHICKEN BROTH
WITH SOUR CHERRIES

The Romanian love for tangy soups bordering on the sour is unusually illustrated in this recipe from Oltenia, the region to the north of the Danube in south west Romania. The recipe is normally cooked with cherry plums (myrobolam) a wild, tart, small plum, yellow or red in colour which ripens in Britain in July or August. In France the Mirabelle liqueur is made from it but in Romania it is mostly eaten raw by children or used, like in this recipe, as a souring agent in preference to the more common 'bran borsh' or vinegar. I have adapted it to Morello cherries* (since they have to be sieved you can use preserved cherries, provided they contain no added sugar) or small, tart, early gooseberries. Another feature specific to this region is the use of leeks instead of onions for the stock base (the leek is the Oltenian 'national' vegetable — see FILLED LEEKS, etc.).

Chop finely the leeks, carrot, parsnip, celeriac, green pepper.

Place the chopped vegetables and chicken pieces in a large saucepan with 2 pts./1 l. water. Bring to the boil, cover and simmer for 1 hour or until the chicken is cooked and the carrots have softened.

In the meantime, boil the Morello cherries or gooseberries in plenty of water until soft. Remove stones and sieve or blend in a food processor to obtain a thin pulp. Reserve.

In the same water, boil the vermicelli for 5 minutes or

2 lb./1 kg. chicken pieces
1 lb./500 gr. unsweetened Morrello cherries* or tart gooseberries
2 leeks
1 carrot
1 parsnip or parsley root
2 oz./60 gr. celeriac
1 small bunch lovage
1 oz./30 gr. chopped green pepper
2 oz./60 gr. egg vermicelli
1 egg yolk
1 tblsp. chopped parsley
1 tsp. salt
12 peppercorns

until soft.

When chicken stock is ready, add cherry pulp, salt and peppercorns. Bring back to the boil mixing and simmer for another 5 minutes.

Beat the egg yolk. Chop the parsley and lovage very finely and mix with the beaten yolk. Place the yolk and herb mixture at the bottom of a tureen, then mix in a ladle of the broth and pour rest of broth on top through a collander. Add boiled vermicelli, adjust seasoning and replace, if you want, some of the chicken meat shredded off the bone and a few slices of carrot. Serve warm but not too hot.

SORREL SOUP 'IASSI'

SERVES 6

Iassi is the ancient capital of Moldavia and was an important cultural centre at the turn of the century: the cradle of influential literary figures as well as of a marked obsession with Western values and traditions, and especially with France. This influence is evident in this Romanian version of a 'noble' French 'cream of...' soup, (in this case a Potage Germiny) served by French-educated Iassi hostesses to their equally cosmopolitan guests, as a contrast to the native soured soups redolent of country cooking. The Romanian taste for a tangy broth wins through, however, both in the choice of sorrel, a fairly sharp plant, and in the use of acidulated soured cream for the creamy finish.

Sorrel can only be used when very young, so this soup is ideally suited to early spring. Chop off all the sorrel roots and wash the leaves several times in running water to eliminate all the sand and grit. Shred the leaves into long thin strips, reserving 5-6 nice whole leaves for decoration. Melt the butter in a saucepan and sweat chopped sorrel leaves, covered, for about 5 minutes over a low flame. Peel and dice potatoes into small cubes.

Bring stock to the boil and place the sorrel leaves in it, together with the salt and

---

8 oz./250 gr. very young sorrel leaves
2 pts./1 l. chicken or veal stock
2 potatoes
2 oz./60 gr. butter
½ tsp. salt
2 egg yolks
5 fluid oz./150 ml. soured cream

---

diced potatoes. Bring back to the boil and simmer for 30 minutes.

Separate the eggs and whisk the cream into the yolks in a large bowl.

When the soup is ready, whisk ½ pt./300 ml. of the liquid into the eggs and cream very slowly at first, then in a steady trickle, until fully blended. Continue stirring and add the rest of the soup in a thin trickle as well.

Pour soup back into the saucepan and return it to the fire, over a moderate flame, stirring continuously, for 5 minutes. Do not allow soup to boil again, as it might curdle eggs and cream.

Blanch reserved whole sorrel leaves in boiling water for 1 minute, cool them under running cold water and add to the soup. Serve warm but not too hot.

A farmhouse. Buzău, Romania.

A fisherman's house and windmill. Dobrudja, Romania.

The Old University Building. Bucharest, Romania c. 1920.

The Athenée Concert Hall, a centre of social life. Bucharest, Romania c. 1920.

The Castle at Bran, reputedly the home of Dracula. Transylvania, Romania c.1920.

The Monastery of Keïa. The Teleajen Valley, Romania c. 1920.

A Street in the old Turkish Quarter, Sarajevo, Yugoslavia c. 1910.

Fruit Market. Bosnia, Yugoslavia c. 1910.

Inside a Romanian home c. 1910.

The Church of the Magi ('Trei Ierarhi')at Jassy, Romania, nineteenth-century engraving.

The Tismana Falls and Monastery. Valachia, Romania c. 1910.

BULGARIAN HOT BEAN SOUP
SERVES 8

Soak the beans overnight. Drain, cover with cold water and bring to the boil. When they start foaming, drain again. Cover with 4 pt./2 l. of well flavoured beef stock. Add the quartered carrots, onions, parsnips, salt, pepper, chillies. Add thinly sliced cabanos sausage and the pork or bacon, cut into large chunks. Simmer over a low flame for about 1½ hours, or until the beans break between your fingers. Add tomato purée and simmer for another 10

A fiery, warming soup for snow bound winter nights on the Danube plains.

1 lb./500 gr. haricot beans
2 oz./60 gr. dried cabanos sausage
6 oz./180 gr. piece belly of pork or smoked bacon
2 carrots
2 parsnips or parsley root
2 onions
4 pt./2 l. beef stock
salt
pepper
2 small dried chilli peppers
2 tblsp. tomato puree

minutes. The liquid will reduce by about half. Drain and reserve liquid. Reserve the pieces of meat and sausage and boiled onions. Discard the other vegetables. Set aside ¼ of the beans and blend the rest while still hot with the onions, to obtain a thick paste. Skim the fat off the reserved liquid. Thin the bean paste with this liquid, then put back meat and cabanos pieces and the reserved beans. Reheat gently and serve.

CAULIFLOWER SOUP WITH SMETANA
SERVES 4

Wash and trim the cauliflower and separate into florets. Boil florets in 2 pts./1 l. chicken stock or salted water.
In the meantime, melt the butter and make a roux by mixing with the flour.
Take a ladle of the soup liquid and pour over the roux, mixing constantly to avoid lumps. Pour the roux into the soup saucepan and simmer until cauliflower has

1 lb./500 gr. cauliflower
5 fluid oz./150 ml. soured cream or smetana
2 pt./1 l. chicken or veal stock
1 egg
1 tblsp. chopped fresh coriander
1 oz./30 gr. flour
2 oz./60 gr. butter
1 tsp. salt
¼ tsp. pepper

softened but is still 'al dente' (about 30 minutes in total).

In a tureen, beat eggs well and whisk in the soured cream or smetana. Pour a ladle of the soup over the smetana, mix well and then pour the rest of the soup over it (this is done to avoid the soured cream breaking up in contact with the hot soup). Add pepper, adjust seasoning and serve sprinkled with chopped fresh coriander.

COURGETTES AND SOURED CREAM SOUP

Grate the carrot on the fine teeth of a manual grater or in a food processor. Chop the green pepper into fine long strips. Peel the courgettes and dice them into ⅓"/1 cm. cubes. Blanch the tomatoes in plenty of boiling water for 1 minute and peel their skins off. Dice them as well.

Chop the onion finely. Heat oil, and sweat onion over a low flame until soft, but not brown. Add grated carrot and sweat for 4 minutes. Add pepper strips and sweat for 5 minutes. Add courgette cubes, cover and sweat on a very low flame for 10 minutes. Finally, add tomato cubes and sweat, covered, for another 5 minutes.

Transfer the contents of the

2 lb./1 kg. white baby marrows or large courgettes
3 pt./1.5 l. chicken or veal stock or water
1 carrot
1 large onion
1 green pepper
4 tomatoes
2 oz./60 gr. rice
3 tblsp. lemon juice or 1 pt./600 ml. BRAN BORSH
2 tblsp. chopped fresh lovage*
2 fluid oz./60 ml. oil
1 tsp. salt
⅓ tsp. white pepper
1 tsp. sugar (optional)
3 tblsp. soured cream
1 egg

frying pan into a saucepan and cover with 3 pts./1.5 l. chicken stock or water. Bring to the boil and add the rice.

Simmer uncovered for 30 minutes. Do not over boil – the courgette cubes must not disintegrate into a purée. Add lemon juice or – if you are using BRAN BORSH – add it now, but use only 2 pt./1 l. stock or water in the first place.

Add salt, pepper, lovage, and sugar if you wish. Boil for another 5 minutes.

In a tureen, mix the egg yolk with the soured cream. Slowly pour 2 tblsp. of the soup onto the soured cream mixture and mix well. Add a ladle of soup and mix again. Now you can pour the rest of the soup into the tureen without fear of the cream curdling. Serve warm but not too hot.

CREAM OF PEA SOUP

Chop the leek and onion roughly. Simmer the peas, leek, onion in the stock or lightly salted water until a pea taken between forefinger and thumb is easily crushed. In the meantime, trim the spinach and wash well in several waters to eliminate any sand or grit. Blanch in boiling water for 2 minutes. Drain the spinach and add to the peas. Simmer for a further 5 minutes. Drain well reserving the liquid and rub the vegetables trough a sieve or blend them in a

12 oz./360 gr. peas
1 onion
1 leek
4 oz./125 gr. spinach
2 pts./1 l. beef stock or water
2 pts./1 l. milk
¼ tsp. sugar
½ tsp. salt
¼ tsp. hot paprika
2 tblsp. fresh dill

food processor. You should get a fairly thick paste.

Mix puréed peas, etc. with 1 pt./600 ml. of the cooking liquid (you can concentrate

the stock by boiling it down to 1 pt./600 ml. or add the entire quantity of stock left and adjust the thickness of the soup when adding the milk). Bring back to the boil, simmer for 2 minutes, remove from the flame and add the milk, finely chopped dill, sugar, salt and paprika. Heat gently over a low flame, without boiling. Adjust seasoning and serve warm, but not hot, with croutons.

FISH DISHES

BAKED BREAM
SERVES 4-6

Preheat oven to G4/180C/355F.
Wash the fish well, gut it but do not scale. Sprinkle it, inside and out, with salt and paprika, place a sprig of parsley inside and place in a buttered ovenproof dish. Pour the vinegar, wine and oil over the fish. Dot all

---

1 sea bream (about 3 lb./1.5 kg.)
3 oz./90 gr. butter
½ tsp. hot paprika
1 tsp. salt
1 tblsp. white wine vinegar
½ tblsp. olive oil
1 tblsp. dry white wine
1 sprig parsley

---

over with butter and bake in the middle of the oven for 40-50 minutes until nicely browned on the outside and the flesh becomes flaky. Serve whole in the baking dish with LEEKS FILLED WITH RICE or MUSHROOMS IN SOURED CREAM.

ROBBERS' CARP
SERVES 8

Traditionally, a whole large carp was impaled on a wooden stick and wedged between two Y-shaped branches of oak. Two shallow holes were dug on either side of this improvised roasting spit and charcoal was burned in them until it glowed faintly. The carp was then rotated slowly and sprinkled continuously with oil and lemon juice until the heat rising from the charcoal, and its distinctive smells, penetrated into the fish.

The glowing spit made a fitting meeting point for a night gathering of 'haiduks': Balkanic highway robbers, occasionally touched by a Robin Hood-like grace.

De-scale the carp thoroughly, gut it and reserve its roe for other dishes (see CARP ROE SALAD). Slit carp on one side, leaving it attached at head and tail ends. Rub its skin all over with coarse salt and crushed garlic, if desired.
Place 2 bay leaves in cleaned belly.
Barbecue the carp on a spit for about 1 hour, rotating slowly and basting constantly with lemon juice and oil. Place fish about

---

1 carp (or pike or pike-perch)
  about 3 ½-5 lb./1½-2 kg.
2 tblsp. coarse salt
2 bay leaves
2 fluid oz./60 ml. lemon juice
2 fluid oz./60 ml. olive oil
2 tblsp. chopped parsley or
  coriander
3 cloves garlic (optional)

3"/9 cm. away from charcoal.
If you prefer barbecuing the fish over a charcoal grill, oil grill well and grill fish for 10 minutes either side on low

heat, making sure skin does not stick to the grill. Wrap the fish, covered in bay leaves, on both sides in tin foil and bake about 1"/3 cm. away from the charcoal for 40 minutes–1 hour (depending on size), opening the foil and basting with oil and lemon juice every 10 minutes.
Remove the bay leaves before serving and serve sprinkled with chopped parsley or coriander.

BAKED CARP
ON A BED OF CABBAGE

This is a superb way of serving carp, where the buttery taste of the fish contrasts with the slightly acid cabbage. It is also one of the best ways of incorporating the classic Romanian BRAISED SOURED CABBAGE (varza calita — literally 'tempered' cabbage) into a dish you can bring to the table to general applause. The colour combination of reddish brown cabbage with the golden fish decorated with lemon slices adds to the effect.

Preheat oven to G4/180C/355F.

Shred cabbage very finely, to vermicelli size. Heat oil in a large frying pan (you may have to do it in two batches) and add bay leaves. When the bay leaves begin to sizzle, add tomato purée and wine, reducing the heat to avoid splashing. Stir vigorously for 30 seconds, then add the shredded cabbage, peppercorns, crushed juniper berries and thyme and mix constantly until cabbage is completely coated with the wine and tomato mixture.

---

1 lb. 4 oz./600 gr. carp
1 lb. 4 oz./600 gr. white cabbage
4 tblsp. oil
2 tblsp. tomato purée
5 fluid oz./150 ml. dry white wine or vermouth
20 peppercorns
4 juniper berries
2 sprigs thyme
2 bay leaves

Place the cabbage in a baking tray or other large ovenproof dish in an even, thin layer. Place in the middle of a preheated oven and leave for 45 minutes or until cabbage is soft.

In the meantime, clean the carp and discard head, tails and fins. With a sharp knife, cut four indentations across, about 2"/6 cm. apart, to allow heat to penetrate easily. (If carp had any roe, you can use it for 'CARP ROE SALAD'.) Rub with 1 tblsp. oil on both sides. Place carp on top of the cabbage and replace in the oven for a further 1 ½ hours or until fish is nicely brown all over.

Serve with POLENTA CAKES or SPICY BEAN HOTPOT.

CARP STEAKS
IN GARLIC VINAIGRETTE

This and the following recipes for a variety of cold fish in sour dressings and marinades are the kind of 'drinking companions' you would expect at a lazy, 'al-fresco' dinner in a country courtyard in the middle of one of those scorching Romanian summers when even the pavements are melting in the cities and anyone with a modicum of sense and means leaves for the seaside, or the mountain villages turned into ad-hoc resorts for the duration. A variety of salads, cold soups and light fish dishes are spread on a trestle table in a shaded part of the courtyard, all designed to tickle the palate into the consumption of large quantities of new white wine brought straight from the cellar while farm dogs, chickens and children all round get drunk imbibing the mid-day sun. In short, they are the Balkans' answer to the Russian 'zakuski', but in order to satisfy the insatiable Romanian taste for sour things, a variety of dressings are used (based on vinegar, lemon juice or brine) as well as two types of 'marinades': one with a base of tomatoes blended into a sauce and the other based on vinaigrette.

Rub the carp steaks with salt and grill over a hot flame for a few minutes on each side until nicely browned. (Alternatively, fry in a hot cast iron pan without any fat).
Wipe the salt off and place the steaks in a shallow dish. Whisk oil, vinegar, paprika and crushed garlic into a

---

1 lb./500 gr. carp (or other firm white fish) cut in 4 steaks
½ tsp. coarse salt
2 fluid oz./60 ml. olive oil
4 fluid oz./120 ml. wine vinegar
¼ tsp. hot paprika
6 cloves garlic

---

homogenous liquid. Pour over the carp steaks and set aside in a cool place to marinate for a few hours. Serve with POLENTA or thick chunks of brown bread and butter.
The dish goes down particularly well accompanied by small glasses of iced vodka or plum brandy.

SERBIAN CARP

This is a traditional method for preparing fish (you can use it for any white juicy fish) characterised by the fact that the carp is first larded and then braised in sour cream on a bed of potatoes. There are several variants of this method, depending on their area of origin. Here is a traditional recipe from the Banat, (a region in Transylvania near the Yugoslav border) which borrows from the Serbs across the Danube the idea of keeping the potatoes moist and sweet by sprinkling grated carrots on them.

Preheat the oven to G5/190C/380F.
Lard the carp by making long shallow slits about 2"/6 cm. from each other across the whole fish. Stick pieces of bacon in the slits, trimming them to fit the size of the slits. Rub the fish with salt and pepper. Peel the potatoes and slice them into triangular, fairly thick slices. Slice green peppers and tomatoes into rings. Grate the carrot. Heat oil in a large frying pan and saute fish on both sides until golden, moving constantly to avoid sticking. Remove with a slotted spoon and reserve.
In the same oil, fry potatoes until slightly brown but not cooked through. Remove with slotted spoon and set aside.
Now fry the pepper rings for up to 5 minutes, until slightly brown. Remove with slotted spoon and set aside.
Finally, chop onion finely, reduce heat and sweat over a

---

2 lb./1 kg. carp, gutted and scaled, with roe (at the famous Gundel's Restaurant in Budapest they use skinless fillets of carp for this recipe – if you prefer your fish boneless ask your fishmonger to remove head, tail and spine and allow about 6 oz./180 gr. per person)
4 oz./125 gr. smoked bacon
2 lb./1 kg. potatoes
1 lb./500 gr. green pepper
2 oz./60 gr. carrots
8 oz./250 gr. onions
8 oz./250 gr. tomatoes
14 fluid oz./420 ml. soured cream
5 fluid oz./150 ml. oil
2 fluid oz./60 ml. dry white wine
2 small sprigs of thyme
2 tblsp. chopped parsley
½ tsp. black pepper
1 tsp. salt
2 tsp. mild paprika

---

gentle flame until soft and gold.
Grease a deep baking tray or other ovenproof dish and line it with the potato slices. Sprinkle the grated carrot over the potatoes. Place the fish on top. Crush the carp roe (optional) with a fork and mix with the wine and onion to make a thin paste. Spread it over the carp. Cover with green pepper rings and with the slices of tomato at the very top. Sprinkle the thyme, lightly chopped, over the tomatoes. If you are not using roe, slice onions in rings rather than chopping them and fry as above. Omit the wine and place onion rings as the first layer over the carp.
Pour 10 fluid oz./300 ml. soured cream on top and around the fish. Sprinkle with paprika.
Bake in preheated oven until fish is brown on top and potatoes are soft inside. (45 minutes–1 hour, depending on the size of the fish).
Before serving, pour another 4 fluid oz./120 ml. soured cream on top and sprinkle with chopped parlsey.

CARP FILLETS IN BRINE (SARAMURA)

SERVES 6 as a starter or 4 as main course

Cold fish fillets or steaks, fried or grilled and served in a brine flavoured with paprika (saramura) are great Romanian favourites, especially when eaten with a piping hot POLENTA. They make ideal party dishes, as the fish fillets become very meaty and are easily sliced into individual portions when served, but look spectacular displayed whole in a shallow serving dish. Carp is the fish most often given this treatment, but you can use any meaty fish like pike, bream or even sturgeon: the flavour of the fish is not spoiled, as the method requires a minimum of cooking, while the sharp brine brings out the meaty texture of a good fish. The method is also suitable for small fish, eaten whole, like whitebait or small sardines.

Brush each fish fillet with oil and grill or fry quickly over a hot flame for 4-5 minutes. Cook the skinless side first, then turn fillets skin-side to the flame.

Bring the water or fish stock to the boil (the latter makes for a far better 'saramura', but the fish will have to be eaten immediately, otherwise

2 large carp fillets (from a 2 lb./1 kg. carp)
1 tsp. olive oil
1 tsp. hot paprika or 1 hot green chilli, chopped
5 fluid oz./150 ml. water or fish stock
1 tsp. salt

the stock will set). Add salt, paprika or chopped chilli and boil for 3-4 minutes. Place fish fillets in a serving dish skin downwards and pour boiling brine over them. Allow them to cool completely and serve with a very hot POLENTA or on a bed of hot BRAISED SOURED CABBAGE.

CARP IN GARLIC ASPIC
SERVES 4

Clean the carp, and cut off the head, tail and fins and set these aside. Remove the triangular, bitter bone between the head and body of the fish, then slice the carp into 4 equal steaks. Set aside.

Chop the onion roughly and boil in the water. When it is soft, drain the water and reserve. Sieve the onion, or purée in a food processor. Replace liquid on the heat and add carrot, bay leaf and peppercorns. Bring back to the boil and add the fish head, tail and fins. Boil on a medium flame for 10-15 minutes. Add the carp steaks and boil for another 5 minutes. Remove steaks carefully with a slotted spoon and set aside on a

1 lb./500 gr. whole carp
8 oz./250 gr. onions
2 pt./1 l. water
1 small carrot
1 small parsnip or parsley root
5 cloves garlic
1 bay leaf
10 peppercorns
1 tsp. salt
2 tsp. mild or medium paprika

deep platter or individual deep dishes.

Try the liquid: if a drop taken between forefinger and thumb feels sticky, the liquid will set well. If not, boil liquid for a further 10-15 minutes.*

Strain and discard vegetables and fish head, etc. (reserving bay leaf and carrot for decoration). Mix in puréed onions and the finely crushed cloves of garlic. Season well with salt and paprika.

Pour seasoned liquid over carp steaks and allow aspic to set in the fridge for a few hours. You can decorate the aspic with boiled carrot cut in thin rounds and bay leaf, placed on top of the fish steaks before pouring the liquid.

If the liquid has not thickened enough and is in danger of reducing too much, you can add a sachet of gelatine, mixed in one cup of the hot liquid. Do not bring liquid to the boil after adding gelatine.

A good sized carp head, however, should provide enough gelatine to allow liquid to set well.

SERBIAN COD
SERVES 4

Preheat oven to G3/170C/335F.

Soak the cod fillets in salt water for about ½ hour (about 2 tsp. salt to 2 pt./1 l. water).

Peel and slice the potatoes into thin slices and onion into thin rings. Line an ovenproof dish with the potato and onion rounds and dot with butter. Slice tomatoes into thin rounds and place on top of the potatoes. Season with the salt and pepper and sprinkle with the wine. Cover with a

1 lb./500 gr. cod fillets
1 onion
4 tomatoes
1 lb./500 gr. new potatoes
2 oz./60 gr. butter
5 fluid oz./150 ml. soured cream
or yoghurt
3 fluid oz./90 ml. Riesling wine
or dry Tokay*
1 tsp. hot paprika
3 tsp. salt
½ tsp. pepper
1 tblsp. chopped parsley

lightly dampened linen cloth making sure the cloth does not touch vegetables. Bake at the top of the oven for about 35 minutes or until potatoes are half-cooked. Rinse fish fillets in running cold water and pat dry with a clean cloth. Place fish on the vegetables, sprinkle with paprika and pour soured cream or yoghurt on top. Increase oven temperature to G5/190C/380F and bake fish for another 35 minutes or until potatoes are soft and moist and fish has become flaky. Serve hot, sprinkled with chopped parsley.

MARINADED HERRINGS

SERVES 4 - 6

Clean the herrings and remove the back bone. (If you get your fishmonger to do it make sure he gives you the roe.) Cut into chunky pieces (about 6 pieces from each fish) and place them in a clean medium size jar (1 lb. 8 oz./700 gr.), alternating layers of fish, onion rings and very finely sliced carrot. Add blanched olives, juniper berries, peppercorns, mustard seeds and bay leaves.
Pound herring roe in a

This recipe is usually made with Danube sweet water herrings, but if you cannot get them sea herrings or mackerel will do.

2 medium herrings (13 oz./400 gr. when cleaned and headless) with their roe
1 small (2 oz./60 gr.) carrot
2 oz./60 gr. thin onion rings
½ tsp. mustard seeds
20 peppercorns
2 bay leaves
6 black olives
5 tblsp. oil
3 tblsp. vinegar
small branch of thyme
10 juniper berries

bowl, adding oil very slowly, to make a thick paste. Thin it with the vinegar until you obtain a whitish liquid. Pour it over the fish and vegetables – it should just cover them. Add 1"/3 cm. oil to top liquid up and tie a cloth or clingfilm tightly around the mouth of the jar to make sure the metal lid does not come into contact with the marinade. Marinate in the fridge for at least 1 month.

DANUBE HERRING IN MUSTARD SAUCE

SERVES 4

Split the fish along its side and remove roe. Soak in water overnight to remove excess salt. Remove the spine with a sharp knife. Cut the fish in 2"/6 cm. wide slices and place in a shallow dish. With a wooden spoon mix roe and mustard until smooth. Add oil, little by

8 oz./250 gr. whole smoked kipper (with roe)
2 tsp. mustard
2 fl. oz./60 ml. oil
2 tblsp. lemon juice
4 black olives

little, to obtain a mayonnaise-like consistency.

Add lemon juice to taste. Pour the sauce over fish and allow to marinate for a few hours. Serve decorated with black olives and sprinkled with coarsely ground black pepper or juniper berries. A potatoe and cumin salad is sometimes served with the herring.

PIKE-PERCH
SERVES 6

Pike-Perch* (Zander) is the great freshwater fish delicacy of the Balkans. It is a ferociously predatory fish and therefore very meaty, with little of the fat one so often finds in lesser lake-bred fishes. It comes in different sizes, from the giant pikes (Fogas) of Lake Balaton in Hungary which can grow to 30 lb./14 kg.; to small, 1 lb./500 gr., pikes caught by amateur anglers all over Romania. There are innumerable Balkanic recipes built around pike and the fish takes pride of place in Hungarian cuisine as well.

Salt the fish fillets with ½ tsp. salt and sprinkle with lemon juice.
Set aside in the fridge.
Boil the fish head, bones, tail and skin together with ½ the pickling onions, bay leaf, peppercorns and ½ tsp. salt, to make about 10 fluid oz./300 ml. concentrated fish stock.
Wash and slice the mushrooms in fine slices.
Melt butter in a frying pan and sweat mushrooms with the remaining onions until the latter have softened.
Scrub potatoes (or peel and cut them into 2″/6 cm. cubes if you cannot get small ones). Place in a saucepan, without water.
Place fish fillets in a large pan on a bed of sweated mushrooms and onions, pour wine over them and

---

2 lb./1 kg. pike-perch or pike, filleted (ask a good fishmonger, he will get it for you on 24 hours notice). Keep skin, head, tail and spine!
10 oz./300 gr. mushrooms
1 lb./500 gr. new, small potatoes
1 bay leaf
4 oz./125 gr. butter
4 oz./125 gr. small (pickling) onions or spring onions
2 fluid oz./60 ml. lemon juice
6 fluid oz./180 ml. dry white wine
1 tsp. salt
12 peppercorns
5 fluid oz./150 ml. thick soured cream
1 tblsp. chopped parsley

---

strain fish stock over them as well. Cook over a low flame for 15 minutes.
Remove fillets gently onto a hot serving plate with a slotted spoon.
Strain liquid through a sieve into the saucepan with the potatoes, bring back to the boil and boil over a moderate flame, uncovered, until potatoes are cooked.
Arrange the mushrooms and onions left in the sieve around and over the fillets.
Discard bay leaf and peppercorns. Place boiled potatoes all around fish fillets when ready.
Away from the flame, mix into the boiling liquid, which should have reduced by about ½, 5 fluid oz./150 ml. soured cream. Sprinkle with coarsely chopped parsley, pour over the fish and potatoes and serve immediately.

STUFFED PIKE-PERCH

To tenderize the pike flesh, rub it inside and out with salt as soon as you have bought it and leave for 2-3 hours in the fridge. Wash it well, both inside and out, scale and trim fins and tail with a pair of scissors.

Make a small incision along the belly and start prizing the skin off by gently introducing a small, fairly blunt knife between skin and flesh with a circular motion, so that at the end the skin is attached only to the head. Alternatively, remove head and start by prising the neck skin first, then hold the neck flesh with one hand and pull skin off with the other hand, like a glove turned inside out. The skin should remain attached in the end only at the tail.

Either way, the aim is to obtain as clean a pike skin as possible. Do not worry if bits of fish remain attached to the skin: simply scrape them off with a knife and reserve – you will soon mince the rest of the flesh as well. Wash skin and sprinkle with a little salt.

With a sharper knife, remove as much of the flesh from the spine as you can. Add it to the scrapings from the skin, if any. Reserve bones and head.

Soak the crustless bread in milk for a few minutes and squeeze out as much of the liquid as you can by hand. Mince fish meat and soaked bread together in a mincer

Because of its meaty, somewhat dry texture, pike is ideally suited for stuffing with a combination of vegetables and minced fatty bacon. Edward VII was a great lover of stuffed pike and it was always prepared for him on his visits to Marienbad, where he went regularly to take the waters. There are two basic recipes for stuffed pike: with a savoury and with a sweetened filling. (see below: 'BUKOVINA' STUFFED PIKE-PERCH).

3 lbs./1.5 kg. whole pike* or pike-perch*, (incl. head)
1 carrot
1 onion
4 potatoes
2 eggs
2 oz./60 gr. mushrooms
2 oz./60 gr. fat bacon
1 slice white bread, crust removed
2 tblsp. milk
2 fluid oz./60 ml. olive oil
1-2 tsp. salt
½ tsp. freshly ground black pepper
½ tblsp. fresh chopped parsley
2 anchovies (optional)
1 tsp. fresh thyme
1 tsp. chopped chives or spring onions
5 fluid oz./150 ml. dry white wine or vermouth
4 oz./125 gr. butter

or food processor. Add oil, mixing well to make a paste. Chop the mushrooms into medium pieces. Chop the bacon, chives and anchovies finely. Heat a little oil in a frying pan and fry bacon for

3 minutes. Add chives, then mushrooms and sweat on a low flame for 5 minutes. Mix eggs into the fish paste, add 1 tsp. salt, pepper, thyme, parsley, anchovies and the contents of the frying pan. Mix well until smooth. Squeeze all remaining water out of the skin and fill it with the fish mixture. Reshape it into its original fish shape and sow the head (or tail) opening as well as any tears that might have occurred. You can now either:

A. bake the fish by rubbing it with butter and placing it in a buttered long ovenproof dish in the middle of a preheated (G4/180C/355F) oven for 1 hour, basting it constantly with butter, or

B. boil the stuffed pike in a mixture of wine and vegetables. Place fish in a long shallow casserole and pour wine diluted in an equal quantity of water all around it. Slice the carrot, onion, and halve potatoes. Place them around the fish with all the fish bones you have reserved and the fish head. Boil, covered, for 1 hour over a low flame. Remove fish with a slotted spoon, boil down cooking liquid to about 4 fluid oz./120 ml. and pour over the fish.

Serve either hot or cold, sliced into individual 'steaks' and surrounded by lemon quarters and the boiled vegetables.

'BUKOVINA'
STUFFED PIKE-PERCH
SERVES 4-6

This traditional recipe comes from Bukovina, a region at the edge of the Balkans proper, which passed in turn through Polish, Austrian and Romanian hands and is now in the Soviet Union. At the turn of the century there was a large Jewish population in Bukovina and sweetened stuffed pike is often eaten to this day at the Passover meal, combining the traditional requirement to eat fish on the festive night with a regional taste for sweetened savoury dishes.

Trim, scale, wash and skin the pike as shown at STUFFED PIKE-PERCH. Remove all the flesh from the spine and add it to the scraps from the skin. Chop 1 onion finely and sweat in a little oil on a low flame until you have obtained a golden purée. Soak the bread in milk and squeeze out excess liquid by hand. Pass the fish, bread, onions, salt, pepper, through a fine mincer or blend in a food processor. Add beaten egg white, parsley, marjoram, sultanas and sugar. Mix well and add the oil little by little at the end. Fill the fish skin with this mixture, reform fish into its original shape and sew opening and any tears that might have occurred.

3 lb./1.5 kg. whole pike* or pike-perch*, including head
2 tblsp. sugar
1 egg white
2 slices white bread, crust removed
2 oz./60 gr. plump sultanas
4 fluid oz./120 ml. milk
2 onions
2 carrots
5 fluid oz./150 ml. oil
1 tsp. salt
½ tsp. freshly ground black pepper
4-6 potatoes
½ tsp. sweet marjoram
1 tsp. fresh chopped parsley
6 peppercorns
5 fluid oz./150 ml. dry white wine or vermouth

In a long saucepan, boil the fish trimmings, chopped second onion, carrots and potatoes, fish bones and head, peppercorns, ½ tsp. salt, covered, for 30 minutes in 1 pt./600 ml. water. Add fish to the stock, prick the skin with a needle to avoid bursting, add wine and simmer for another 30 minutes. Allow the fish to cool in the boiling liquid, slice into 4-6 'steaks' and reshape on a platter, adding head if you wish. Strain cooking liquid over the fish and serve cold, surrounded by boiled potatoes and decorated with carrot slices and chopped parsley.

STURGEON

Romania has some of the best sturgeon* fishing grounds in the world, at the confluence of the Danube Delta with the Black Sea. Up until fairly recently, sturgeon and its family (sterlet – the small type, with the best caviar; 'nisetru' the larger type, with the best flesh; and the lesser prized 'morun' and 'cega' varieties which can grow up to 30 lb./60 kg. in weight) could be ordered at two or three of the best restaurants in Bucharest, either as 'batog' – that is smoked and sliced very thinly, like a salami; or fresh, cooked more or less in the way that a good Western chef might treat turbot: grilled, fried or steamed with great respect for the superb white, meaty flesh of the fish which spurns any fussy additions. In this country sturgeon has been a 'royal' fish since a mediaeval decree ordered that only the Sovereign could eat a sturgeon caught in English waters. As this is nowadays an extremely rare occurrence (the first sturgeon of the season is still offered to the Queen, nevertheless) you can safely indulge this great luxury on the (not so rare) occasions when sturgeon* is on sale at Billingsgate.

My favourite way of eating sturgeon, ever since the times in my childhood when I used to be taken by my father for a grand treat at 'Capsha's' – the grandest and most famous of all Bucharest restaurants – is to simply grill the fish, cut in thick steaks and then either eat it hot with melted butter or with a tangy sauce 'à la grecque' or cold, as sturgeon ZAKUSKA. In an old, eighteenth century 'Fanariot' recipe, sturgeon was steamed on a bed of bay leaves, sprinkled with lemon juice and stuffed with olives.

Sturgeon is easier to clean if you place the fish in a long pan and pour boiling water on top of its skin. The scales will then come off easily when scraped with a knife. The black, shiny skin should become smooth. When fish is clean, cut it into four thick steaks with a sharp knife. Brush with olive oil, sprinkle with salt and grill over a hot grill for 5-7 minutes on each side, taking care the flesh does not burn. Brush both the fish and the grill constantly with oil. The fish should become a reddish-brown colour, criss-crossed by the black grill lines. Sprinkle with chopped parsley and lemon juice and

2 lb./1 kg. sturgeon*
1 tsp. salt
2 fluid oz./60 ml. olive oil
1 lemon
1 tblsp. fresh chopped parsley

For the sauce
a. 4 oz./125 gr. unsalted butter

or

b. 3 fluid oz./90 ml. olive oil
3 fluid oz./150 ml. soda water
1 lemon
¼ tsp. freshly ground black pepper
2 tblsp. fresh chopped parsley
½ tsp. salt

either pour melted butter on top and serve decorated with lemon slices or make the sauce 'à la grecque':

Place the soda water in a bowl and add chopped parsley, oil, pepper, the juice of the lemon and the salt. Whisk sauce with a wire whisk until frothy. The sauce should be quite tangy and sharp to contrast with the hot, meaty fish.

If you want the sturgeon to go a little further, you can cut the raw fish into cubes and place the fish cubes on up to 6 skewers, alternating with lemon slices. Grill as above and serve with the tangy sauce in a bowl for dipping the sturgeon cubes. The sturgeon zakuska is made as shown at FISH ZAKUSKA.

MARINADED TROUT

Preheat oven to G5/190C/ 380F.

Chop the onion and carrots into fine slices.

Clean the trout inside and out and rub with a little salt. Heat the oil until it is smoking and sauté the trout for 3-4 minutes on each side, making sure skin does not stick to the pan, then remove with a slotted spoon and set aside in a casserole large enough to take fish in one layer.

In the same oil, fry chopped onion and carrot for 4-5 minutes, lowering heat to moderate. Add flour and mix well to make a roux. Fry for a further 5 minutes. Mix tomato paste with a little water and add it to the pan. Add paprika, salt, bay

In the Balkans, steaks of carp, bream, cod, even sturgeon are used for this aromatic cold or hot dish. Trout is excellent in the wine and tomato sauce which sets off its delicate flavour.

---

4 medium trout, about 8 oz./250 gr. each
3 oz./90 gr. carrots
1 onion
3 fluid oz./90 ml. oil
3 fluid oz./90 ml. dry white wine or vermouth
3 oz./90 gr. flour
2 tblsp. tomato paste
2 bay leaves
10 peppercorns
1 tsp. salt
1½ tblsp. white wine vinegar
½ tsp. hot paprika
1 sprig thyme or ½ tsp. dry thyme
2 oz./60 gr. of the tiniest button mushrooms (optional)

---

leaves, peppercorns, vinegar, wine or vermouth and thyme. Reduce heat to low, cover and simmer for ½ hour. The resulting marinade should be fairly sharp and tangy. Add optional mushrooms for the last 5 minutes.

Pour the marinade over the trout in the casserole and adjust seasoning. Bring back to the boil, then place at the top of the preheated oven for 10-15 minutes, or until trout is nicely browned and the flesh comes easily away from the bones. Serve hot with POLENTA CAKES or even better, cold with TOMATOES FILLED WITH PEPPERS and AUBERGINE CAVIAR.

TROUT IN SOURED CREAM

Clean, gut and wash the trout well. Remove heads if you wish. Rub the fish with salt and fill their bellies with chopped herbs. Roll them in breadcrumbs and fry them in the heated oil over a moderate flame for about 5 minutes on each side. Remove with a slotted spoon, turn up the heat and sauté pine kernels over a

---

4 trout (about 8 oz./250 gr. each)
10 fluid oz./300 ml. soured cream
1 tblsp. chopped dill
1 tblsp. chopped parsley
2 tsp. salt
4 fluid oz./120 ml. oil
2 tblsp. breadcrumbs
1-2 oz./30-60 gr. pine kernels

---

lively flame for about 3

minutes, shaking pan to avoid sticking.

Place the fried trout in a pan large enough to take them side by side, pour cream on top, add pine kernels but not any remaining oil and simmer over a low flame, covered, for 5-6 minutes. Serve with boiled new potatoes and a BULGARIAN 'SHOPSKA' SALAD.

BRAISED WHITEBAIT WITH GREEN HERBS

SERVES 6-8

Preheat oven to G6/200C/
400F.
Wash the fish and pat dry.
Sprinkle with pepper and
place in an ovenproof dish,
preferably in one layer.
Chop onion finely and
spread over the fish. Crush
the garlic, mix with the
vinegar and the salt to make
a paste and spread it over

2 lb./1 kg. whitebait or fresh
  small sardines
6 cloves garlic
4 fluid oz./120 ml. fish stock
4 fluid oz./120 ml. dry white
  wine
5 fluid oz./150 ml. olive oil
2 fluid oz./60 ml. white wine
  vinegar
1 tblsp. chopped fresh parsley
1 tblsp. chopped fresh coriander
4 oz./125 gr. onions
2 tblsp. lemon juice
1 bay leaf
½ tsp. pepper
2 tsp. salt

the fish.
Around it pour the oil,
chopped coriander and
parsley, fish stock, wine and
lemon juice.
Place in the preheated oven
for 40 minutes. The dish can
be eaten hot, although it is
traditionally served cold,
with wedges of lemon.

THE 'SCAPET'S' FISH 'ZAKUSKA'

SERVES 4

'Zakuska' is a Russian word meaning 'snack'. In Romania the word was used until 1860 as the general term for lunch, but has now reverted to its more specialized use to describe a cold snack of fish or vegetable cooked in a rich tomato sauce and often flavoured with wine or vodka. This tradition was maintained in the Romanian repertoire by the small Russian minority living in Romania. Most of these live in the Danube Delta and work mainly as fishermen there and along the Black Sea. A small sect of Russians, however, the 'scapet', moved to the cities where they monopolized the trade of coach driving until the advent of the car. These mysterious, hugely fat coachmen were said to follow the strict rules of their sect which required the men to castrate themselves as soon as they had children. They could still be seen driving their black victorias in small towns until the late fifties, taciturn, sallow complexed and forbidding – the ideal eunuchs to lead clandestine amorous rides in their coaches in summer and in horse-drawn sledges in winter.

Preheat oven G4/180C/355F. Rub fish steaks with salt. Heat 2 tblsp. oil in a frying pan and sauté fish steaks until slightly brown on both sides and firm to the touch. (Alternatively, grill fish steaks under a fierce flame until lightly brown and firm).

Cut the carrots, parsnips and pickled cucumber into thin rounds and boil until carrots are almost soft. Chop onion into quarter rings and fry lightly in the rest of the oil. Blanch the tomatoes in boiling water and sieve or blend to make a thin tomato sauce.

Mix the boiled carrot, parsnip, fried onion and cucumber into the tomato sauce. Adjust seasoning, adding salt if needed. Bring to the boil and bubble for 20 sec. Add fried or grilled fish, bay leaf, peppercorns and pour wine or vodka diluted in tomato sauce on top. Place in preheated oven for ½ hour. Cool and serve cold. As with VEGETABLE 'ZAKUSKA' the dish will keep for several weeks or even months if you allow it to cool, place it in a jar, tie the jar mouth with greaseproof paper and boil the jar in a saucepan of boiling water for ½ hour. Keep in the fridge.

---

4 fish steaks (about 6-8 oz./180-250 gr. each) – in the Balkans bream, carp or pike would be used, but any meaty white fish will do. Try grey mullet, cod, or – my favourite – conger eel.

3 tblsp. oil

2 carrots

2 parsley roots or parsnips

8 oz./250 gr. tomatoes

1 onion

1 cucumber, pickled in vinegar

2 tblsp. dry white wine (or 1½ tblsp. tomato sauce with ½ tblsp. vodka)

1 bay leaf

12 peppercorns

1 tsp. salt

FISH RATATOUILLE
('GHIVECI')
SERVES 4

Preheat oven to G4/180C/ 355F.

Clean the fish and remove tail and head. Rub the skin with coarse salt and leave for as long as it takes to prepare the vegetables. Chop onion finely and fry lightly in 1 tblsp. oil. When it starts to brown, add carrot, celery, parsnip, all finely sliced. When they begin to soften, add tomatoes or tomato paste (diluted in a cup of water) and bay leaf, peas, beans and peppercorns. If you have used fresh tomatoes, add a cupful of water, cover and simmer on a low heat until almost soft (about 30

'Ghiveci' is the Balkanic form of ratatouille. But whereas in a good, Provençale ratatouille every vegetable is cooked separately, a good 'ghiveci' is appreciated for the mellow blending of the ingredients, slowly simmered together in a tomato sauce.

---

1 lb./500 gr. white firm fish (traditionally carp, pike or sturgeon, but you can use brill, grey mullet or halibut with excellent results)
3 tblsp. vegetable oil
1 medium onion
1 carrot
1 parsnip or parsley root
1 celery stalk
2 ripe tomatoes or 1 tblsp. tomato paste
2 oz./60 gr. green peas
1 oz./30 gr. green beans, sliced in length
2 peppercorns
salt
1 bay leaf

---

minutes). Cut the fish into 2"/6 cm. thick steaks. Test the beans, and when they are almost cooked, place the fish steaks on top of the vegetables, adding 2 tblsp. oil. Either cover and simmer over a medium flame for 15 minutes or place at the top of the preheated oven for 15 minutes. The liquid ought to evaporate almost completely, but if the dish is getting too dry add a little water.

Place on a serving dish, allow to cool. Serve cold, with POLENTA. The dish will improve left overnight to mellow and for the flavours to blend into each other.

POULTRY
AND
GAME DISHES

TRANSYLVANIAN CHICKEN PAPRIKA WITH DUMPLINGS

SERVES 4

'Paprika' dishes have spread all over the Balkans from their Hungarian roots. There are, however, distinct differences, as in this Transylvanian version in which the 'paprika' method — cooking meat or poultry with onions smothered in paprika and small quantities of liquid which are gradually absorbed — is complemented by a tomato sauce rather than the Hungarian soured cream sauce. I am a great fan of the soured cream version, however, (used in Romania as well, of course, but in a different recipe, flavoured with dill, rather than paprika) so here is a recipe for spring chicken cooked by the 'paprika' method, but with two different finishes.

As for the dumplings, they are traditionally 'galushka'-type dumplings, that is small (bite-sized), flour based dumplings (see TRANSYLVANIAN GALUSHKA DUMPLINGS).

Joint the chicken into 4 pieces. Chop the onion very finely. Melt the fat in a large frying pan and brown chicken pieces in it until the skins turn golden brown. Remove with a slotted spoon and sprinkle with salt. Put chopped onions in the frying pan, reduce heat and sweat onions until they are soft and resemble a golden purée.

Take the pan away from the flame (paprika burns easily) and mix in the two kinds of paprika powder. Replace chicken pieces over the onions and either

A: pour ½ the chicken stock, increase the flame and simmer for about ½ hour or until chicken is cooked through, replenishing stock from time to time, or

---

1 spring chicken, up to 3 lb./1.5
   kg. in weight
1 large onion
2 oz./60 gr. lard or oil
1 tblsp. mild paprika
¼ tsp. hot paprika
1 tblsp. tomato paste or 10 fluid
   oz./300 ml. soured cream
1 tsp. salt
5 fluid oz./150 ml. chicken stock

B: dissolve tomato paste in the whole quantity of chicken stock, pour it over the chicken and place, uncovered, in the middle of a preheated oven (G6/200C/400F) for ½ hour. The tomato sauce will be fairly thick. Mix in the dumplings for the last 5 minutes of cooking and serve immediately.

If you have chosen the first method, remove the chicken from the pan when ready and keep on a heated plate. Increase heat to full and bubble up cooking juices for 5 minutes. Remove from fire, skim off any fat that has risen to the surface, and mix in the soured cream. Replace on a gentle flame, add galushka dumplings and allow sauce to bubble only once more. Pour ½ the sauce over the chicken pieces, decorate with dumplings all around (their bright white should contrast with the golden chicken and the light pink of the sauce) and serve immediately with the remaining sauce on the side and accompanied by a CUCUMBER AND DILL SALAD.

COUNTRY SPRING CHICKEN WITH TOMATOES

SERVES 4-6

Clean the chicken and rub with salt and pepper. Quarter the chicken and brown pieces in the heated oil until brown on all sides and the juices are sealed in. Remove from the pan with a slotted spoon and set aside. Chop the leeks or spring onions finely. Sweat in the same fat as the chicken, lowering the flame, until soft but not brown. Blanch the tomatoes in plenty of boiling water for 3-4 minutes. Peel skins and

1 young spring chicken, about 2 lb./1 kg., preferably corn fed
2 lb./1 kg. ripe tomatoes
1 lb./500 gr. young leeks or spring onions
3 fluid oz./90 ml. oil
4 fluid oz./150 ml. soured cream
7 fluid oz./200 ml. chicken stock or water
1 tsp. salt
½ tsp. pepper
1 tsp. taragon or fresh thyme
2 tsp. lemon juice
2 tblsp. chopped parsley
6 black olives (optional)

add to the frying pan together with the lemon juice and taragon or thyme. When the tomatoes have collapsed pour stock over them, add chicken pieces, cover and simmer for ½ hour or until chicken pieces have cooked through. Remove the pan from the heat, mix in the soured cream and serve generously sprinkled with coarsely chopped parsley and black olives if you wish.

SPRING CHICKEN WITH PEARS

SERVES 4-6

Preheat oven to G5/190C/380F.
Joint the spring chicken into 4-6 pieces, and rub them with salt. Melt ½ the butter in a large frying pan and brown chicken pieces on both sides, until skin turns golden brown.
Wash the pears, without peeling. Quarter them, discard the hard middle bits and the seed boxes. Slice into thin slices.
Melt the remaining butter in the frying pan and fry the pear slices for 5 minutes on

1 good size spring chicken, about 3 lb./1.5 kg., preferably corn fed
1 lb./500 gr. pears
4 oz./120 gr. butter
1½ tblsp. sugar
2 fluid oz./60 ml. dry white wine or vermouth
1 tblsp. lemon juice
1 tsp. salt
1 tblsp. fresh chopped coriander
¼ tsp. freshly ground black pepper

each side or until half softened.

Place a layer of pears in a saucepan, put the chicken pieces on top and cover with remaining pear slices. Dissolve the sugar in the wine and pour sauce into the casserole. Add fresh coriander, pepper and braise in the preheated oven for 45 minutes or until chicken is fully cooked.
Just before removing from the oven sprinkle with lemon juice. Serve hot with a BULGARIAN 'SHOPSKA' SALAD.

CHICKEN BREAST BAKE
SERVES 4

Preheat oven to G5/190C/ 380F.

Chop the onion finely and sweat in a little oil until soft but not brown. Mince the chicken breast. Remove crust from bread and soak in milk for a few minutes.

In a bowl, mix well the chicken, onion, bread, dill, eggs, 1 tblsp. breadcrumbs, tomato, until mixture is

6 oz./180 gr. chicken breast, boned, skinned and trimmed
1 tblsp. vegetable oil
1 onion
1 slice white bread
2 fluid oz./60 ml. milk
2 eggs
1½ tblsp. breadcrumbs
2 heaped tblsp. chopped fresh dill
1 tomato, blanched and cubed
¼ tsp. salt
¼ tsp. freshly ground black pepper or cayenne
4 fluid oz./120 ml. soured cream (optional)

smooth. Add salt and pepper.

Grease a 7"/18 cm. flan dish with oil or butter and sprinkle with the rest of the breadcrumbs. Place mixture in flan dish and bake for 1 hour. Serve piping hot with a dollop of soured cream and surrounded by a green salad with capers and red MARINADED PEPPERS.

CHICKEN BREASTS IN WALNUT SAUCE
SERVES 4

Preheat oven to G6/200C/ 400F.

Place the chicken breasts in a casserole, pour oil around them and cover with sprigs of parsley and dill. Cover and roast in oven for about 1 hour, until tender.

In the meantime, make this sauce:

Pound the walnuts till fine. Melt butter in saucepan, add flour to make a roux. Add ground walnuts and crushed garlic. Mix well.

4 chicken breasts
1 lb./500 gr. walnuts
¼ tsp. salt
¼ tsp. freshly ground black pepper
1 fluid oz./30 ml. oil
1 lemon
2 sprigs parsley
2 sprigs fresh dill
2 oz./60 gr. butter
2 oz./60 gr. flour
4 cloves garlic

10 minutes before chicken is

ready, remove from the oven, remove skins and cover breasts with the walnut sauce. Replace in oven for 10 minutes.

Squeeze the juice of 1 lemon over breasts before serving (use plenty of lemon juice to cut across the rich sauce). Serve with a CUCUMBER SALAD WITH DILL to contrast further with the thick, rich sauce.

DUCKLING ON A BED OF BRAISED CABBAGE

SERVES 6-8

Preheat oven to G6/200C/ 400F.

Clean the duckling (try to get a very young one) and rub it all over with salt and paprika.

Place it in a baking tray and pour ½ the oil over and around it.

Add 3 tblsp. water and place tray in the middle of the preheated oven for 45 minutes–1 hour or until the bird is ¾ done. Keep basting with the gravy in the baking tray.

In the meantime, prepare the braised cabbage:

Shred the cabbage very finely, to vermicelli size.

Heat remaining oil in a frying pan and add bay leaves. When bay leaves begin to sizzle, add tomato purée and wine, reducing heat to avoid splashing. Stir well for 30 seconds, until all

---

3 lbs./1.5 kg. young duckling
2 lbs./1 kg. cabbage
6 fluid oz./180 ml. oil
1 tsp. hot paprika
2 tblsps. tomato paste
12 peppercorns
2 bay leaves
6 juniper berries
1 tsp. salt
5 fluid oz./150 ml. dry white
  wine or vermouth
1 sprig thyme
2 tsp. lemon juice

---

the tomato purée has dissolved. Now add the shredded cabbage, peppercorns, juniper berries (crushed if you like) and thyme. Mix constantly until the cabbage is completely coated with the tomato sauce. Add lemon juice, and continue braising for 5-10 minutes until cabbage begins to soften. Remove from

flame and set aside.

When the duckling has started to brown and is beginning to soften, remove it from the tray. Place shredded cabbage in one layer in the baking tray, mix it with the duckling juices, replace duckling in the tray on top of the cabbage and put it back in the oven, this time at the top, for another 30-45 minutes or until cabbage is soft, the duckling is brown and crispy and a fork plunged in the thigh of the bird produces golden rather than pink juices.

Allow the bird to rest in the turned off oven, with the door ajar, for 15 minutes and serve on its own or with FRIED CHEESE DUMPLINGS (unsweetened) or GARDEN NUGGETS.

DUCK WITH MORELLO CHERRIES

SERVES 6-8

Remove the giblets from the duck and simmer them in the red wine for 5 minutes. Chop the onions finely, clean and slice carrots and add them to the giblets. Add salt, pepper, marjoram, rosemary and simmer for another 5 minutes. Add 15 fluid oz./450 ml. water. Bring to the boil, skim and simmer on a very low flame, covered, for 2¼ hours. Remove lid and boil the wine stock down on a strong flame for another 10 minutes until it reduces to about ⅓rd. Strain through a fine sieve.

Butter a roasting tin. Preheat oven G5/190C/380F.

Brush the duck with the oil and roast in the preheated oven for 30 minutes.

Drain off fat from the roasting tin, reserving 1 tblsp. Pour the strained stock over duck. Return to the oven for another 45 minutes. Remove the duck gently with a slotted spoon, strain stock again through a fine sieve or through muslin and set aside to cool, until all fat has risen to the surface. Remove as much of the fat as possible.

Lower oven temperature to G3/170C/335F, pour the stock around the duck and

This recipe comes from Bessarabia, the old northern Romanian region now in the Soviet Union. It has, however, a distinct Oriental flavour and I suspect it may have been brought from as far away as Persia by the invading Tartars who swept northern Romania in destructive waves over several hundreds of years, before finally settling in the Crimea, on the Russian shore of the Black Sea.

---

1 medium duck (about 5 lb./2.5 kg.)
5 fluid oz./150 ml. red wine
5 fluid oz./150 ml. white wine
1 lb./500 gr. Morello cherries*
2 onions
2 carrots
1 tsp. chives
rind of 1 lemon
1 tsp. salt
1 tsp. black pepper
2 tblsp. brown sugar
1 tblsp. flour
1 oz./30 gr. butter
1 tsp. sweet marjoram
½ tsp. rosemary
1 tblsp. flour
1 fluid oz./30 ml. walnut oil

---

braise duck for another 1 hour until bird is nicely browned on all sides and crisp. Remove the duck, keep hot in the oven turned off and with the door slightly ajar, and strain stock

once more through muslin. In the meantime, stone the cherries trying not to tear the flesh more than strictly necessary. Simmer the cherries for 10 minutes in the white wine with the lemon rind and the sugar (omit sugar if you are using preserved Morello cherries already sweetened). Remove the cherries with a slotted spoon, and boil down cooking liquid for another 5 minutes, increasing the flame to medium.

Melt the reserved tblsp. of duck fat in a frying pan, add flour and make a roux by cooking for 5 minutes, stirring, until flour begins to brown. Add the stock to the roux, little by little, whisking all the time.

Add the liquid in which the cherries have been boiled, and simmer for 10 minutes stirring continuously.

Remove from the flame and pour sauce into a large sauce boat or similar vessel.

Serve the duck on a serving platter surrounded by the Morello cherries with the sauce served separately.

Serve with roast potatoes or CABBAGE LEAVES FILLED WITH MAIZE.

DELTA WILD DUCK

The Danube Delta must be one of the largest and richest hunting grounds in the world. Thousands of acres of reed-covered canals, linking a myriad small islands, create the breeding ground for all manner of fish and fowl, including an amazing variety of wild duck and geese. This recipe for wild duck is the traditional way of eating duck (as well as rabbit and hare) of the 'Lipoveni', the Russian-speaking, hard-drinking fishermen of the Delta. You can use this recipe equally well for domesticated duck (omit the barding bacon) or for rabbit.

It is not strictly necessary to marinade the duck, but it will remove any remnant of fishy taste. If you decide to marinade it, proceed as follows:

Dry the duck in a clean towel. Rub it inside and out with ½ a lemon dipped in salt. Bring the marinade ingredients to the boil and pour them over the duck which has been placed in a large saucepan. Cover and leave for 1 hour. Drain and dry again with the towel. Quarter the duck. Rub it with salt and tie a slice of bacon around each piece. Heat the oil in a frying pan and brown the duck pieces well on all sides.

Chop the onions finely and add them to the duck. Add flour to make a roux and fry until slightly brown. Pour the wine over the roux and the duck and add tomato paste, crushed garlic, salt, peppercorns and bay leaf. Cover and simmer until the duck is soft and the juices inside are no longer pink (about 30 minutes). Add vinegar for the last 5 minutes of the cooking and allow to bubble up a few times. Serve immediately, with POLENTA or SOURED BRAISED CABBAGE.

1 medium wild duck (mallard or teal) or 2 widgeons: plucked, drawn and trussed
4 slices of fat smoked bacon
3 onions
½ tblsp. flour
1 tblsp. tomato paste
2 cloves garlic
2 tsp. salt
12 peppercorns
1 bay leaf
2 tblsp. wine vinegar
4 fluid oz./120 ml. oil
2 fluid oz./60 ml. red wine

For the marinade (optional):
½ lemon
5 fluid oz./150 ml. wine vinegar
2 bay leaves
6 peppercorns
1 small onion
1 tsp. salt

WILD DUCK WITH QUINCES

SERVES 4

Wild duck and quinces go extremely well together: first because quinces come into season in the autumn, during the duck shooting season; and then because the rich duck meat needs a sharp, tangy contrast and quinces are ideally suited to provide it. In this country this contrast is usually provided by an orange or lime salad – both Mediterranean fruit, rare in the northern parts of the Balkans. Quinces, however, are thirteen to the dozen in Romania in the autumn and are used accordingly (see also BEEF STEW WITH QUINCES).

Preheat the oven to G5/ 190C/380F.
Joint the duck into 4 pieces. Tie a slice of bacon around each piece. Melt ½ the butter in a large frying pan, and brown duck pieces well on all sides. Remove with a slotted spoon and sprinkle with salt.
Wash the quinces without peeling and quarter them. Remove hard inner core and seed boxes. Slice quinces into thin slices, like apple slices. Melt the remaining butter in the same frying pan and fry quince slices in the butter and duck/bacon juices for 5 minutes on each

---

1 good size mallard or teal or 2 widgeons, plucked, drawn and trussed
4 slices fat, smoked bacon
1 lb./500 gr. quinces
4 oz./125 gr. butter
1 tblsp. sugar
4 fluid oz./120 ml. white port or dry white wine
1 tsp. salt
1 tsp. sweet fresh marjoram
½ tsp. freshly ground black pepper
1 tblsp. lemon juice

---

side or until half soft.
Line a casserole with quince slices, then place duck pieces on top, sprinkle with marjoram and pepper and cover with remaining quince slices.
Heat the wine in a small saucepan and dissolve the sugar in it to make a caramel sauce. Pour the sauce into the casserole and braise in preheated oven for 45 minutes or until the duck is cooked but still pink.
Sprinkle with lemon juice and fresh coriander or lovage just before serving. Serve with GARDENER'S MOUSSAKA or a light summer salad like the YUGOSLAV OR BULGARIAN 'SHOPSKA' SALADS.

PHEASANT WITH CHERRIES

SERVES 6

Turkish in origin, this Bulgarian recipe for pheasant makes excellent use of two of the country's best products: cream and cherries. My grandfather, a great maker and drinker of liqueurs, would have used the alcohol-soaked Morrello cherries* left after the fermentation process of home-made cherry brandy (Vishniak/Visinata) If you feel less extravagant you can use preserved Bulgarian Morrello* or red cherries (if you cannot get fresh ones), as the recipe calls for them to be soaked and sweetened anyway.

Soak the cherries in the sweet wine for 2-3 hours. Remove stones carefully trying not to break cherries too much. Drain and reserve.

Sprinkle or brush pheasant with the dry white wine. Chop onion finely and sweat in the melted butter until soft but not brown. Add pheasant, increase flame to moderate and fry on all sides for about ¼ hour shaking pan and turning frequently to avoid sticking.

After about 15 minutes, when the bird is nicely

1 pheasant
5 fluid oz./150 ml. soured cream or smetana
1 lb./500 gr. morello or red cherries
2 fluid oz./60 ml. dry white wine
3 oz./90 gr. butter
½ tsp. salt
½ tsp. pepper
2 tblsp. sweet wine (Tokay*, Romanian Cotnari* or Marsala)
2 onions
½ tsp. mild paprika

browned on all sides, add cream (use double cream if you prefer), although the slightly acidulated taste of the smetana goes well with the rich pheasant) by pouring slowly all around the pheasant. Lower heat and braise for a further 15 minutes basting constantly. Add salt and pepper and set on a hot plate, pouring sauce over it.

Arrange soaked morello cherries all around the bird, sprinkle bird and cream with a light powder of mild paprika and serve.

STUFFED QUAILS 'NEGRUZZI'

Preheat the oven to G8/ 230C/450F.

Pluck the quails and singe them over a flame. Pat them dry with a clean cloth but do not wash. Remove their eyes and innards, reserving the intestines and livers which are very tasty.

Make the stuffing:

Chop finely the intestines, half the bacon, onion, mushrooms and liver.

Melt ½ the butter in a frying pan and sauté the mixture for 15 minutes over a moderate flame. Add salt, pepper, marjoram and parsley. Allow mixture to cool a little, then add the egg. Mix well.

Fill each quail with the mixture, but do not pack it too tightly. Bend the quails' necks towards their legs and tie them with string into neat parcels.

Wrap the vine leaves and the rest of the bacon or larding fat all around the birds and

This classic Romanian recipe was named after Costache Negruzzi, a famous literary figure of the nineteenth-century Renaissance. He was also a renowned gourmet and the co-author of one of the first Romanian cookery books, published in Moldavia in 1841.

---

6 quails, hung for at least 24 hours
6 large vine leaves
8 oz./250 gr. smoked fat bacon
4 oz./125 gr. mushrooms
2 oz./60 gr. chicken, goose or calf's liver
1 egg
1 onion
4 oz./125 gr. butter
1 tsp. salt
½ tsp. pepper
½ tsp. sweet marjoram
1 tblsp. fresh chopped parsley
6 slices white bread

---

tie them or secure with small skewers or toothpicks. Place the wrapped birds in a tray large enough to take them all in one row.

Roast the quails in the preheated oven for 20-30 minutes, until bacon has shed most of its fat and quails are nicely browned all over.

In the meantime, fry the thin slices of bread in butter until golden.

Remove the wrapping of bacon and vine leaves, discard the string and place each quail on a piece of toast. Serve immediately, with bacon on the side.

If you have some stuffing left, mash it finely with a fork, and serve with it.

In Moldavia, where quails were traditional autumn fare, they would probably be served on a bed of BRAISED SOURED CABBAGE and accompanied by PEPPERS FILLED WITH AUBERGINE CAVIAR or a simple MARINADED PEPPER SALAD.

BRAISED RABBIT
IN SOURED CREAM
SERVES 6-8

This traditional recipe was made famous at a Bucharest restaurant and 'garden' called 'Cina', perhaps not as prominent as 'Capsha's', but still a fashionable meeting place, due in part to its position directly opposite the Royal Palace. The head chef at 'Cina' before the war was Mr. Fritz, German in name but Romanian in cooking, whose great speciality was rabbit fillets in a soured cream sauce, served with a preserve of green apricots. Mr. Fritz was generous with his recipes and would distribute them freely on request, often signed by himself at the table, as a sign of supreme favour: 'He would appear in the dining room dressed in his chef's hat, flattened to resemble a sponge cake, and wearing his chef's knives across the shoulders, like a cow-boy's bandolier. He would shake your hand, like a doctor, and ask you full of solicitude whether his cooking had been to your liking. Slowly withdrawing his hand he would then tell you, for the umpteenth time, how the Emperor Franz Joseph himself had shaken that very hand after a visit to Pelesh Castle (the summer residence of the Kings of Romania) before the Great War.' (Ion Dulgheru in *Almanah Literar Gastronomic*, Bucharest 1982).

Dilute the vinegar in an equal quantity of water. Bring to the boil and place all other marinade ingredients into the liquid. Simmer for 10 minutes. In the meantime, clean all loose skin from the rabbit fillets if necessary. Cut several long slits into the skin and stuff with slices of bacon (trimmed to fit the slits) and slivers of garlic. Place rabbit in an earthenware pot, pour boiling marinade on top, cover and set aside at room temperature for 12-24 hours. Turn rabbit every few hours.
Preheat the oven to G5/190C/380F.
Dry the rabbit in a clean cloth and rub the outer skin with coarse salt and pepper. Place in a deep, well greased

---

1½ lb./750 gr. rabbit (the back fillets, either side of the spine)
4 oz./125 gr. smoked bacon or smoked belly of pork
2 cloves garlic
2 oz./60 gr. butter
1 pt./600 ml. beef stock
10 fluid oz./300 ml. thin soured cream (smetaña)
2 tsp. salt
2 tsp. pepper
8 fluid oz./240 ml. red wine

For the marinade:
4 fluid oz./120 ml. wine vinegar
1 fluid oz./30 ml. olive oil
1 carrot cut in very thin rounds
1 onion cut in thin rings
1 bunch parsley
1 branch thyme
2 bay leaves
½ tsp. salt
¼ tsp. pepper

---

roasting tray, skin upwards, and pour wine and ½ the stock around it. Braise in the preheated oven for 1½-2 hours, basting constantly with the liquid. Add more stock if liquid evaporates. When the rabbit is ready, remove it from tin and keep covered in a warm place. Boil braising liquid down to 10 fluid oz./300 ml. (add stock if you have not got enough). Mix soured cream with the deglazed liquid and simmer over a low flame, stirring constantly and scraping, to remove the roast bits stuck at the bottom of the tray.
Strain the sauce through a fine sieve and pour over the rabbit on a platter. Serve with GREEN HERB MOULDS and a CUCUMBER AND DILL SALAD.

RABBIT WITH OLIVES
SERVES 6-8

Clean and marinate the rabbit as described at BRAISED RABBIT IN SOURED CREAM omitting, if you prefer, the larding and the garlic.

Remove the fillets and chop the rest into good sized pieces.

Chop the onion and sweat in 2 fluid oz./60 ml. oil until soft but not brown.

When onion begins to yellow, add rabbit pieces, increase flame and brown well on all sides. Pour in stock or water a little at a time until rabbit is soft.

½ a rabbit (the back side, including the fillets either side of the spine)
3 fluid oz./90 ml. oil
5 fluid oz./150 ml. stock or water
4 onions
8 oz./250 gr. large black olives
5 fluid oz./150 ml. red wine
8 oz./250 gr. small (pickling) onions
1 tblsp. tomato paste
2 tsp. salt
2 tsp. hot paprika

Blanch the olives in boiling water for 10 minutes. Drain and reserve.

In the meantime, fry lightly the pickling onions in the remaining oil. Add them to the rabbit. When rabbit is almost soft, add tomato paste diluted in wine, the blanched olives and remaining stock (or rabbit blood, if you can get some, mixed with 2 tblsp. wine). Add salt and paprika and adjust seasoning. Simmer on a moderate flame until sauce has boiled down quite a lot. Serve warm with POLENTA.

HAUNCH OF VENISON IN SOURED CREAM

SERVES 8

In Romania venison is rarely hung, as the red deer of the Carpathians is hunted early (Romanian winters are very severe and mountain trails often become impassable) and tends to be young and tender. The huntsman's treatment for a young buck carcass is to rub it with a mixture of 3 parts oil to 1 part rum and leave it in the warm for 4-5 hours. The venison you are likely to buy in this country, however, will in all probability be hung already, especially if you are buying the farmed deer meat sold widely by city butchers and supermarkets. Marinade this meat for 24 hours in the mixture below or, if you need to keep it for up to 8 days, boil marinade first and keep venison in it at room temperature (not in the fridge, the cold slows the marinade process). Use a covered stone or earthenware pot.

Preheat the oven to G8/230C/450F.

Drain the marinaded haunch of venison and remove the thin skin covering it. With a sharp knife, cut thin shallow slits into the meat, at regular intervals. Lard the venison by stuffing a slice of fat bacon into each of these slits. Brush the haunch with oil and rub with salt, thyme and marjoram.

Place the venison in a baking tray and place it at the top of the oven. Turn on all sides for the first 20 minutes, brushing continuously with oil. Pour the rest of the oil over it, reduce heat to G5/190C/380F and roast at the top of the oven for 1¼ hours (allow 25 minutes per 1 lb./500 gr. of meat. Baste often with the oil and juices in the pan. Sauce will probably dry out during cooking – add a little stock or wine from time to time.

When the venison is ready, set it aside to rest on a hot dish in the turned-off oven, with the door slightly ajar. Pour the cooking juices into a saucepan, scraping off all the residue at the bottom of the tray. Bring them to the boil, add remaining wine or stock and boil rapidly down for about 5 minutes. Remove from the flame, allow to cool for 2 minutes and stir in soured cream, little by little. Add chopped dill and strain some sauce through a fine sieve over the venison haunch. Serve remaining sauce separately in a sauce boat. Serve with roast potatoes and with a little ROSE PETAL or ROTTED WALNUTS PRESERVE.

---

4 lb./2 kg. haunch of venison (preferably buck venison)
8 oz./250 gr. fat bacon
2 tsp. salt
4 fluid oz./120 ml. oil
10 fluid oz./300 ml. thick soured cream
7 fluid oz./200 ml. beef stock or red wine
1 tsp. sweet marjoram
2 branches fresh thyme or 1 tsp. dry thyme
1 tblsp. fresh chopped dill

For the marinade:
5 fluid oz./150 ml. dry white wine
5 fluid oz./150 ml. white wine vinegar
2 fluid oz./60 ml. oil
1 carrot, sliced
1 stick celery, chopped
2 onions, cut into rings
1 bay leaf
12 peppercorns
1 branch thyme
1 tsp. salt

WILD BOAR

The fir-tree forests of the Carpathians used to be full of wild boars until fairly recently. To this day boar hunts are organized for V.I.P.s and one can occasionally buy boar meat, especially in Yugoslavia. One restaurant in Ljubliana boasts of both boar and bear sausages, but I must confess the latter proved somewhat disappointing. Wild boar, however, is a different matter: well marinaded and prepared it can be delicious. The best meat comes from a young animal (up to 18 months old) and it can be roasted, braised or grilled like pork. The meat does need to be marinaded first, however.

The boar meat needs to be skinned and have all veins and bristle removed. Rub it with coarse salt and set aside while you prepare the marinade.

Bring the wine and vinegar to the boil. Chop the carrot, parsnip, onions into coarse slices and add them to the boiling marinade. Add all the other marinade ingredients. Simmer for 3 minutes and set aside to cool for 5 minutes.

Place meat in a large earthenware or stone pot and pour marinade on top. Cover and allow meat to marinate for 24 hours, turning it 3-4 times. Preheat the oven to G8/ 230C/450F.

Take the boar meat out of the marinade and drain well. Pat it dry with a clean towel and place in a roasting tin large enough to take the whole leg comfortably. Place

---

4 lb./2 kg. leg of wild boar
1 tblsp. coarse salt
½ tsp. freshly ground pepper
1 tsp. rosemary
5 fluid oz./150 ml. soured cream

For the marinade
8 fluid oz./240 ml. dry white wine or vermouth
8 fluid oz./240 ml. wine vinegar
1 carrot
1 parsnip or parsley root
2 onions
3 cloves garlic
3 cloves
1 bay leaf
1 stick celery (with leaves)
12 peppercorns
1 tsp. salt

---

at the top of the preheated oven and let it brown well on all sides (about 30 minutes). When the meat is nicely sealed, turn oven down to G6/200C/400F and pour the marinade all around it. Allow boar to braise in the middle of the oven for 1 ½ hours, adding a little wine if the liquid evaporates too quickly. When the boar is roasted through, drain marinade into a saucepan, turn oven off and keep the meat in it, with the door slightly ajar.

Skim the fat off the top of the sauce. Bring it back to the boil, adding freshly ground pepper, rosemary and 2 tblsp. of water if necessary. Pass the sauce through a fine sieve and mix soured cream slowly in. Place leg of boar on a serving platter, carve a few fairly thick slices and pour some of the sauce on top. Serve immediately, with the rest of the sauce on the side and a little QUINCE or BITTER CHERRY SHERBET on each plate. You can roast potatoes in the meat gravy or serve a MOLDAVIAN CHEESE PIE with the roast.

MEAT DISHES

GOLDEN NUGGETS IN A SOURED CREAM SAUCE

SERVES 4

This recipe comes from the small town of Huedin in northern Transylvania. Huedin is situated near the river Koros sacred to the memory of the Hungarian Gypsies of old and revered as the 'river of gold'. Gold has been mined in Transylvania since pre-Roman times and in the bed of that river the 'gold-washing Gypsies used to gather the alluvial gold and in return for this toil they were given special privileges by the Empress Maria Theresa in the eighteenth century'. (W. Starkie – *Raggle-Taggle*, 1929).

Mince the beef or white meat finely, together with the onion.

Soak the bread in milk for 2-3 minutes. Mix minced meat in a bowl with the soaked bread, egg, 1 tblsp. of the mixed herbs, 1 tblsp. flour, salt and pepper.

Dip your hands in flour, take about a tblsp. of the mixture at a time and roll into a small ball the size of a walnut. Roll the balls lightly in flour and fry in ½ butter and ½ oil on a medium flame. When they are nicely

---

12 oz./360 gr. lean beef (or chicken breasts, skinned boned and trimmed or veal, but these tend to be rather bland)
1 small onion
1½ tblsp. mixed chopped dill, parsley or coriander
1 fluid oz./30 ml. milk
1 slice white bread, crust removed
1 egg
3 oz./90 gr. flour
8 fluid oz./240 ml. soured cream
1 oz./30 gr. butter
2 fluid oz./60 ml. oil

---

browned on all sides add 3 fluid oz./90 ml. water and simmer, uncovered, for about 10 minutes. Shake the pan occasionally to avoid sticking. Drain off any excess liquid, but leave about 2 tblsp.

Add soured cream and the rest of the chopped herbs and simmer for another 2-3 minutes. Serve hot, with freshly boiled egg noodles and a cucumber salad. (See CUCUMBER AND DILL SALAD and BALKAN NOODLES).

BELGRADE CIGARS

Preheat the oven to G6/ 200C/400F.

Grate carrots, parsnip and celery on the fine teeth of a manual grater or using the grater of a food processor. Heat ½ the oil and sweat the grated vegetables over a low flame for 10-15 minutes until soft. Add salt, pepper, coriander and cumin seeds. Remove from the flame and add 1 raw egg. Boil rice in a little water until soft. Drain and add to the vegetable mixture.

Beat the meat slices with a heavy mallet to obtain slices as thin as pressed ham. Put 1 tblsp. of vegetable mixture inside each slice, roll them to make fat 'cigars' and fix their edges with small skewers or tooth picks. Heat the remaining oil and

1 lb./500 gr. lean beef brisket or sirloin cut in very thin slices (ask your butcher to cut it, or use a very sharp knife)
2 carrots
1 parsnip
4 oz./125 gr. red cabbage
2-3 sticks celery
1 oz./30 gr. onion
3 eggs
½ tsp. cumin seeds
1 tsp. pepper
1 tsp. chopped coriander
2 bay leaves
3 fluid oz./90 ml. oil
1 oz./30 gr. flour
1 oz./30 gr. rice
2 tblsp. tomato paste
4 fluid oz./120 ml. beef stock or water
½ tblsp. finely chopped parsley

sweat meat 'cigars' on a low flame until thoroughly cooked and soft (cca. 15-20 minutes). When ready remove them, add flour to the oil still in the frying pan and mix to make a roux. Dilute the tomato paste in the stock or water and pour over the roux. Add salt and bay leaves and simmer for 5 minutes.

Pour the sauce over the 'cigars' and place at the top of the preheated oven for 10 minutes.

Boil the remaining 2 eggs until hard. Peel and slice into thin rounds. Dip each slice of egg in finely chopped parsley and decorate each meat 'cigar' with an egg slice.

Serve with MARINADED RED PEPPERS.

SOFIA BOILED BEEF

Boil the beef in 2 pts./1 l. water for 30 minutes or until it is half cooked. Clean the vegetables and add them to the beef, together with the bay leaf and peppercorns. Boil for a further 30 minutes–1 hour or until meat is very soft.

Remove the meat from the stock with a slotted spoon, and slice into 1"/3 cm. thick slices if you had it in 1 piece. Arrange neatly in an ovenproof dish which takes all the slices in one layer. Make a roux by mixing the

1½ lb./750 gr. rolled sirloin of beef in one piece or sliced into 1"/3 cm. thick slices
2 carrots
1 onion
2 sticks celery
2 parsnips
1 bay leaf
12 peppercorns
2 oz./60 gr. flour
2 eggs
3 fluid oz./90 ml. yoghurt
2 fluid oz./60 ml. oil
2 tblsp. grated cheddar

flour in the heated oil. Pour meat stock through a sieve over the roux and discard vegetables. Mix well and boil over a fairly lively flame for 10 minutes. Aim to reduce to about 10 fluid oz./300 ml.

Beat the eggs well and mix into the stock, away from the flame. Add yoghurt, mix well again and pour sauce over the meat. Sprinkle with grated cheese and brown in the oven for 10 minutes. Serve hot.

BEEF STEW WITH QUINCES

Quinces are a familiar sight in Romanian markets all through the autumn. As one cannot eat them raw, Romanians have devised a variety of recipes to make good use of the plentiful crop. They are familiar enough in the West as the basis for tangy jellies and jams (according to one theory, their Portuguese name – Marmelo – is the root for marmalade), but they are also ideally suited, because of their sharp yet pungent flavour, for use in meat and poultry stews. See also SPRING CHICKEN WITH QUINCES.

Preheat the oven to G6/ 200C/400F.
Dice the meat in 1"/3 cm. cubes. Heat ½ the butter in a frying pan and seal meat cubes until brown on all sides. Add salt and 3 tblsp. wine. Cover and simmer over a low flame until meat begins to soften (about 20-30 minutes, depending on the cut of meat). Add a little wine every 5 minutes or so, up to about 4 fluid oz./120 ml.
Wash the quinces well, but do not peel. Cut them in halves and remove the hard centres and the seed boxes.

---

1 lb./500 gr. lean stewing beef or lamb fillet
1 lb./500 gr. quinces
4 oz./125 gr. butter
4 fluid oz./120 ml. dry white wine (or 8 fluid oz./240 ml. if you are using wine for the caramelized sauce)
4 tsps. sugar
½ tsp. salt
½ tsp. sweet marjoram
1 tsp. fresh chopped sage
1 tsp. paprika

Slice them in thin slices, like apples.
Heat the rest of the butter and fry quince slices for about 5 minutes on each side or until half softened.
Brown the quince pieces well, however, or they will fall apart.
Melt sugar in 4 fluid oz./120 ml. water or white wine to make a thin caramel sauce. Pour it over the quinces and the meat placed in a casserole. Add paprika, sage and marjoram and place at the top of preheated oven for ½ hour or until meat is fully softened. Serve immediately with CHICORY IN SOURED CREAM or GREEN HERB MOULDS.

A U B E R G I N E   M O U S S A K A

Slice the aubergines in 1"/3 cm. thick slices. Blanch them in salted boiling water, salt lightly and place on a flat surface under a wooden chopping board or similar. Place a weight on top and leve 15-30 minutes to drain as much of the water as possible.

In the meantime, mince the beef, raw carrot and potato as finely as possible. Chop the onion and sauté in 1 tblsp. oil together with the minced meat and vegetables. When the meat and onion are nicely browned, drip slowly over them 4 fluid oz./120 ml. mixed water and red wine. Simmer over a low flame until all liquid has evaporated. Set aside to cool.

Preheat the oven to G6/200C/400F. Retrieve aubergines and either:
A: roll them in 2 tblsp. flour and sauté them, slice by slice, in oil or a mixture of butter and oil. They will absorb a lot of oil and should come out nicely browned on both sides, or
B: briefly brown the aubergine slices without any fat in a very hot cast iron

---

2 medium sized aubergines (1 lb. 8 oz./750 gr.)
1 lb./500 gr. lean beef, finely minced
1 tblsp. chopped parsley
½ carrot
½ potato
2 fluid oz./60 ml. red wine (optional)
1 onion
2 eggs
2 tblsp. soured cream
⅓ tsp. salt
⅓ tsp. pepper
oil
2 tsp. flour (optional)
2 tblsp. breadcrumbs
1 tblsp. tomato purée
5 fluid oz./150 ml. beef stock or water
1 tblsp. chopped green peppers (optional)
1 tomato (optional)

---

pan or similar. Place in a colander on top of a saucepan with boiling water and steam the browned aubergine slices for about 10 minutes. This method makes for a lighter end result.

Mix the cooled minced meat with 1 tblsp. soured cream, 1 tsp. chopped parsley, 1 egg and season with salt and pepper.

Brush the bottom of a 6"/15 cm. round casserole with oil and sprinkle with breadcrumbs. Place alternate layers of aubergine and meat mixture, starting and finishing with the aubergine (use the slices at either end of the aubergine, which show more of the purple skin, for the bottom and top layers).

If you want to tip the casserole inside out and serve it in cake shape, then place the moussaka in the preheated oven now. Alternatively, slice the tomato and green pepper and place on top of the moussaka. Whisk 1 egg into 2 tblsp. soured cream and spread over the moussaka. I prefer it this way, but you will not be able to tip the moussaka cake over. Either way, bake in the preheated oven for 45 minutes.

It is essential to allow the moussaka to 'rest' for at least 15 minutes before serving, to allow the flavours to blend into one another.

Cut up in slices like a cake and serve warm.

109

CAULIFLOWER MOUSSAKA
'CERNEA'
SERVES 6

This recipe was one of the great specialities of Andrei Cernea, the 'maestru' or head chef at the 'Continental' restaurant in Bucharest in the 1930s and 1940s. Andrei Cernea was the best modern exponent of Romanian regional cooking and under him the 'Continental' became a veritable Mecca of traditional cooking, despite its cosmopolitan name. He decorated the main dining room in traditional country style, with embroidered table cloths and wooden kitchen utensils and suceeded in getting the incomparable Maria Tanase, folk singer extraordinaire, mistress of Cabinet ministers and the idol of the whole nation, to come and sing in his restaurant, accompanied by the resident Gypsy 'taraf' (folk band). She came just as much for Cernea's moussakas as for his 'joie de vivre' — the 'maestru' was famous for dividing his favours equally between his slow moussakas and the quick-witted Gypsy girls who baked them.

Preheat the oven to G6/200C/400F.

Separate florets from a nice cauliflower and discard the stalk. Wash the florets and blanch in plenty of boiling water, (salted with 1 tsp. salt) for 15 minutes or until florets are half cooked but still crisp. Drain well. Beat 1 egg. Dip each floret in turn in flour, then in beaten egg and fry in 2 oz./60 gr. melted butter until gold all over.

Chop the onion finely and sweat in 1 oz./30 gr. of the remaining butter until soft but not brown. Pass the softened onion and meat through a mincer or mince finely in a food processor.

---

1 lb./500 gr. cauliflower
8 oz./250 gr. lean beef
1 onion
6 oz./180 gr. butter
2 tsps. salt
1 tsp. black pepper
2 oz./60 gr. flour
3 eggs
1 clove garlic
½ tsp. nutmeg
½ tblsp. fresh chopped coriander
2 tblsp. breadcrumbs
5 fluid oz./150 ml. soured cream

Fry mince in 2 oz./60 gr. butter until brown and crumbly (about 20 minutes). Add 1 fluid oz./30 ml. water every 5 minutes (4 fluid oz./120 ml. in all) and mix well. Add 1 tsp. salt, pepper, nutmeg, parsley and crushed garlic.

Grease a casserole with 1 oz./30 gr. butter, sprinkle with ½ the breadcrumbs and place one layer of cauliflower florets on the bottom.

Spread meat mixture on top, then cover with the second layer of florets. Separate the remaining 2 eggs.

Beat the soured cream with 2 egg yolks and spread over the moussaka.

Sprinkle with remaining breadcrumbs and place in preheated oven for ½ hour or until nicely set and brown on top. Serve in the baking dish.

MARINADED LEG OF LAMB

Preheat the oven to G8/ 230C/450F.

Trim excess fat and skin off leg of lamb. Score ½"/2 cm. deep slits across lamb about 2"/6 cm. apart. Slice garlic cloves finely and place a few slices in each slit. Cut bacon rashers to fit slits and stuff on top of the garlic.

Prepare the marinade: bring the wine and vinegar to the boil. Add carrot, onion, celery – all sliced. Bring back to the boil and add thyme, bay leaf, peppercorns, salt. Simmer for 5 minutes. Allow to cool slightly. Place leg of lamb in

3 lb./1½ kg. leg of lamb
6 bacon rashers
4 cloves garlic
1 tblsp. oil or lard

For the marinade:
12 fluid oz./375 ml. dry white wine
6 fluid oz./180 ml. wine vinegar
1 carrot
1 onion
1 stick celery
1 small branch thyme or ½ tsp. dry thyme
1 bay leaf
10 peppercorns
1 tsp. salt

a stone or earthenware pot big enough to take it comfortably.

Pour marinade on top, cover and keep in a cool place for 48 hours. Turn leg around 3-4 times a day.

Grease a roasting tin with oil or fat. Drain leg well and dry in a clean towel. Brush with oil and place in oven for 1 hour 15 minutes (rare) to 1 hour 35 minutes (well done). Brush from time to time with oil or fat. Serve with SPICY BEAN HOTPOT in winter or with a SPINACH SALAD and DILLED PEAS or mange tout in spring.

LAMB 'SHOP-KEBAB'

Preheat the oven to G6/ 200C/400F.

With a very sharp knife, trim all visible fat off the leg of lamb and slice meat off the bone into thin slices and small cubes. Chop spring onions and green peppers into thin strips. Add oil and mix well to coat meat pieces with the oil. Place everything in a baking tray or other ovenproof dish and place at the top of the preheated oven for 15-20 minutes or until meat is

1½ lb./750 gr. leg of lamb (not including bone) or lamb fillet
8 spring onions
1 lb./500 gr. green peppers
4 fluid oz./120 ml. olive oil
3 eggs
4 fluid oz./120 ml. yoghurt
1 tsp. hot paprika
1 tsp. salt

sealed outside but still juicy and pink inside. When meat is sealed, add salt and

sprinkle with paprika. Add 2 fluid oz./60 ml. water.

In the meantime, beat the eggs into the yoghurt and pour over the meat.

Replace in the oven, increase flame to G7/220C/430F and braise for another 15-20 minutes or until meat is fully cooked and soft (the braising time will depend on the cut of meat used and on how well done you like your lamb). Serve with SPICY BEAN HOTPOT or FILLED TOMATOES.

BRAISED LAMB WITH SPINACH
SERVES 4

Dice the meat into 1"/3 cm. cubes. Heat oil and fry meat quickly until browned and sealed on all sides. Remove with a slotted spoon.
Chop onions and garlic finely and fry in the same fat as the meat until soft. Slice leek or spring onions and add to the onions. Fry until leeks become translucent. Transfer to a casserole with a tight lid and add meat, rice, paprika and salt. Mix well.
Add ⅓ of the combined wine and stock, cover well and simmer for at least 2 hours

Lamb and spinach, a spring favourite in my childhood, come together in this unusual stew from Yugoslavia.

1 lb./500 gr. lamb fillet
2 fluid oz./60 ml. oil
1 medium onion
2 cloves garlic
4 oz./125 gr. brown rice
6 oz./180 gr. leeks or spring onions
1 tsp. rosemary
1 tblsp. mild paprika
8 oz./250 gr. spinach
1 egg
4 fluid oz./120 ml. soured cream
½ tsp. salt
10 fluid oz./300 ml. dry white wine
10 fluid oz./300 ml. stock or water
1 tomato, to garnish
2 tblsp. lemon juice (optional)

or until lamb is tender. The rice will gradually absorb all the liquid, so you will need to replenish it from time to time.
Towards the end, trim the spinach and wash leaves well. Blanch spinach and rice and add raw egg. Allow stew to reheat for 5 minutes, then serve garnished with sliced tomatoes and soured cream.
The dish is much tastier when reheated. Pour 2 tblsp. lemon juice over stew just before serving, if you like.

LAMB WITH SORREL
SERVES 4

Preheat the oven to G5/190C/380F.

Clean the sorrel, by washing several times in running cold water, and chop off any roots and stringy bits.

Blanch sorrel leaves in boiling water for 4-5 minutes. Drain well and reserve.

Dice the lamb fillet in 1″/3 cm. cubes. Trim, wash and chop finely the white part of the leek.

Heat the oil and fry the lamb cubes on all sides until juices are sealed inside and they are brown all over. Remove with a slotted

Like **LAMB WITH SPINACH**, this dish definitely belongs in the spring. To be suitable for use in stews, sorrel must be very young (picked in May–June). Its distinctive acid taste goes well with spring lamb and is enhanced in Romania by the addition of lemon juice.

---

1 lb./500 gr. lamb fillet
2 lbs./1 kg. fresh, young sorrel
   leaves
1 tsp. flour
3 fluid oz./90 ml. oil
1 leek or 2 oz./60 gr. shallots or
   spring onions
1 tblsp. tomato paste
4 fluid oz./120 ml. dry white
   wine
1 tsp. salt
1 tsp. freshly ground black
   pepper
1-2 tsp. lemon juice

---

spoon and set aside.

In the same frying pan sweat chopped leeks until soft but not brown.

Add tomato paste, wine, salt and pepper and simmer for 2 minutes, stirring until tomato paste has dissolved. Place the meat in a casserole and add the sorrel leaves. Pour tomato sauce over them, cover and place in the preheated oven for 45 minutes–1 hour or until meat has softened. 10 minutes before stew is ready add lemon juice. Serve with small boiled potatoes and new buttered carrots.

LAMB AND OKRA

SERVES 4

Preheat the oven to G3/ 170C/335F.

Cut the lamb into 1"/3 cm. cubes. Slice the onion finely. Slice tomatoes into quarters and green peppers into long strips.

Melt butter in a cast iron pan and fry lamb cubes on a high flame until brown on all sides. Remove the lamb with a slotted spoon and set aside.

Reduce the heat and fry onion until golden brown, adding a little butter if necessary. Replace the lamb over onion and add tomatoes, peppers, cloves, rosemary, lemon slices, salt and paprika.

1 lb./500 gr. lamb fillet
2 medium tomatoes
2 oz./60 gr. green pepper
6 oz./180 gr. okra
1 large onion
2 oz./60 gr. butter or mixed oil and butter
4 cloves
2 lemon slices
½ tsp. salt
¼ tsp. hot paprika
½ tsp. dry rosemary or sprig of rosemary
1 fluid oz./30 ml. beef stock or water
1-2 tblsp. lemon juice

Cover lamb and stew in preheated oven for 2 hours or until lamb is soft. Add 1 fluid oz./30 ml. stock if necessary, but the stew should be as dry as possible. When lamb is soft add lemon juice.

In the meantime, chop the ends off okra pieces. Blanch in 2 pt./1 l. boiling water mixed with 3 tblsp. vinegar for 2 minutes. Wash several times in cold water and drain well. Add okra to lamb at the last minute and reheat in oven for a further 2 minutes. Serve sprinkled with parsley.

DOBRUDJA KEBABS

SERVES 6

Dobrudja is the Black Sea coastline shared between Bulgaria and Romania. A favourite settling place for the Turks when the two countries were part of the Ottoman Empire, it still has a significant muslim minority (ethnic Turks and Tartars) with their middle-eastern, almost Arabic, tradition of cooking.

Mutton in its various forms figures large, of course, in this tradition.

Ask your butcher to give you a young, tender leg of mutton which has hung in a cool place for at least 2-3 days after it was cut. Discard carefully any filaments and remove any visible fat (mutton fat has a particularly unpleasant taste).

Dice the mutton leg in 1"/3 cm. cubes. Sprinkle with salt, pepper and thyme. Slice the garlic cloves into thin slivers and cut a little slit in each meat dice. Place

2 lb./1 kg. mutton leg
4 cloves garlic
8 oz./250 gr. tomatoes
12 bay leaves
1 fluid oz./30 ml. olive oil
2 onions
2 green peppers
1 tsp. salt
3 sprigs thyme or 1 tsp. dried thyme
½ tsp. pepper

a garlic sliver in each slit. Slice the tomatoes, onions and green peppers in large rings.

On six long skewers, place the meat cubes separated by alternate rings of tomatoes, onions, peppers and bay leaves. Brush skewers and grill with oil and grill on a hot barbecue or grill, rotating constantly and brushing occasionally with oil. Serve with FILLED LEEKS or RED CABBAGE AND APPLE RELISH.

SERBIAN MUTTON 'TOKANA'

'Tokany' is the Hungarian word describing a stew made with onions and paprika, in which the meat is braised by gradually absorbing small quantities of water. The Balkans have countless variations on this theme and even their names are almost identical, regardless of national boundaries ('tocana' in Romania, 'tokana' in Serbia). Here is a Serbian 'tokana' using mutton and the traditional Serbian combination of green peppers, potatoes and tomato sauce.

Preheat the oven to G5/ 190C/380F.

Wash meat well, and cut off all visible fat. Blanch the meat in 2 pts./1 l. boiling water for 5 minutes. Drain and cut into finger-sized pieces.

Heat fat in a frying pan and fry meat until brown all over. Remove with a slotted spoon and set aside.

Chop the onions into quarter rings. Peel and chop potatoes into 1"/3 cm. cubes. Remove the stalks and seeds from the peppers and chop into long strips. Slice the tomatoes. Fry the onions in the fat left from the meat until transparent. Add paprika and the tomato paste diluted in 4 fluid oz./120 ml. of meat stock or water. Add the potatoes, peppers, tomatoes, then the meat pieces on top and cover with wine, thyme, crushed garlic, salt, pepper and chopped parsley. Place the dish in the middle of the preheated oven and braise covered for 1 ½ hours or until mutton pieces are soft and the potatoes are cooked through. Add a little stock or water mixed with wine if the dish gets too dry. Serve very hot, with POLENTA or RED CABBAGE RELISH.

---

1 lb./500 gr. mutton
3 medium onions
1 lb./500 gr. green peppers
4 tomatoes
1 lb./500 gr. potatoes
2 oz./60 gr. lard or oil
4 cloves garlic
1 oz./30 gr. mild paprika
4 fluid oz./120 ml. meat stock or water
2 tblsp. tomato paste
1 tsp. salt
1 tsp. pepper
2 small branches of thyme or 1 tsp. dried thyme
4 fluid oz./120 ml. dry red wine
1 tblsp. chopped parsley

SERBIAN PORK CHOPS

SERVES 4

Preheat the oven to G6/200C/400F.

Sprinkle the meat with ½ the salt and pepper. Heat oil well and brown chops on both sides for 10 minutes. (You can also grill the meat under a hot grill if you prefer).

Remove them with a slotted spoon and set aside.

Chop the onion very finely and sweat it in the hot oil (reduce heat). Add the mild paprika and 4 fluid oz./120 ml. water and mix well.

Slice the tomatoes into thin rounds, chop peppers into long strips. Add them to the

This recipe displays the traditional Serbian love for meat or fish cooked first and then braised on a bed of tomatoes and green peppers.

4 pork chops
8 oz./250 gr. onions
1 lb./500 gr. tomatoes
1 lb./500 gr. green peppers
3 oz./90 gr. rice
3 fluid oz./90 ml. oil
1 tsp. salt
1 tsp. freshly ground black
  pepper
1 tsp. mild paprika
1 tblsp. chopped fresh dill
1 tblsp. chopped fresh parsley

frying pan together with the rice, salt and ¾ of the chopped herbs.

Boil, uncovered, over a low heat until rice has softened. Add a little water if necessary. Mix ingredients lightly and shake the pan from time to time. Season with the remaining salt and pepper.

Return the meat to the pan and braise in the preheated oven for another 15-20 minutes or until pork chops are done. Serve hot, sprinkled with remaining chopped herbs.

PITTA MEAT PIE

Preheat the oven to G5/190C/380F.

To make the dough:

Place the flour in a bowl and make a space in the middle. Put the eggs, oil, salt in the space and mix with a wooden spoon. Add the water, little by little, mixing continuously, until all the water has been absorbed and there are no lumps. You should get a fairly soft dough. Keep mixing the dough clockwise with your hand, slapping it against a board every now and then, until it starts to bubble up and it peels off your hand and the board. Divide it into three round cakes, brush with oil and replace on the board (sprinkled with a little flour) covered with a cloth. Allow dough to rest for 20 minutes.

To make the filling:

Mince the meat finely together with the onions. Heat the oil and sauté minced meat in it until brown all over and all the oil has been absorbed. Allow it to cool, add salt, pepper,

This is a Yugoslav meat speciality, made with the so-called Katmer dough and filled with either minced meat or cheese. In Yugoslavia it is often eaten at the end of the meal, but it makes an ideal party or light supper dish. Use bought filo pastry if you cannot be bothered with making the dough.

for the 'Katmer' dough:
1 lb./500 gr. flour
2 eggs
¼ tsp. salt
7 fluid oz./210 ml. warm water
1 fluid oz./30 ml. oil

For the filling:
12 oz./375 gr. veal
12 oz./375 gr. pork
2 large onions
3 fluid oz./90 ml. oil
2 eggs
1 tsp. salt
½ tsp. pepper
½ tsp. marjoram
1 tblsp. fresh chopped dill
4 oz./125 gr. butter
5 fluid oz./150 ml. soured cream

eggs, marjoram and dill and mix well.

Divide each one of the 3 dough cakes into 3 and roll them with a pin on a floured table top until you get sheets as thin as cigarette paper. Cut the resulting sheets to the size of your baking tray. Place the sheets you have obtained from the first big dough cake in your well buttered baking tray, dotting liberally with butter in between the sheets.

Put ½ the meat mixture over these sheets. Cover meat layer with the sheets obtained from the second dough cake, dotting with butter as above.

Spread a second layer of meat using the remaining mixture and cover it with the sheets derived from the third dough cake, again dotting with butter in between.

Pour the remaining butter, melted, on top.

Pierce the pie with a fork in a few places and place in the preheated oven to bake for 1 hour or until gold all over. Serve hot with dollops of soured cream on the side.

MOLDAVIAN MEAT FRITTERS

Chop the onion very finely and sweat in a little oil until soft but not brown. Soak the crustless slice of bread in water for a few minutes and squeeze out as much of the water as you can by hand. Pass the meats, bread, softened onion, raw carrot and raw potato through a fine mincer twice, or mince finely in a food processor. Add the raw egg, chopped crushed bay leaf, herbs, salt and pepper. Mix all the ingredients well with a wooden spoon.

Dip your hands in cold water and make small, round meat balls – the size of a

8 oz./250 gr. pork
8 oz./250 gr. lean beef
1 onion
1 slice white bread
1 carrot
1 potato
1 egg
1 bay leaf
1 tsp. salt
1 tsp. pepper
1 tsp. fresh chopped dill
1 tsp. fresh chopped coriander
2-3 tblsp. fine brown breadcrumbs
2 oz./60 gr. butter or mixed butter and oil

large walnut – by taking ½ tblsp. of the mixture at a

time and rolling it between your palms. Roll the meat balls in the breadcrumbs and flatten them into an oval shape.

Heat the fat in a frying pan and fry meat fritters over a moderate heat until dark brown on the outside and fully cooked inside. Serve sizzling with mashed potatoes and a CUCUMBER AND DILL SALAD.

You can also serve them in a sauce made of 10 fluid oz./300 ml. soured cream heated gently and mixed with ½ tblsp. finely chopped dill and a little salt.

MEAT FRITTERS IN AUBERGINE SAUCE

Make meat fritters as shown at MOLDAVIAN MEAT FRITTERS.

Place the aubergines under a hot grill about 3″/9 cm. from the flame. Grill on all sides until skin has turned black and they are soft to the touch. Split them, scoop out flesh and seeds and mash with a wooden or plastic spatula until you obtain a grey-green 'aubergine caviar'. Place on a slanted wooden board and drain as much of the inner water as possible by pressing aubergine flesh gently with

1 lb./500 gr. lean beef
3 medium aubergines (1 lb./500 gr.–1½ lb./750 gr.)
4 fluid oz./120 ml. oil
4 tomatoes
1 tsp. pepper
1 tblsp. fresh chopped coriander
1 hot dried chilli (optional)

the palm of your hand. Allow to drain while you prepare tomatoes.

Blanch the tomatoes in boiling water for 3-4 minutes. Peel the skin off the tomatoes and crush them in a mortar with a wooden

pestle or similar.

Heat the oil in a pan, and sauté the mashed aubergines, together with the crushed tomatoes, salt and pepper. Add 4 fluid oz./120 ml. water and simmer for 3 minutes over a low flame, uncovered.

Place the meat fritters into the sauce, sprinkle with chopped coriander and add the crushed dried chilli if desired (or ½ tsp. pepper if you prefer). Allow to simmer for another 10-15 minutes over a low flame and serve immediately.

MEAT RATATOUILLE ('GHIVECI')

SERVES 6-8

Preheat the oven to G4/ 180C/355F.

Chop finely: carrot, cabbage, parsnip, celery, green pepper, onions.

Cut into round slices: aubergine, courgettes. Chop ends off okra and green beans. Separate cauliflower into florets. Peel and cube potatoes.

Slice tomatoes.

Blanch the aubergine slices in boiling water for 3 minutes. Drain well and place in a large bowl together with all the other vegetables, except the onions. Add salt and pepper, mix and set aside for 15 minutes.

In the meantime, cube the pork and beef into ⅔"/2 cm. pieces. Heat oil in a pan and brown meat on all sides. Add chopped onions and paprika. Mix well to avoid sticking. When onions begin to brown, add 3 fluid oz./90 ml. water and boil gently until meat has started to soften (20-30 minutes, depending on the meat cuts you are using). Add a little warm water if needed.

As with the FISH 'GHIVECI', this Balkan version of ratatouille is based on vegetables sweated together for hours until their flavours blend into each other and into the meat they surround. In Yugoslavia, the 'Djuvec', as it is spelled, will probably be made with mutton or lamb, but I prefer this Romanian version, with a mixture of pork and beef and including an astonishing array of autumn vegetables.

8 oz./250 gr. pork
8 oz./250 gr. beef
4 oz./125 gr. cabbage
1 carrot
1 parsnip
4 oz./125 gr. celery
4 oz./125 gr. okra
4 oz./125 gr. peas
4 oz./125 gr. green beans
2 courgettes or a medium baby marrow
1 medium aubergine
4 oz./125 gr. cauliflower
3 tomatoes
1 green pepper
2 potatoes
2 onions
2 tsp. salt
1½ tsp. ground black pepper
1 tsp. hot paprika
3 fluid oz./90 ml. oil
1 oz./30 gr. butter

Butter a large casserole and place ½ the vegetables in it. Put meat pieces on top and cover with remaining vegetables. Pour 2 fluid oz./60 ml. oil and 4 fluid oz./120 ml. water or stock on top and set in the middle of the preheated oven, covered, for 2 hours or until vegetables are cooked through. If the 'ghiveci' gets too dry before the vegetables are fully cooked add a little warm water, but there should be very little sauce left at the end.

Do not stir dish at any stage to avoid vegetables sticking to the bottom crumbling or getting mushy. Do, however, shake casserole slightly from side to side every 30 minutes or so, to avoid vegetables sticking to the bottom. 15 minutes before the end, remove lid and place casserole at the top of the oven to brown the top layer of vegetables. Dot with little slivers of butter and serve warm but not too hot. The dish is incomparably better left overnight and reheated.

SAXON 'TOKANY'

SERVES 6

In Transylvania, especially around the town of Sibiu, there is a sizeable German speaking population – descendants of Saxon and Schwabian farmers and craftsmen brought in as settlers over the centuries, first by the native Transylvanian princes and later by Austro-Hungarian administrators. The beginnings of these settlements are clouded in legend. According to one version, the Saxons of Sibiu (Hermannstadt in German) are the descendants of poor Baron Hermann, the courtier of fair Gisela, the German princess who became the bride of Stephen I, King of the Magyars. Besotted with his princess and determined to be with her in her new land, Hermann brought all his family from Nurenberg to make a Saxon-land in Transylvania. Another legend maintains that a Gypsy pipe player (the Pied Piper of Hameln) took all the children of the town of Hameln on the river Wesser in Hanover to Sibiu through subterranean passages known only to the Gypsies, as revenge for not being paid after drowning the Hameln rats in the river. Whatever the truth this very unusual, rich 'tokany' (stew) is a childhood favourite, brought to Bucharest by the young Transylvanian girls who used to come south in search of service and fortune. I am indebted to the marvellous *'Gundel's Hungarian Cookbook'* for setting out clearly a famous traditional dish.

Scrape all remaining fat off the kidneys and discard the membrane. Cut in halves, lengthwise, and remove veins. Blanch the kidney halves in boiling water for 3-4 minutes. Drain and reserve.

Chop the kidney, pork and beef into long strips, about 1"/3 cm. wide. Slice mushrooms thinly. Chop onion very finely.

Heat the fat in a pan and sweat onion over a low flame until soft but not brown. Away from heat, add the paprika (it burns easily!) and mix well.

Replace over a medium flame and add beef strips, crushed garlic, ⅔ of the salt and pepper and all the marjoram. Sauté for 5 minutes until beef is brown

---

8 oz./250 gr. calf or pig kidney
3 oz./90 gr. smoked bacon
12 oz./360 gr. stewing beef
12 oz./360 gr. stewing pork
6 oz./180 gr. mushrooms
4 oz./120 gr. onions
1 tblsp. mild paprika
1 tsp. sweet marjoram
2 cloves garlic
1 tsp. salt
1 tsp. pepper
3 oz./90 gr. lard or oil
10 fluid oz./300 ml. thick soured
   cream

---

and sealed all over.

Add 3 fluid oz./90 ml. water and braise covered, over a low flame until beef has softened (about 20 minutes). Add pork strips and replenish liquid if necessary. Cover and continue cooking over a low flame.

Chop bacon into small pieces and fry them over a low flame in a separate pan until they have shed most of their fat. Add kidney pieces, mushroom slices and the remaining salt and pepper. Sauté over a lively flame for 5 minutes or until kidney pieces have shed all the blood.

When the pork strips are almost done (white and soft inside), tip the contents of the frying pan over the meats. Mix well and continue cooking for another 5-10 minutes or until all the different meats are done. Add soured cream, stir and heat gently without allowing it to boil. Adjust seasoning and serve with POLENTA CAKES or COURGETTES 'CELJE'.

THREE-MEAT BOSNIAN HOT-POT

Preheat oven G5/190C/380F. Dice the meats into 1″/3cm. cubes. Remove the rind from bacon and fry bacon pieces in oil. Add the pork first, then after 3 minutes the lamb and beef. Brown meats to seal on all sides. Remove from pan with a slotted spoon and set aside.

Fry the chopped onions and chopped garlic in the fat left from the meat until soft. Add paprika and mix gently away from the flame. Mix with the meat.

Clean the vegetables and chop into medium sized pieces.

This is a warming, rich 'meal-in-one', to be eaten on cold nights, served with chunks of brown bread, dipped without inhibitions into the sauce.

8 oz./250 gr. pork fillet
8 oz./250 gr. lamb fillet
8 oz./250 gr. beef
4 oz./125 gr. smoked bacon
1 pt./600 ml. white wine
1 pt./600 ml. beef stock or
  water
2 fluid oz./60 ml. oil
3 oz./90 gr. carrots
2 medium onions
4 cloves garlic
3 oz./90 gr. celery
3 oz./90 gr. cauliflower
3 oz./90 gr. bobby beans
3 oz./90 gr. green peppers
3 oz./90 gr. aubergines
3 oz./90 gr. tomatoes
½ tblsp. chopped fresh dill
½ tblsp. chopped fresh coriander
½ tblsp. chopped fresh parsley
2 tsps. mild paprika
1 tsp. salt

In a large earthenware pot, place alternative layers of vegetables and meat, starting and finishing with diced vegetables. Sprinkle the finely chopped herbs on top. Pour the wine and stock or water and cover with greaseproof paper. Tie a wet muslin cloth on top of the greaseproof paper and place in the middle of oven for 2½-3 hours or until the meat is tender. Dampen muslin occasionally to prevent paper from cracking.

Adjust seasoning and serve in earthenware bowls, steaming hot.

SPICY ROMANIAN SAUSAGES (MITITEI)

SERVES 8 (about 20 pieces)

Mince the meat and suet together 3 times, or blend very finely in a food processor. Add salt and place in a bowl in the fridge for 24 hours, tightly packed and covered.

Mix in black pepper, cumin powder, bicarbonate of soda, hot paprika, 4 fluid oz./125 ml. beef stock. Crush the garlic cloves and make a paste mixing them into ½ fluid oz./15 ml. beef stock. Mix the garlic paste into the

---

2 lb./1 kg. neck of beef
4 oz./125 gr. beef suet
2 tsp. black pepper
2 sprigs thyme or 2 tsp. dry thyme
½ tsp. cumin powder
1 tsp. hot paprika
⅛ tsp. bicarbonate of soda
2 oz./60 gr. crushed garlic
2 tsp. salt
10 fluid oz./300 ml. beef stock

---

meat.

Take 1 tblsp. of the meat

mixture at a time and, dipping your hands in cold water, shape into thick, short sausages, about 2"/6 cm. long and 1"/2 cm. thick. Pour the rest of the stock in a bowl and grill sausages over a hot charcoal grill or similar, brushing constantly with stock or fat and turning on all sides. They should be very dark brown outside and a rosy pink inside.

CEVAPCICI

SERVES 12 (about 30 pieces)

Remove all blood vessels from the meat and cut into small cubes. Salt and leave to stand for a few hours. Mince the meat finely and add pepper. Make a paste out of the crushed garlic and water and mix it into the minced meat. Knead well to bind and leave in the fridge for at least 2 hours.

This is a Yugoslav variety of the spicy Romanian sausages above.

---

2 ½ lb./1.2 kg. neck of beef
1 lb./500 gr. neck of mutton or lean pork
3 tsp. pepper
2 tsp. salt
2 fluid oz./60 ml. water
3 cloves garlic

Knead once more and shape finger-thick sausages from it (thinner than the Romanian version, about the size of a forefinger). Replace in fridge for 1 hour.

Grill on a moderate barbecue or similar, keeping juices in. Turn carefully, without piercing.

STUFFED CABBAGE (SARMALE)

SERVES 8

Cabbage leaves, either pickled in brine or raw and blanched, filled with a mixture of minced pork and beef, are — together with Polenta — the best known Romanian foods. They are eaten all through the year, but are traditional at Christmas, when huge cauldrons full of stuffed cabbage are brought to the family table, to form the centre

piece of an all-night meal, supplemented by filled vine leaves, smoked meats and a variety of fish and pork cuts in garlic aspics. All these dishes are, of course, designed to make good use of the pig which every self-respecting Romanian farmer slaughters before Christmas. They are also meant to sustain the family through a

night of revelry centred around the midnight Orthodox Church service, thus making the Christmas Eve supper and not the following day's lunch, the main meal of the festivities. There is a 'luxury' filling for this dish as well: you can replace the mince and rice mixture with 1 ½ lb./750 gr. breast of goose, finely minced.

Preheat the oven to G4/180C/355F.

Chop the stalk off the cabbage and undo the leaves carefully, in order not to tear them. Set aside the thick outer leaves and blanch the nice inner ones for 5 minutes in 2 pts./1 l. salted boiling water mixed with 3 tblsp. vinegar. When leaves are softened and elastic but not mushy, remove from acidulated water with a slotted spoon and set aside. Chop onions finely and sweat in butter until soft but not brown. Add the rice and fry lightly for 3 minutes. Add 2 tblsp. water and simmer until the rice has absorbed the water.

Soak the crustless slice of bread in water and squeeze out as much of the water as you can by hand.

Mince the two kinds of meat together in a mincer or in a food processor. Mix in rice, onion, chopped herbs, soaked bread, salt, pepper and add 3 tblsp. water. Mix well to obtain a smooth filling.

Take each leaf of cabbage, place it flat with the thick 'vein' inside and put about 1 flat tblsp. of filling in. Roll leaves tightly, taking care not to tear them. If the

---

3 lbs./1.5 kg. white cabbage
11 oz./350 gr. lean beef
11 oz./350 gr. lean pork
8 oz./250 gr. smoked bacon
1 slice white bread, crust removed
2 onions
2 oz./60 gr. butter
2 tblsp. rice
3 oz./90 gr.
1 tsp. salt
½ tsp. pepper
1 tblsp. fresh chopped dill
1 tblsp. fresh chopped parsley
2 branches thyme
2 tomatoes
2 tblsp. tomato paste
3 tblsp. vinegar
2 tblsp. lemon juice

---

leaves are very large, cut them in half. You should get a cylinder about 3"/9 cm. long and 1"/3 cm. thick. In Moldavia the filled cabbage is walnut size – if you want them as small as that (they will be small enough to eat one with each mouthful) simply cut the leaves into ⅓ of their normal size and use about 1 tsp. of filling for each one. Either way, tuck ends under the leaves to avoid opening while cooking.

Chop the remaining cabbage the size of macaroni. Line a large saucepan with a layer

of cabbage strips, place a slice of bacon over them, add a few slices of tomatoes and cover with a tight layer of stuffed cabbage.

Cover them with a second layer of chopped cabbage and repeat procedure until you have exhausted all the ingredients, ending with a layer of chopped cabbage (this is important, as the top layer will get dry and burnt in the oven).

Dilute the tomato paste in 4 fluid oz./120 ml. water and add lemon juice. Pour this tomato sauce into the saucepan cover and bring to the boil. Simmer for ½ hour on a low flame, then place in the middle of the preheated oven, uncovered, for 2 hours, or until the meat inside the cabbage leaves is fully cooked. This dish is much better left overnight and reheated. Serve with POLENTA and soured cream on the side.

You can also use PICKLED CABBAGE leaves for this recipe. The procedure is identical, but omit blanching (just dip leaves in boiling water for 1 minute if they are too sour) and use sauerkraut* to layer the bottom of the saucepan.

STUFFED VINE LEAVES

Blanch the vine leaves in boiling water for 5 minutes, until they start to change colour. Separate them gently and place them spine upwards on a board, ready for stuffing.

Prepare the stuffing: soak crustless bread in water for a few minutes. Squeeze out as much water as you can by hand. Mince meat with soaked bread.

Chop the onion finely and fry in oil until soft. Add rice, fry gently for 2-3 minutes and cover with 2 fluid oz./60 ml. water. Reduce heat further and simmer for 5 minutes. Mix rice and onion with the minced meat. Add chopped herbs, salt, pepper, cinnamon. Mix well and add 3 fluid oz./90 ml. water.

Fill the vine leaves with the mixture and fold to make a neat parcel.

Making sure the loose ends

Vine leaves stuffed with a mixture of pork and beef or with rice and pine kernels are traditional dishes for the Christmas supper, where they accompany STUFFED CABBAGE and POLENTA. I prefer, however, this spring version, eaten at Easter, in which the leaves are filled with lamb meat flavoured with cinnamon. This produces an altogether lighter and more pungent effect.

½ lb./250 gr. vine leaves
1 lb./500 gr. lean lamb or veal
1 slice white bread, crust removed
1 onion
4 oz./125 gr. rice
1 tsp. ground cinnamon
1 tsp. salt
½ tsp. black pepper
2 tblsp. chopped dill or mixed chopped dill and coriander
1 small sprig of rosemary or 1 tsp. dry rosemary
2 tblsp. olive oil
2 tblsp. tomato purée or 6 ripe tomatoes
3 fluid oz./90 ml. lemon juice
5 fluid oz./150 ml. soured cream or yoghurt

---

are placed towards the bottom of the saucepan, place vine leaves in tight rows. Pack the vine leaves even tighter by placing a plate or lid on top and pressing down gently. Make a sauce out of the blanched and blended tomatoes or tomato purée diluted in enough water to cover leaves. Salt to taste, add 1 tblsp. olive oil, the sprig of rosemary and simmer covered for 1 hour on a low flame. Remove from heat, add lemon juice (do not add anything sour from the beginning as it will cause vine leaves to harden), cover and place in a moderate oven for a further ½ hour. Allow to cool a little, add soured cream or yoghurt to the sauce and serve with POLENTA CAKES or a RED CABBAGE AND APPLE SALAD.

FILLED CABBAGE LEAVES 'STANIMASHK'

SERVES 6-8

Chop the onions finely. Fry them in the lard until soft but not brown. Mix the peppercorns with softened onions. Add salt.

Slice the pork into thin rectangles about 1″/3 cm. long.

Cut the cabbage stalk off and undo leaves carefully. Set aside the thicker outer leaves and pick the nice inner ones. Slice them into 2-3 pieces if they are too big and wrap a piece of meat and 1 tblsp. of onion with 2-3 peppercorns in each leaf. Fold the leaves

This is a Bulgarian version of stuffed cabbage, unusual in that it uses whole slices of pork fillet for the stuffing, instead of the customary mince-and-rice mixture.

1½ lb./750 gr. pork fillet
1 head of cabbage pickled in brine (see PICKLED CABBAGE)
6 onions
4 oz./125 gr. lard
24 peppercorns
10 fluid oz./300 ml. pickling brine from the cabbage
1 tsp. salt
4 oz./125 gr. smoked bacon

carefully.

Chop the rest of the cabbage into long thin strips. Line the bottom of a saucepan with the chopped cabbage and place filled cabbage leaves on top, placing a slice of smoked bacon between the layers.

Dilute pickling brine with enough water to cover the cabbage leaves and boil, uncovered, over a moderate flame until all liquid has evaporated and meat inside the leaves is soft. Serve on a bed of rice or POLENTA.

LEEKS FILLED WITH MEAT

SERVES 4

Preheat the oven to G5/190C/380F.

Cut the green stalks off the leeks and discard. Place the white stems in a bowl of cold water for ½ hour until all grit has been eliminated. With a sharp knife scoop out as much of the white inner flesh as possible, leaving 2-3 outer layers and a plug at the stalk end. Chop the scooped-out flesh into fine pieces. Heat the oil in a frying pan and gently fry the rice. Add 4 fluid oz./120 ml. water and simmer gently to allow the rice to absorb most of the water. Remove

4 large leeks (about 1 lb./500 gr. after discarding green stalks)
8 oz./250 gr. minced pork
3 oz./90 gr. rice
3 fluid oz./90 ml. oil
½ tsp. salt
1 tblsp. tomato paste
1 tblsp. chopped dill or coriander
½ tsp. cumin seeds (optional)
1 egg
½ tsp. pepper

rice from the fire and reserve. Place the minced pork in the frying pan. Turn up the heat and sauté

the pork for about 10 minutes. Towards the end add the chopped dill, salt and pepper. Mix with rice and allow to cool. Mix in the egg.

Fill the leek stems with the mixture. Place in a long covered ovenproof dish. Make a sauce as follows: Lightly sweat chopped-up white leek flesh. Add 4 fluid oz./120 ml. water, tomato paste, cumin seeds, salt. Bring to the boil and adjust seasoning. Pour sauce over leeks, cover and braise in the middle of the oven for 20 minutes.

STUFFED PEPPERS

Preheat the oven to G3/ 170C/335F.

Cut a lid in the peppers and remove stalks and seeds. Place on a rack or board, hole downwards and drain. Soak the bread in 1 fluid oz./30 ml. water. When water has been entirely absorbed, squeeze it out and mix with the minced meat. Heat ½ the oil in a frying pan and gently sweat chopped leeks or chopped onion until soft. Add finely chopped garlic and rice. Increase heat to medium and fry rice quickly for 2 minutes. Pour 1 fluid oz./30 ml. water, mix well and add

4 large peppers (14 oz./400 gr. in weight)
8 oz./250 gr. lean beef, finely minced
1 slice white bread, crust removed
½ onion or 2 oz./60 gr. chopped leeks
1 clove garlic, finely chopped
2 oz./60 gr. rice
1 tblsp. chopped coriander
¼ tsp. salt
2 fluid oz./60 ml. oil
1 tblsp. tomato paste
⅓ tsp. flour
2 tblsp. soured cream

to the meat. Add chopped coriander and mix all

ingredients well.

Fill the peppers with the mixture. Heat the rest of the oil and fry peppers lightly on all sides until slightly brown. Place the peppers in an ovenproof covered dish. Add 4 fluid oz./120 ml. water or stock to the fat from the frying pan and stir in the tomato paste. Bring to the boil, pour over peppers and place in the middle of the oven. Braise covered for 1½ hour. The dish is even better when left overnight and reheated.

Before serving, mix the sauce with the soured cream and pour over peppers.

COURGETTES/BABY-MARROWS STUFFED WITH BEEF

Preheat the oven to G5/ 190C/380F.

Scrub the courgettes well and if their skins are too thick, scrape them with a knife. Cut them in half, lengthwise, and scoop out with a teaspoon about ¾ of the inner flesh. Now make this mixture:

Soak the slice of bread in a little water for a few minutes.

Squeeze out as much of the water as you can by hand. Mince the meat in a fine mincer or in a food processor. Chop the onion finely and sweat in butter until soft but not brown.

6 young, medium-sized courgettes or baby marrows
12 oz./360 gr. lean beef
1 slice bread, crust removed
1 small onion
1 egg
4 oz./125 gr. rice
½ tsp. salt
¼ tsp. hot paprika
½ tblsp. chopped dill
2 tblsp. tomato paste or 4 ripe tomatoes
2 oz./60 gr. butter

For the sauce:
1 small onion
1 tsp. cumin seed
5 fluid oz./150 ml. soured cream
½ tblsp. fresh chopped dill

Add scooped-out courgette flesh and rice, fry for 3 minutes on a low heat and add 3 fluid oz./90 ml. water. Allow the rice to absorb the water, then mix together minced meat, the contents of the frying pan, soaked bread, egg, salt, paprika and chopped dill.

Fill the courgette halves with the mixture. Place the halves on top of one another to re-form into whole courgettes, removing any stuffing coming out of the sides. Place in a casserole wide enough to take them in one row side by side. Make a sauce by blanching and then sieving or blending tomatoes or by mixing the tomato paste with 4 fluid oz./120 ml. water. Add cumin seed, chopped second onion and a little salt. Pour this sauce over the courgettes in the casserole and braise in the preheated oven for 45 minutes-1 hour until filling is cooked through. Before serving, sprinkle with chopped dill and mix soured cream into the tomato sauce. Serve hot, with a salad as a main course or as a side dish.

STUFFED SPINACH LEAVES
SERVES 6

Preheat the oven to G5/190C/380F.
Cut the stalks off spinach leaves and wash well in plenty of water. Blanch leaves in boiling water for 1 minute only. (The leaves are very delicate and tear easily if boiled too long.) Remove them one by one from the boiling water with a slotted spoon and drain well.
Prepare the stuffing: Soak the bread in water for a few minutes. Squeeze out as much water as you can by hand. Mince finely the two kinds of meat with the soaked bread. Chop the onion finely and fry in 1 tblsp. oil until soft and golden brown. Add rice, lower flame and fry gently for 3 minutes. Add 2 fluid oz./60 ml. water and simmer covered for a further 5 minutes, on a very low flame. Mix rice and onion

8 oz./250 gr. large spinach leaves (use the Cyprus variety, with leaves large enough to stuff. You can also use dock leaves for this recipe)
8 oz./250 gr. lean beef
8 oz./250 gr. lean pork
1 slice bread, crust removed
1 onion
2 tblsp. olive oil
4 oz./125 gr. rice
1 tsp. salt
1 tsp. nutmet
½ tsp. pepper
2 tblsp. chopped dill
1 sprig thyme
2 tblsp. tomato purée or 6 ripe tomatoes
2 tomatoes
5 fluid oz./150 ml. soured cream or yoghurt
1 tblsp. lemon juice or vinegar

with the minced meat. Add chopped dill, salt, pepper, nutmeg. Mix well and add 3

fluid oz./90 ml. water or stock. Fill the spinach leaves and make small sausage shaped rolls. Place the rolls in a casserole, loose ends downwards, with slices of tomatoes in between. Make a sauce out of the 6 tomatoes blanched and blended or tomato purée diluted in enough water to cover spinach rolls. Add 1 tblsp. oil, sprig of thyme, cover and place in preheated oven for about 1 hour or until meat inside is soft. (If you have some stuffing left over, make a few meat balls and place between spinach leaves – they will give you an indication of how cooked the meat is without having to undo the spinach rolls). Add lemon juice and cook for a further 15-30 minutes. Allow to cool slightly, mix the soured cream or yoghurt with the sauce and serve.

BLANCHED CALF'S BRAINS

SERVES 4-6

Brains are frowned upon to some extent in this country, but in the Balkans and especially in Romania (displaying here the French influence) they are considered a great delicacy and are widely used. Blanching them is the essential preparation for all the recipes which follow, so treat this procedure as a master recipe to be followed before you attempt any of the variants and combinations. Brains are not readily available in this country but look for a good butcher who supplies restaurants and he will easily get them for you on 24 hours notice. Cook them within 24 hours of purchase. If you need to keep them longer, soak and blanch them and they will keep in the fridge for up to 3 days.

Wash the brains thoroughly in running cold water to remove as much of the blood as you can. Soak the brains in a bowl with cold water for at least 1 hour, but preferably for 2 hours, changing the water every 20 minutes or so. Remove the thin filament covering them – this may be a little laborious, but if you have soaked them well the filament should be soft enough to peel off easily. Wash them again.
Gently heat 2 pt./1.2 l. water mixed with the salt and vinegar in a saucepan. Plunge the brains into the warm water and simmer

---

1 lb./500 gr. calf's brains or
   beef brains
1 tblsp. vinegar
1 tsp. salt
1 tblsp. capers
1 crisp lettuce
1 tblsp. lemon juice
1 oz./30 gr. butter (optional)
2 tblsp. tomato paste (optional)

---

allowing the water to bubble gently for 20 minutes (for beef brains – 30 minutes; for lamb brains only 15 minutes). Remove from heat and allow them to cool in the cooking liquid for another 20 minutes. Drain well.
The brains are now ready to be served 'nature', sliced and placed on a bed of crisp lettuce sprinkled with capers and lemon juice or to be used as the basis for other recipes.
Blanching will make them firm, white and easy to slice with a sharp knife.
In Romania, blanched brains will also be served hot (do not cool them in their liquid, just remove with slotted spoon when ready) whole or in slices, with melted butter mixed with lemon juice or 2 tblsp. tomato paste diluted in a little of the boiling liquid.

BRAIN CROQUETTES
SERVES 4

Clean and blanch the brains as described at BLANCHED CALF'S BRAINS. Slice in 1″/3 cm. wide slices.

Melt the butter over a low flame. Add the flour and milk and mix until you get a thick mixture which starts to come away from the walls of the saucepan. Remove from the heat, allow to cool for 3 minutes then mix in the eggs, brain slices, salt and pepper. Separately fry in a little butter the red pepper shredded very finely, until soft but not brown. Mix the

1 lb./500 gr. beef brains
2 fluid oz./60 ml. milk
2 oz./60 gr. butter
2 tblsp. flour
2 eggs
½ tsp. salt
½ tsp. pepper
2 oz./60 gr. red pepper (optional)
2 fluid oz./60 ml. oil

For the sauce (optional):
1 tblsp. tomato paste
½ tsp. sugar
¼ tsp. cumin seeds
¼ tsp. black pepper

red pepper into the brain mixture. Mix well for a few minutes to obtain a smooth white paste, shot through with the red pepper shreds. Dip your hand in a little flour and, taking ½ tblsp. of the mixture at a time, shape finger-long croquettes. Fry the croquettes in heated oil and serve with a salad or covered with a tomato sauce made from 1 tblsp. tomato paste diluted in 2 tblsp. water and flavoured with the pepper and cumin seeds.

BRAINS GOUJONADE
SERVES 4

Clean and blanch the brains as described at BLANCHED CALF'S BRAINS. Slice them into finger-thick slices. Season the flour with the salt and pepper. Beat the egg. Roll the brain slices into flour, then egg and

1 lb./500 gr. beef or calf brains
1 tblsp. flour
1 egg
1 tblsp. breadcrumbs
2 oz./60 gr. butter
½ tsp. salt
½ tsp. pepper

finally in the fine breadcrumbs. Shake off excess breadcrumbs and fry in very hot butter or ½ butter and ½ oil until golden all over. Serve on a bed of DILLED PEAS.

BAKED BRAINS WITH MUSHROOMS

SERVES 2

Preheat the oven to G6/ 200C/400F.
Prepare brains as shown at BLANCHED CALF'S BRAINS. Slice them into thin slices. Wash and trim the mushrooms and slice thinly. Blanch the tomatoes for 2 minutes in boiling water and peel off their skins.
Slice them, with a sharp knife, into thin rounds. Sprinkle with salt.

4 oz./125 gr. calf's or beef brain
4 oz./125 gr. mushrooms
5 oz./150 gr. ripe tomatoes
2 oz./60 gr. butter
1 tblsp. breadcrumbs
1 tblsp. grated cheddar
¼ tsp. pepper
¼ tsp. salt

Sweat the mushrooms in ½ tblsp. of the butter until soft and brown. Sprinkle with freshly ground pepper.
Butter a small ovenproof dish well, and line it with alternating layers of brain slices, mushrooms and tomatoes. Finish with brains. Melt remaining butter and pour over the brains. Sprinkle on top with breadcrumbs and grated cheese and bake in preheated oven for 25 minutes. Serve hot.

TOMATOES FILLED WITH BRAINS

SERVES 4-6 (each 2 oz./60 gr. tomato will take 1 oz./30 gr. of stuffing)

Preheat the oven to G5/ 190C/380F.
Prepare brains as shown at BLANCHED CALF'S BRAINS. Chop into small pieces. Cut a lid in the tomatoes, scoop out the inner flesh with a grapefruit knife and put a pinch of salt and one of pepper in each tomato. Place them hole down on a rack and drain for ½ hour. In the meantime, chop the chives very finely and soften in a little butter mixed with oil. Add the brains and sauté for 5 minutes. Add the egg

1 lb./500 gr. medium tomatoes
8 oz./250 gr. brains
1 egg
1 oz./30 gr. grated parmesan cheese
1 oz./30 gr. chopped chives or spring onions
1 oz./30 gr. butter
1 fluid oz./30 ml. oil
¼ tsp. black pepper
¼ tsp. salt
½ tsp. mild paprika

and scramble together brains and egg until the egg is solid but not too dry. Add salt and pepper and mix well.
Fill each tomato with the brain mixture. Butter an ovenproof dish and arrange the tomatoes in it. Sprinkle each tomato with parmesan and paprika. Replace lids on the tomatoes.
Bake in preheated oven for 15 minutes, but do not allow tomatoes to get soggy: their still crisp and fresh taste should act as a foil to the buttery, soft brain mixture.

SAVOURY BRAINS PUDDING IN PEPPER SAUCE

SERVES 4-6

Clean and blanch brains as shown as BLANCHED CALF'S BRAINS. Slice into finger-thick slices.

Separate the eggs. Soak crustless bread in the milk and squeeze as much of the liquid as you can by hand. Mix together the butter, egg yolks, soaked bread and grated cheese. Add the chopped brains. Beat egg whites until stiff and fold gently into the mixture. Butter a bowl. Pour the mixture into the bowl and place it in a saucepan with boiling water. Cover and

---

1 lb./500 gr. beef brains
2 oz./60 gr. butter
3 eggs
1 slice white bread
3 tblsp. grated cheddar
1 fluid oz./30 ml. milk
½ tblsp. mild paprika

for the sauce:
2 medium red peppers
1 tsp. salt
1 tblsp. medium or hot paprika
2 fluid oz./60 ml. dry red wine
1 oz./30 gr. butter

---

simmer for 50 minutes. Tip the pudding over onto a shallow serving dish.

While pudding is cooking in the bain-marie, make the sauce:

Remove stalks and seeds from the peppers and slice into small pieces. Sweat them in 1 oz./30 gr. butter until soft, adding salt and paprika. Add wine and simmer for 10 minutes. Sieve or blend in a food processor to obtain a fairly thin sauce. If this sauce is too thick, add a little wine to thin it out. Pour around brains pudding and sprinkle with mild paprika. Serve very hot.

CLUJ LIVER PATE

SERVES 6

Cluj is the ancient capital of Transylvania and has been for centuries a centre of excellence for things pleasurable, including cooking. Cluj cuisine at its best is a successful blend of Austro-Hungarian sophistication with the more rustic tastes of the surrounding countryside. Walter Starkie calls it 'the Oxford of the East of Europe, with its students and its traditional buildings. There is an air of pride about Cluj: It stands surrounded by its mountains as a strong bulwark to countless wars waged between East and West. Cluj was the birth place of Mathias Corvinus, the Hungarian King of the Renaissance era, who brought great art, and high aesthetic standards to his lands.'

Clean all the meats. Soak the brains for at least 2 hours in cold acidulated water (see BLANCHED CALF'S BRAINS). Boil the liver and pork in SEPARATE saucepans of lightly salted water for about 30 minutes. Boil brains for 30 minutes until white and firm. Mince together in a fine mincer or blend in a food processor: bacon, boiled liver, boiled brains, boiled pork. Chop the mushrooms and

---

1 lb./500 gr. pig's liver
5 oz./150 gr. smoked bacon
5 oz./150 gr. pork
5 oz./150 gr. beef brains
1 oz./30 gr. mushrooms
2 eggs
1 tblsp. rum
1 tblsp. red wine or madeira or port
1½ tsp. salt
¼ tsp. pepper

---

boil in 3 fluid oz./90 ml. water for 15 minutes or until soft. Drain well reserving the liquor and sieve or blend in a food processor.

Mix the meat paste with the mushroom paste and add the liquid in which the mushrooms boiled.

Mix in the eggs, rum, wine, salt and pepper. Mix well to obtain a smooth paste. Serve slightly warm with chunks of brown bread or chill and serve cold with toast.

TONGUE WITH OLIVES

Wash the tongue well and scrub it with a brush to eliminate any dirt from the pores. Place it in a saucepan with 3 pts./1.5 l. water, and add 1 onion, carrot, parsnip, peppercorns and salt. Simmer, covered, for 3 hours (2¼ hours for the veal tongue). Skim occasionally. Drain, and peel the outer skin while still hot, starting at the tip and scraping towards the root with a sharp knife. Slice it into 4 equal pieces and place them on a serving dish.

Wash the olives and boil them for 5 minutes in some of the tongue stock. Chop

---

1 lb./500 gr. beef or veal tongue
2 onions
1 carrot
1 parsnip
6 peppercorns
2 tblsp. tomato paste
4 fluid oz./120 ml. red wine
4 oz./125 gr. black olives
1 tsp. salt
1 oz./30 gr. butter
½ tsp. mild paprika
½ tsp. cumin seeds
1 tblsp. fresh chopped parsley

---

the remaining onion finely. Heat the butter in a frying pan and sweat onion over a low flame until soft and golden. Dissolve the tomato

paste in 2 fluid oz./60 ml. of the tongue stock and add it to the onions. Add a little salt, paprika and cumin seeds. Bring sauce to the boil and add wine and olives. Boil over a moderate flame for 5 minutes and pour sauce over tongue on the serving dish. Traditionally, this dish is served cold, but I have always liked it hot. Either way, serve sprinkled with parsley and accompanied by POLENTA CAKES or DILLED PEAS or, if you feel very adventurous, with a little LEMON SHERBET on the side.

STUFFED VEAL TRIPE

Preheat the oven to G6/ 200C/400F.
The stomach of veal (tripe) should be washed well and scrubbed with a brush until white. Sprinkle with salt. Chop the kidneys, liver and meat into 1"/3 cm. cubes and boil them for ½ hour in plenty of lightly salted water. Drain and set aside. Chop the onions finely. Heat the oil and sweat onions until soft. Add the rice and fry over a medium flame for 3 minutes, shaking the pan. Add the chopped and boiled meats and fry for another 5 minutes. Bring ½ the stock

---

1 whole stomach of veal (ask
   your butcher to clean it for
   you without slicing it)
3 lb./1.5 kg. mixed veal liver,
   kidneys, veal meat
12 spring onions or 4 medium
   onions
5 fluid oz./150 ml. oil
4 oz./125 gr. rice
1 pt./600 ml. veal or beef stock
3 tsp. hot paprika
1 tsp. pepper
4 tsp. salt
1 tblsp. fresh chopped parsley
½ tblsp. fresh chopped mint
   leaves

---

to the boil and add it to the pan. Simmer over a low flame until the rice has softened and is beginning to swell. Add 1 tsp. salt, paprika, pepper, parsley and mint.
Stuff the stomach of veal with the mixture and sew the opening with thread or close it with a few small skewers. Place the tripe in a baking tray, pour the remaining stock around and add 3 tblsp. oil. Roast in the preheated oven for 1–1½ hours, basting occasionally with the liquid in the tray. Serve hot.

A Bosnian gypsy woman, c. 1910.

Going to the Sunday dance. Romania c. 1910.

Peasants in Traditional Dress. Transylvania, Romania.

Peasants and Turks in Plevljie, Yugoslavia c. 1910.

Romanian country women with oxen at Huedin, Romania c. 1910.

'Hora' – the Romanian national dance. <u>c.</u> 1910.

Traditional costume of the Oltenian street seller as worn by actors in 'The Lute Player' ('Cobzarul'), a musical drama of <u>c.</u> 1900.

A farmer from Bessarabia, Romania, in everyday clothes c. 1900.

VEGETABLE
DISHES

BULGARIAN AUBERGINES

Prick the aubergines with a fork in a few places, taking care not to tear skin more than necessary. Place under a hot grill about 3"/9 cm. from the flame and grill on all sides until skin becomes black and soft to the touch. Do not allow them to burst open.

Slice the aubergines in two in length with a sharp knife, scoop out the flesh and reserve skins. Place the flesh on a wooden board poised at an angle and allow as much as possible of the water to drain away.

In the meantime, chop the mushrooms and shred pepper finely. Slice garlic into thin slivers. Heat butter in a pan and sauté garlic for

Aubergines are widely eaten in the Balkans, but they are mostly associated with Bulgarian cooking. Bulgarian chefs will wax lyrical on the innumerable merits and uses of the aubergine and would boast proudly of a repertory of hundreds of recipes based on them. Here are a few:

3 aubergines (about 2½ lb./1.250 kg.)
8 oz./250 gr. mushrooms
3 cloves garlic
1 large red pepper
4 oz./125 gr. butter
½ tsp. salt
1 tsp. freshly ground black pepper
1 tblsp. breadcrumbs
1 tblsp. grated parmesan cheese
10 fluid oz./300 ml. live yoghurt

2-3 minutes. Add mushrooms and red pepper, salt and freshly ground black pepper. Sweat in the butter for 7-10 minutes on a low flame, or until soft.

Mash the drained aubergine flesh coarsely with a fork (do not blend or sieve – the mixture should not be too fine). Mix in the contents of the frying pan, pouring out excess liquid, but allowing enough in to make a moist mixture. Adjust seasoning. Fill the aubergine skins with the mixture, sprinkle with mixed parmesan cheese and fine breadcrumbs and place under a hot grill for 5-10 minutes or until nicely browned. Serve with live yoghurt on the side.

AUBERGINES WITH MUSHROOMS

Chop the onion and garlic finely. Heat 2 tblsp. oil in a sauté pan and fry onion and garlic gently until golden brown.

In the meantime, cut the aubergine lengthwise into 8 parts and then across into ½"/1.5 cm. cubes. Add the aubergine cubes to the pan, cover and fry for 3 minutes, until almost soft.

Chop the mushrooms into chunky pieces and add them

8 oz./250 gr. aubergines
3 tblsp. oil
1 onion
2 cloves garlic
3 fluid oz./90 ml. milk
3 oz./90 gr. mushrooms
2 tblsp. soured cream
¼ tsp. freshly ground black pepper
½ tsp. salt

to the pan. Add another tblsp. oil and leave, covered,

for another 3 minutes. Add milk, salt, pepper. Boil on a moderate flame until milk has almost evaporated. Add soured cream, allow it to warm up but not to boil, stirring all the time. Check seasoning. Serve sprinkled with chopped parsley, as an accompaniment to pork or lamb dishes.

FILLED AUBERGINES (IMAMBAIALDI)

SERVES 6

Choose smaller, stocky aubergines. Cut their stalks off, and, using a small sharp knife, cut a slit in length, leaving about 1″/3 cm. uncut at either end. Repeat 4 times, on all sides of the aubergines.

Bring plenty of water to the boil in a large saucepan and blanch aubergines for 8-10 minutes. Drain, place in a row on a wooden board and cover with another flat board, weighted down with about 2 lb./1 kg. of weights. Leave for ½ hour to squeeze the water out of the aubergines.

Cut the onions in quarter rings. Grate finely the carrot, celery, parsnip, green pepper. Crush 6 cloves of garlic.

Fry the onion and garlic in 1 tblsp. oil and sweat on a low flame for 8-10 minutes. Add

This was originally a Turkish recipe (Imambaialdi means 'the Imam has fainted' – presumably because of the extravagant amount of olive oil the harem cooks had used for the dish), but I prefer this lighter and more varied Romanian version.

6 small aubergines (about 1½ lb./750 gr.)
3 onions
7 cloves garlic
1 parsnip
1 carrot
½ head celery
1 green pepper
6 oz./180 gr. red or white cabbage
4 tblsp. olive oil
2 tblsp. tomato paste or 8 oz./250 gr. ripe tomatoes
½ tsp. sugar
1½ tsp. salt
1 tsp. black pepper or hot paprika

1 tsp. salt and the pepper or hot paprika and mix.

Fill the slits in each aubergine with the grated vegetables. Chop the remaining clove of garlic and add a sliver of garlic in each slit.

Place aubergines in a casserole.

Make a sauce with the tomato paste diluted in 8 fluid oz./250 ml. water and ½ tblsp. oil or the blanched and sieved/blended tomatoes with oil. Add sugar, ¼ tsp. salt and ¼ tsp. pepper. Pour sauce over aubergines, cover and simmer on a moderate to low flame for ½ hour.

If you have some vegetable mixture left, stuff some peppers or tomatoes with it and place between the aubergines.

In Turkey the dish is served cold, but I prefer it warm.

GREEN BEANS WITH SMETANA

SERVES 6-8

Wash the beans and chop off stringy bits at either end. Boil in lightly salted water for 20-30 minutes until soft but not soggy. In the meantime, make a sauce by heating the oil, mixing in flour to make a roux and whisking in milk, making sure there are no lumps.

2 lb./1 kg. green beans or bobby beans
5 fluid oz./150 ml. smetana or soured cream thinned with yoghurt
1 tblsp. fresh chopped dill
1 oz./30 gr. flour
2 oz./60 gr. olive oil
3 fluid oz./90 ml. milk
½ tsp. salt
⅛ tsp. pepper

Add salt and pepper, remove from the flame and mix in the smetana. Drain the beans well, add them to the smetana sauce in the saucepan, heat gently and simmer uncovered for 5 minutes. Serve sprinkled with chopped dill.

SPICY BEAN HOTPOT
SERVES 2

Soak the beans in water overnight. Drain and cover with cold water. Place over a low heat and bring slowly to the boil. When water has begun to bubble, drain again and replace over the flame, covering this time with hot salted water. Add the wine. Boil over a medium flame for 10-15 minutes, skimming.

In the meantime, chop finely the onion, carrot, pepper and the bacon or belly of pork and fry in oil for 10

8 oz./250 gr. haricot or butter beans
4 oz./125 gr. belly of pork or smoked streaky bacon mixed with cabanos sausage
4 fluid oz./120 ml. red wine
1 small carrot
1 onion
1 tblsp. chopped red or green pepper
1 tblsp. tomato paste
1 bay leaf
½ tsp. salt
1 sprig thyme
1 small dried red chilli

minutes. Add the sausage cut in thin rounds, for the last 3 minutes. Add the contents of the frying pan to the beans in the pot. Add the salt, tomato paste, bay leaf and small chilli. Simmer for 2 hours until beans are soft (if liquid evaporates too much, add a little mixture of water and wine). Serve hot, sprinkled with chopped parsley and dill on its own, or with POLENTA or garlic paste (see ROMANIAN GARLIC DRESSING).

GREEN BEANS 'PLAKIA'
SERVES 6-8

Bulgarian cuisine has a wide range of dishes bearing Greek or Turkish names, but using vegetables (Bulgaria is the "market garden" of Eastern Europe) where their southern counterparts would use meat or fish. You may know 'plaki' in its Greek embodiment, as a method of cooking Meditteranean fish like red mullet (Barbounia) – here is a Bulgarian vegetarian version using very young green beans instead.

Chop stringy ends off the bobby beans. If you are using young yet slightly larger beans, chop them in two as well. Chop the peppers, de-seed and discard stalks. Chop the onions very finely. Chop garlic finely. Heat ½ the oil and sweat the onions and garlic over a low flame until soft but not brown. Add the peppers and soften for another 10 minutes. Mix the contents of the frying pan with the beans, add remaining oil,

1½ lb./750 gr. bobby beans
2 onions
3 large green peppers
2 tomatoes
2 cloves garlic
3 fluid oz./90 ml. olive oil
1 tsp. hot paprika
1 tsp. salt
3 fluid oz./90 ml. milk
½ tblsp. chopped fresh dill
½ tblsp. chopped fresh parsley or coriander

salt and pepper. Place in a saucepan, add 3 fluid oz./90 ml. water and bring to the boil. When beans begin to soften (10-15 minutes) add the milk. Lower the heat and simmer over a low flame for another 10 minutes, uncovered. Chop the tomatoes into small cubes and add them to the beans. Add finely chopped herbs, simmer for another 5 minutes, give a few good but gentle stirs and serve immediately.

CABBAGE LEAVES
FILLED WITH MAIZE
SERVES 6

An (almost) vegetarian version of the famous STUFFED CABBAGE (SARMALE) in which the meat filling is replaced by coarsely ground maize (not to be mistaken for maize flour – 'polenta'). Coarse maize looks like a smaller version of sweet corn and is a great favourite in White Russian cooking, from where it passed into Moldavia and was adapted to Romanian tastes by being cooked inside pickled cabbage. It is also popular in the United States and you will find it in this country under its American name: hominy*.

Preheat the oven to G4/ 180C/355F.
You should make this dish with whole leaves of CABBAGE PICKLED IN BRINE, but if you are using a fresh cabbage proceed as follows: Cut some of the hard stalk and undo the cabbage leaves one by one, taking care not to tear them. Discard the coarser outer leaves and blanch the rest for 5 minutes in plenty of boiling water acidulated with the vinegar. Remove with a slotted spoon and drain well. The leaves should become flexible but not too soft. If you are using pickled cabbage, simply undo the leaves and wash them under running cold water to remove the excess salt. Chop the onions very finely. Melt ½ the butter and sweat the onions until soft but not brown. Add the crackling or chopped smoked bacon. Add 'hominy' maize and pour 5 fluid oz./150 ml. water on top. Keep mixing and simmer for about 10 minutes until maize has started to

■■■■■■■■■■■■■■■■■
2 lb./1 kg. cabbage (either fresh or pickled – see CABBAGE PICKLED IN BRINE)
5 oz./150 gr. coarsely ground maize (hominy*)
2 tblsp. pork crackling or chopped smoked bacon
4-5 slices smoked bacon
2 onions
5 oz./150 gr. butter or mixed butter and oil
1 tsp. salt
½ tsp. black pepper
1 tsp. hot paprika
2 fluid oz./60 ml. vinegar
2 tblsp. tomato paste
3 tomatoes
1 tblsp. lemon juice
■■■■■■■■■■■■■■■■■

absorb the water and to swell a little (hominy maize will behave like rice when boiled). Remove from the flame, add salt and pepper and set aside to cool a little. Lay out a leaf of cabbage, spine upwards, and fill it with about ½ tblsp. of the maize and onion mixture. Roll the cabbage leaf to make a parcel like a small, fat cigar. Repeat procedure until you have exhausted all the filling (do not put too much in as the maize will swell a lot when cooked). Chop the rest of the cabbage into thin strips or shred it the size of vermicelli. Place cabbage leaves in a large casserole, over a layer of shredded cabbage. Place slices of tomatoes and smoked bacon between each row of filled cabbage, divided from the one below by a row of shredded cabbage. Dilute tomato paste in 5 fluid oz./150 ml. water. Add lemon juice and hot paprika. Pour sauce over the cabbage (omit lemon juice if you are using pickled cabbage). Bring to the boil on a moderate flame and simmer, covered, for 15 minutes. Place in the preheated oven and braise slowly for 1 hour 45 minutes. The dish is much better kept overnight and reheated. Serve on its own or with a rich game dish like DUCK WITH MORELLO CHERRIES.

CABBAGE CROQUETTES

Blanch the cabbage leaves in boiling water for 15 minutes. Shred cabbage finely, till the size of vermicelli.
Soak the bread in the milk and squeeze out as much of the liquid as you can by hand. Mince the meat finely, together with the onions and the soaked bread. Mix the meat and shredded cabbage. Add 2 eggs, salt, paprika, and finely chopped dill. Mix well for a few minutes until

2 lb./1 kg. white cabbage, broken into leaves
8 oz./250 gr. lean beef
3 eggs
2 slices white bread, crust removed
2 fluid oz./60 ml. milk
3 oz./90 gr. flour
4 fluid oz./120 ml. oil
2 medium onions
2 oz./60 gr. fine white breadcrumbs
½ tsp. salt
⅛ tsp. hot paprika
1 tblsp. fresh chopped dill

smooth.
Beat the remaining egg in a bowl and spread flour and breadcrumbs onto 2 plates. Form small (2"/6 cm. long) croquettes taking 1 tblsp. of the mixture at a time. Roll each croquette first through flour, then through beaten egg and finely coat with breadcrumbs.
Heat oil on a very high flame and fry croquettes until golden-brown all over.

BRAISED SOURED CABBAGE (VARZA CALITA)

Shred the cabbage finely on the fine teeth of a manual grater or in a food processor until you get strands the size of vermicelli.
Melt butter (or better still mixed butter and oil) in a large frying pan and fry cabbage in it for 15 minutes, covered and on a low flame. Dilute tomato paste in 2 fluid oz./60 ml. water to make a thick tomato sauce.

2 lb./1 kg. white cabbage
12 peppercorns
1 bay leaf
½ tsp. salt
2 tblsp. tomato paste or 6 ripe tomatoes, blanched and blended
1 tblsp. lemon juice
3 oz./90 gr. butter or oil

Pour it over the cabbage, add peppercorns, crushed

bay leaf, lemon juice and mix well for 5 minutes until every cabbage strand has been thoroughly coated with the tomato sauce. Cover and fry on a very low flame for a further 20 minutes or until the cabbage is soft but not dry or browned. Serve hot with venison, STUFFED PEPPERS or COURGETTES; or with a grilled fish like CARP FILLETS IN BRINE.

SAVOURY CABBAGE PUDDING

Pick a nice, smooth head of cabbage with large leaves. Cut some of the hard stalk out and prize off 6 outer leaves. Reserve.
Shred rest of the cabbage as finely as you can on the fine teeth of a manual grater or using the grater of a food processor. Chop the mushrooms, onions and bacon if you are using any. Sweat the cabbage in 2 oz./60 gr. butter, covered, on a low flame, for 20 minutes until soft but not browned. Stir from time to time, to avoid sticking. Add the chopped onion, mushrooms and parsley and sweat them as well for another 5 minutes, until onion has softened. Remove from flame.
(Alternatively, you can boil the whole cabbage in plenty of lightly salted water, shred it when it is soft and sweat mushrooms, onion and parsley separately. Mix the boiled cabbage with onion, mushrooms, parsley.)

2 lb./1 kg. cabbage
2 oz./60 gr. mushrooms
3 eggs
3 slices bacon (optional)
3 oz./90 gr. butter
3 onions
1 tblsp. chopped fresh parsley
3 tblsp. breadcrumbs
2 oz./60 gr. grated cheddar or similar cheese
1 tsp. salt
½ tsp. pepper
1 tblsp. tomato paste (optional)
½ tsp. cumin seeds (optional)

Allow the cabbage to cool a little, then mix in 2 tblsp. breadcrumbs, cheese, eggs thoroughly beaten, salt and pepper. Mix well.
Line a glass or earthenware bowl with a linen cloth or with enough silver foil to hang all around the outside of the bowl as well. Line the inside of the cloth with the reserved cabbage leaves. They should curve inwards towards the top. Place the cabbage mixture in the middle of the leaves and gather their tops and the hanging sides of the cloth on top to re-create the round cabbage shape. Tie well with string to keep the top of the cloth in place. Place bowl in a large saucepan of boiling water. Cover and boil on a fairly high flame for 1 hour. Turn the cabbage once. Replenish water if it evaporates too much.
Lift the cabbage ball out of the bowl, allow to cool a little, then undo string and remove cloth. Place on a hot serving dish. Pour 1 oz./30 gr. melted butter on top and sprinkle with the remaining breadcrumbs. If you prefer, mix 1 tblsp. tomato paste with 2 fluid oz./60 ml. of the boiling water and the cumin seed and pour over the cabbage instead of the melted butter and breadcrumbs. Serve very hot, surrounded by slices of hard boiled egg sprinkled with parsley.

CHICORY WITH SMETANA

Preheat the oven to G4/ 180C/355F.
Wash the chicory well, trim, then blanch them whole in lightly salted water for 5 minutes.
Butter an ovenproof dish. Drain the chicory and place them in the buttered dish. Dot them with the rest of

1 lb./500 gr. chicory
5 fluid oz./150 ml. soured cream or smetana
2 oz./60 gr. butter
1 tblsp. fresh chopped dill
1 tsp. salt

the butter. Sprinkle with salt.

Pour smetana or soured cream (thinned with a little milk if too thick) over the chicory and braise in the preheated oven for 10 minutes. Serve hot, sprinkled with finely chopped dill.

COURGETTES 'CELJE'

Celje is an ancient Slovenian city, situated at the hub of Central Europe, a few hours' travel from the Austrian, German, Hungarian and Italian Borders.

Peel and de-seed some larger baby-marrows or courgettes. Grate them on the large teeth of a manual grater, add salt and mix in the vinegar. Set them aside for 3-4 hours. Place them in a colander and squeeze as much of the juice out as you can by pressing them down with the palm of your hand.
Heat the oil over a lively flame, add flour to make a

Grated marrow (Tokfozelek) is, of course, a well known Hungarian speciality, and this Slovenian variation, using baby-marrows or courgettes is an interesting adaptation. The

2 lbs./1 kg. large baby marrows or courgettes
3 fluid oz./90 ml. oil
8 oz./250 gr. tomatoes
2 oz./60 gr. flour
4 fluid oz./120 ml. soured cream
10 fluid oz./300 ml. veal or chicken stock
1 tsp. salt
2 tblsp. vinegar

roux and add grated

Hungarian marrows are huge and produce shreds the length and width of double macaroni. The courgettes in this recipe, however, will give you shorter, less even shreds.

courgettes, stirring gently. Pour stock over them. Slice the tomatoes and add them to the saucepan. Reduce heat and simmer on a very low flame, uncovered and without stirring, for 15-20 minutes. Shake the pan lightly from time to time. Away from the flame, stir soured cream in and serve warm on their own or with SERBIAN CARP.

STUFFED COURGETTES
SERVES 6

Preheat the oven to G5/ 190C/380F.

Trim and clean the courgettes and cut in two, lengthwise. Scoop inner flesh with a teaspoon and re-use or discard. Blanch the courgette shells in boiling water for 4 minutes. Drain well and place in a colander to drain as much of the water as possible.

Mix cheese with eggs and butter. Add dill and salt. Fill the courgette shells. Butter an ovenproof dish, place the courgettes tightly packed in it and pour melted butter over them. Place in the middle of the oven and bake, uncovered, for 30-40 minutes, until brown on top. Add a little water to the dish if needed. Pour soured cream around the courgettes and sprinkle with chopped dill.

Serve immediately, in the cream and dill sauce.

6 baby-marrows or 6 large courgettes (about 1½ lb./750 gr.)
6 oz./180 gr. curd cheese
1 tblsp. flour
2 eggs
2 oz./60 gr. butter
1 oz./30 gr. melted butter
1 tblsp. chopped dill
2 tblsp. soured cream
½ tsp. salt

FRIED CUCUMBER 'BISTRITZA'
SERVES 4-6

The Bistritza river in Moldavia is a mountain river famous for its clear, fast waters. The Bistritza region is chiefly known for two things: its timber and its small, lightly coloured striped cucumbers which keep the fresh taste of the mountain river. These two elements come together in this unusual treatment for cucumbers: the timber from the forests upstream is sent to the yards in the valley tied up into large rafts steered by three or four people. The journey can take several days, so the foresters build a primitive fireplace made of bricks and river stones at one end of the raft and cook on it the easily available foodstuffs like mountain woodcock or these lightly fried cucumbers.

Peel the cucumber and dice into 1"/3 cm. cubes. Salt well and set aside for ½ hour in a colander to drain.

Mix the flour and black pepper. Crush the garlic and mix with the cucumber pieces. Dip the cucumber in the seasoned flour, shake off excess flour and fry in the olive oil until gold on all sides (not longer than 4 minutes).

Sprinkle with chopped chives and serve immediately as a light appetizer or with grilled and smoked meats. The cucumbers will be hot and crunchy on the outside but still fresh and moist inside.

1 lb./500 gr. cucumber
4 fluid oz./120 ml. olive oil
2 tblsp. finely chopped chives
2 tblsp. plain flour
1 clove garlic
2 tsp. salt
1 tsp. pepper

GARDEN NUGGETS

SERVES 6

Clean the vegetables and shred finely on the grater or in a food processor. Melt ⅓ of the butter and sweat the mixed vegetables in it adding a little warm water from time to time, until they are soft.

In the meantime, soak the bread in the milk. Squeeze out as much of the milk as you can by hand and mix bread with the vegetables. Beat eggs and flour well and add the vegetable mixture to the batter. Mix in pepper, salt and fennel seeds.

Dip your hands in flour and, taking ½ tblsp. of mixture at

10 oz./300 gr. each of:
cabbage
carrots
potatoes
cauliflower
mushrooms
5 oz./150 gr. butter
1 egg
2 fluid oz./60 ml. milk
3 slices white bread, crust removed
5 oz./150 gr. flour
1 tsp. salt
1 oz./30 gr. breadcrumbs
½ tsp. freshly ground black pepper
1 tsp. fennel seeds

a time, roll it between your palms to form small round balls, the size of a large walnut.

Bring a saucepan of water to the boil and plunge the balls in the bubbling water. Boil them for about 10 minutes. In the meantime melt remaining butter and fry the breadcrumbs in it. Take the balls out of the water with a slotted spoon, drain well and roll in buttered breadcrumbs. Serve immediately as a starter, or as an accompaniment to meat dishes.

GREEN HERB MOULDS

An unusual combination for what the Romanians call a 'little stew', that is any combination of meat with vegetables or of vegetables alone, cooked in small quantities of liquid until the various flavours blend into each other. These 'little stews' are traditionally served in their thick sauce over a stodgy base like POLENTA, rice or brown bread. I have adapted this particular stew, made — unusually — of herbs, into a more decorative arrangement inside spinach leaves moulded in ramekins, elevating it to accompany more delicate dishes than it had originally been devised for.

Chop stalks off the herbs and discard them. Wash the herbs thoroughly in plenty of water, making sure all the sand and grit is removed. Bring milk to the boil and boil herbs over a moderate flame, uncovered, for 30 minutes. Drain excess liquid well by placing herbs in a colander and pressing them with a fork. Reserve 4 tblsp. milk.

In the meantime, separate the spinach leaves from the stalks, taking care not to tear them and wash several times in plenty of water. Blanch the spinach leaves for 5 minutes in lightly salted water. Line 6-8 ramekins with the spinach leaves, allowing as much of the leaves as possible to hang on the outside of the ramekins. Chop the onions and sweat gently in the oil, until soft but not brown.

---

1 lb./500 gr. fresh parsley
1 lb./500 gr. fresh dill
8 oz./250 gr. large leaved (Cyprus) spinach
8 oz./250 gr. onion
4 fluid oz./150 ml. oil
1 pt./600 ml. milk
1 tsp. freshly ground black pepper
1 tsp. hot paprika
2 tblsp. tomato paste
1 tblsp. red pepper sauce or 1 red pepper (optional)
1 tsp. salt
1 oz./30 gr. butter (optional)

Remove the stalk and seeds from the red pepper, chop into long strips and sweat gently in butter until soft but not brown. Sieve or blend pepper strips to obtain a cream-like, red sauce. Mix together the boiled herbs, onions, pepper sauce, tomato paste diluted in the reserved milk, paprika, peppers and salt. Sieve or blend in a food processor. This mixture should not be too dry, so add a little milk or cream if necessary (especially if you did not bother with the pepper sauce).

Fill each ramekin with the herb mixture.Cover on top with the hanging spinach leaves and place in a saucepan with water reaching ¾ way up the ramekins. Simmer for 20 minutes. Remove from saucepan, turn ramekins upside down and unmould the spinach and herb moulds. In Romania, this kind of herb 'little stew' is eaten cold, but I prefer it hot as an accompaniment to a delicate fish like PIKE-PERCH, to a rabbit dish (see BRAISED RABBIT IN SOURED CREAM) or to another vegetable dish.

LEEKS IN SOURED CREAM

Preheat the oven to G5/ 190C/380F.
Clean the leeks, remove green parts and place in a bowl of cold water, stalks down, for at least ½ hour to remove grit.
Cut the cleaned leek stems into 2″/6 cm. long pieces. Blanch them in boiling water and drain well.
Cover them with the milk, add salt and allow to simmer for 10-15 minutes. Drain off

1 lb./500 gr. leeks
4 fluid oz./120 ml. milk
2 oz./60 gr. butter
4 fluid oz./120 ml. soured cream
1 oz./30 gr. grated cheddar or
   parmesan cheese
½ tsp. salt
½ tsp. hot paprika
½ tsp. cumin seeds or ½ tblsp.
   fresh chopped dill (optional)

the milk, reserving it in case it is needed at the next stage.

Grease an ovenproof dish. Place leeks in it, pour soured cream, (thinning it out with a little of the drained milk if necessary) season with paprika and cumin seeds or dill if you wish, sprinkle with grated cheese, cover and place in the middle of the oven for 10 minutes until leeks are soft but still a little crunchy. Serve with MARINADED LEG OF LAMB or MOLDAVIAN MEAT FRITTERS.

FILLED LEEKS WITH RICE

Preheat the oven to G5/ 190C/380F.
Cut green section of the leeks and place white bulbs in a bowl of cold water, stem down, for at least ½ hour, until all grit has been eliminated.
In the meantime, lightly fry rice in 2 oz./60 gr. butter in a saucepan for 2 minutes. Pour 8 fluid oz./240 ml. water over rice. Simmer until rice has absorbed most of the water. Remove from saucepan and reserve in a bowl.
Wash the leeks well and remove with a sharp knife as much of the inner white flesh as you can, leaving 2-3 outer layers and a solid plug

4 large leeks (about 5 oz./150
   gr. of white leek stalk each)
   or 8 smaller leeks
4 oz./125 gr. rice
½ tsp. salt
¼ tsp. hot paprika
2 onions
1 tsp. flour
1 tsp. sugar
1 tblsp. tomato paste
1 tsp. cumin seeds
8 slices smoked bacon (optional)

at the green (stalk) end. Finely chop the scooped-out white flesh and sweat in 1 oz./30 gr. butter until soft. Season with salt and paprika. Mix the sweated leek flesh with the rice and fill the leek shells.

Grease a casserole and place filled leeks in it.*
Finely chop onions and sweat in remaining butter until soft and beginning to brown. Add flour and mix. Add 2 fluid oz./60 ml. water, tomato paste, sugar, paprika, cumin seed and bring to the boil, stirring.
Pour sauce over leeks, cover casserole and place in the middle of oven for 20 minutes until they are soft but still crunchy. Serve hot.
*You may, if you wish, wrap 1 slice of smoked bacon around each leek and fix it with a small skewer, before placing in the oven.

LEEKS WITH OLIVES

Preheat the oven to G5/190C/380F.
Clean the leeks, remove green parts and place the white stems in a bowl of water for ½ hour to remove grit. Cut them in ½"/6 cm. pieces and blanch in boiling salt water. Drain well. Heat the oil and sauté leeks until they start to brown. Place in a covered ovenproof dish. Make the sauce:

1 lb./500 gr. leeks
4 oz./125 gr. black olives
2 fluid oz./60 ml. oil
1 tblsp. tomato paste
1 tsp. flour
1 tsp. vinegar or lemon juice
½ tsp. salt
1 oz./30 gr. butter
½ tsp. cumin or fennel seeds

Make a roux by melting butter and adding the flour. Mix well. Add 3 fluid oz./90 ml. water, tomato paste and vinegar or lemon juice. Add the fennel or cumin seeds and pour over the leeks in the casserole. Allow to braise for 15 minutes.
In the meantime, blanch the olives for 3 minutes in boiling water. Add them to the leeks, adjust seasoning and replace in oven for a further 5 minutes. May be served hot or cold.

MUSHROOMS IN SOURED CREAM

SERVES 2 as a starter or 4 as a sauce

Cut the mushrooms (very finely for the sauce, in thicker slices if to be used as a starter). Sweat in half the butter until soft.
In the meantime prepare a roux with the rest of the butter and the flour. When roux is foaming, pour stock over it and stir. Add the sweated mushrooms, pepper, salt, dill. Bring to the boil, mixing occasionally. You

This is a delicious and easily made dish which can be used as a starter or as a sauce for roast meats or venison, based on the contrast between the slight acidity of the cream and the buttery mushrooms.

6 oz./150 gr. button mushrooms
3 fluid oz./75 ml. chicken or
   veal stock
2 tsp. flour
2 tsp. chopped dill
½ tsp. freshly ground black
   pepper
½ tsp. salt
2 generous tblsp. soured cream

can add a little more stock if sauce is too thick. Add the soured cream stirring all the time and bring back to the boil on a very low flame. Adjust the seasoning, then allow to cool a little if served as a starter or pour very hot over cold venison or beef. You can also serve it with cauliflower or boiled potatotes.

NETTLE PURÉE

Like all peasant cultures, the Balkans have their share of dishes based on nettles – 'the poor man's spinach'. Far from looking down on them, I find nettles both extremely health-giving and equal in taste to more 'noble' green leaved vegetables. You will have to pick your own of course – Fortnum and Mason's do not stretch to nettles these days – but they are well worth a try. Only the very young nettles you can pick in early spring are suitable for eating- and use some old gloves when you go after them. Here are a couple of basic recipes from Romania:

Trim the nettle leaves from stalks and discard the stalks. Place the nettle leaves in an earthenware bowl under the tap. Fill it with water, stir nettles vigorously with a spoon and lift them out of the water with a slotted spoon, so that the grit and sand are left at the bottom of the bowl. Wash the bowl out and repeat procedure 3-4 times until the nettles are perfectly clean.
Blanch the nettles in a saucepan of salted boiling

1 lb./500 gr. young nettles, picked in early spring (April-May)
½ flat tblsp. flour
½ tsp. salt
1 small onion
1 fluid oz./30 ml. oil
1 small horseradish root

water for about 10-15 minutes until soft. Drain (reserving a little of the boiling liquid) sieve or blend in a food processor or mash coarsely on a wooden board.

In the meantime, chop the onion finely, sweat gently in the oil until soft and mix flour in. Continue frying for 2 more minutes, stirring all the time. Add the puréed nettles, mix well, pour 2 tblsp. of the boiling liquid over them and fluff them up over a moderate flame until they gain quite a lot in volume. Serve hot, with grated horseradish on top; on their own, as a side dish with meat dishes, or spread over POLENTA CAKES.

NETTLE PILAU

Trim and clean the nettles as for NETTLE PURÉE. Blanch them in salted water for 10 minutes, drain (reserve the liquid) allow to cool and chop coarsely on a wooden board.
Chop the onion and garlic finely and sweat in the oil over a low flame until soft but not brown.

2 lb./1 kg. very young nettles, picked in April-May
4 oz./125 gr. rice
2 oz./60 gr. small (pickling) onions
1 onion
3 cloves garlic
1 tsp. hot paprika
1 tsp. salt
1 fluid oz./30 ml. oil

Add the rice and fry lightly for 2 minutes, shaking the pan. Add the chopped nettles, pickling onions, and 10 fluid oz./300 ml. of the liquid in which the nettles were boiled. Add salt and paprika. Simmer for 20-30 minutes over a low flame, until rice is soft. Serve hot or cold.

TRANSYLVANIAN FILLED ONIONS

Peel 1-2 outer layers off the onions. Boil the onions, whole, in plenty of water for about 10 minutes or until soft but not mushy. Chill the onions well and scoop out the inner flesh with a grapefruit knife or a small sharp knife, leaving 2-3 outer layers.

Chop or grate walnuts to pinhead size. Soak the crustless bread in water for 5 minutes and squeeze out as much of the water as you can by hand.

Cut the olives in two and discard stones. Chop well the onion flesh which you have scooped out. Chop dill

---

6 large (Spanish) onions – about 1½ lb./750 gr.
4 oz./125 gr. small black olives
4 oz./125 gr. walnuts
5 fluid oz./150 ml. dry white wine
3 slices white bread, crust removed
½ tsp. sugar
2 tblsp. tomato paste
½ tblsp. chopped fresh dill
½ tblsp. chopped fresh parsley
5 fluid oz./150 ml. soured cream
1 tsp. salt
½ tsp. mild paprika
½ tsp. caraway seeds

---

and parsley finely.
Mix together the walnuts,

bread, olives, salt, paprika, onion flesh and herbs. Mix well with a wooden spoon until smooth. Fill the onion shells with the mixture. Bring the wine to the boil and whisk in the tomato paste, caraway seeds and sugar. Boil on a medium flame for 3 minutes. Lower the heat and gently place onions in the wine and tomato sauce. Simmer on a very low flame for 5 minutes or until filling has warmed up. Serve onions on individual plates with sauce around them and ½ tblsp. of thick soured cream on top of each onion.

DILLED PEAS

Chop the dill finely. Melt ½ the butter and add ½ the dill to it. Add the green peas, stir for 2 minutes and cover with stock or water. Add salt, cover and simmer for 15 minutes or until peas are half cooked.

Make a roux from the remaining butter and flour, add the rest of the dill and the milk, whisking or

---

2 lb./1 kg. green peas
4 tblsp. fresh chopped dill
6 fluid oz./180 ml. veal/chicken stock or water
2 oz./60 gr. butter
5 fluid oz./150 ml. milk
1 oz./30 gr. sugar
½ tsp. salt
2 oz./60 gr. flour
⅛ tsp. pepper

---

stirring continuously until smooth. Add the white sauce to the peas. Add the sugar and pepper and bring back to the boil.

Boil over a moderate flame until peas are soft. Discard some of the liquid if there is too much left and serve with poultry or SOFIA BOILED BEEF.

RED PEPPER SURPRISE

Place the peppers under a hot grill at about 3″/9 cm. from the flame and grill on all sides until skin browns and starts to bubble up. The skin should come off the flesh easily, but do not overcook as the pepper flesh should not be burned and should retain an al-dente texture to contrast with the creamy filling. Peel skin off peppers and discard stalks and seeds. Wash in cold water and drain well.
Prepare the filling:
Mix well, with a fork, the cheese, creme fraiche,

4 large red peppers (about 6 oz./180 gr. each)
1 lb./500 gr. ricotta cheese (or any unsalted white cheese: curd, sheep's cheese, etc.).
4 tblsp. creme fraiche
2 eggs
¼ tsp. salt
1 tsp. hot paprika
1 tblsp. chopped fresh dill
2 tblsp. flour
2 tblsp. oil
4 fluid oz./120 ml. soured cream

paprika, finely chopped dill, salt and one egg yolk. Resist the temptation to blend in a

food processor – the mixture should not be too thin. Stuff the peppers with the cheese mixture, taking care not to split them. Roll the stuffed peppers in the flour and dip in one beaten egg. Fry the coated peppers in very hot oil (if your peppers were too undercooked after the grilling, they will soften a little more now), for 2-3 minutes, until golden brown on all sides. Serve immediately, topped with dollops of soured cream and accompanied by a fresh green or cucumber salad.

TWO-PEPPER 'ZAKUSKA'

Boil the tomatoes until soft (about 10 minutes). Sieve or blend in a food processor. Place red and green peppers under a hot grill at about 3″/9 cm. distance from the flame and grill on all sides until skin starts to brown and bubble away from the flesh, taking care not to let the flesh itself burn. Dip your hands in cold water, then skin the peppers, remove stalks and seeds and wash peppers under cold water making sure no skin or black bits remain. Cut peppers into long strips about ⅓″/1 cm. wide and 2″/6 cm. long.
Clean the carrot and slice into thin rounds. Slice onion into quarter rings. Sweat lightly the carrot and onion

A well known dish of Russian inspiration, designed to use and preserve autumn vegetables for the long Balkan winter ahead. The same method is used for FISH 'ZAKUSKA'.

1 lb./500 gr. ripe tomatoes
8 oz./250 gr. red peppers
8 oz./250 gr. green peppers
1 carrot
½ onion
2-3 cloves garlic
1 tblsp. oil
1 tsp. sugar
½ tsp. salt
⅓ tsp. freshly ground black pepper

in the oil, over a low flame, until carrot is soft and onion strips have become transparent but not browned.

Add the carrot, onion, red and green peppers and crushed garlic to the tomato sauce. Add the sugar, salt and pepper. Adjust seasoning, allow to cool and serve cold as an accompaniment to grilled meats or fish. It has a refreshing taste. If you prefer a more fiery taste, try 'PINDZUR', a Yugoslav version of 'zakuska'.
To keep for several months: place 'zakuska' in a jar, tie mouth well with clingfoil or greaseproof paper and place in a large saucepan. Pour water around the jar to ¾ height. Bring to the boil and boil 'zakuska' in the jar over a medium flame for ½ hour. Remove from saucepan, cool and keep in a cold place.

THE BOYAR'S STRUDEL

SERVES 6

C. Negruzzi tells the story of a minor Moldavian noble who was desperate for high Court position. His manoeuvres were constantly frustrated, however, by the indifference of the Greek Fanariot Prince, whose interests could be summed up in one word: pies. A glorious host of pies, with yoghurt, with cream, 'alivanca', 'baclava', sweet and savoury; they were all buried daily in the Prince's bottomless stomach. Every morning, before going into the Council chamber, the Prince would spend two happy hours with his stewards deciding the kind of pies to be had at dinner.

Our poor courtier, at his wits' end, sits day after day on his verandah, puffing at his hookah pipe and turning his head in despair at all the delights, pies and doughnuts his lady wife brings to the table. Wishing to please him, his lady presented him one day with a magnificent creation: 'a fat, pot-bellied pie crowned by a garland of doughnuts, an Empress of pies, a gastronomical masterpiece'.

"Wife!" – shouts our courtier jumping from the table – "wife, I have just made High Steward!"

"When?"

"This moment."

"How?"

"You see this pie? Out of the belly of this pie will rise my stewardship."

The pie was instantly despatched to the Court.

It so happened that on that very day, His Highness was sitting at his table with a face of thunder. The entire Court stood shaking in front of him: there was talk of sending six of the boyars to the salt mines, of putting the Court chefs in the stocks and of nailing the High Steward to the public pillory ... by his ear! Why this terror? Because the rascals had forgotten in their knavery to bake a pie for His Highness's table. Oh, treacherous and unpardonable omission.

The Despot's mind seemed to be made up, the Court was already in mourning, when, held high on a silver platter, our boyar's masterpiece of a pie made its entrance. I will not attempt to describe the cries of relief and joy uttered by sovereign and courtiers alike. Suffice it to say that our clever boyar achieved his life's ambition: the following day he was summoned to Court to don the robes of the High Steward. (C. Negruzzi: *The Story Of A Pie*, 1858).

Preheat the oven to G5/ 190C/380F. Grease a deep, ovenproof dish about 8"/20 cm. in diameter.

Place a layer of pastry all around the dish, leaving the extra pastry to hang down on the sides of the dish. Dot all over with small knobs of butter. Place a second layer of pastry on top.

Prepare the filling:

Wash, trim and boil the spinach for 10 minutes. Blend or sieve it with nutmeg, ¼ tsp. black pepper and ¼ tsp. salt. Set aside to cool, grate the cheddar. Mix with creme fraiche and 2 egg yolks. Add the remaining salt and pepper. Mix well with the blended spinach.

---

10 oz./300 gr. filo pastry
4 oz./125 gr. butter
11 oz./330 gr. grated cheddar
9 oz./270 gr. creme fraiche
2 eggs
5 oz./150 gr. spinach
2 tblsp. soured cream
4 fluid oz./120 ml. double cream
½ tsp. ground nutmeg
½ tsp. salt
½ tsp. black pepper or cayenne

Beat the egg whites until stiff and fold into spinach and cheese mixture. Add 2 tblsp. soured cream and mix well.

Spread a layer of this mixture over the pastry layers in the dish. Repeat the procedure, alternating layers of pastry and spinach (2 layers pastry in between each layer of spinach mixture) and finishing with a layer of mixture. Spread 2 fluid oz./60 ml. double cream on top.

Fold the layers of pastry hanging on the sides of the dish on top, making sure they cover the mixture completely. Pour 1 more tblsp. double cream on top. Cover with greaseproof paper, place in the middle of the preheated oven and bake for 1½ hours, basting with cream every 15 minutes. Remove greaseproof paper after 1 hour to brown the top.

THE GARDENER'S MOUSSAKA

SERVES 4-6

Preheat the oven to G6/ 200C/400F.

Clean all the vegetables and grate them or chop them the size of thin vermicelli. Heat oil in a large frying pan and sweat the vegetables for 10-15 minutes, stirring constantly, until soft. Add 3 fluid oz./90 ml. water and simmer for a further 5 minutes. Boil the rice separately in 4 fluid oz./125 ml. water and add to the vegetables when soft.

Another example of a classic dish in its Bulgarian-vegetarian form. The result should gladden any vegetarian's heart.

2 large onions
1 carrot
1 medium celery
¼ head of cabbage
2 courgettes or 1 largish baby
   marrow
3 potatoes
1 lb./500 gr. tomatoes
4 oz./125 gr. grean beans
4 oz./125 gr. rice
3 eggs
7 fluid oz./210 ml. milk
2 ½ oz./45 gr. flour
3 fluid oz./90 ml. olive oil
1 tsp. salt
1 tblsp. chopped fresh parsley

Add the salt, pepper and ½ the chopped parsley.

Grease a cake tin well, place mixture in it.

Mix the flour, eggs and milk into a thin batter and pour over the vegetable mixture. Sprinkle remaining chopped parsley over the batter.

Bake in a preheated oven for 30 minutes or until nicely browned all over.

Allow to cool a little and serve cut in slices.

POLENTA,
PASTA
AND
DUMPLINGS

POLENTA (MAMALIGA)

SERVES 6

Mamaliga, a form of maize porridge similar in many ways to the Polenta of Northern Italy, is the Romanian national dish, but it is eaten widely all over the Balkans. On a recent visit to Yugoslavia, I was surprised to be offered polenta (with a braised rabbit dish) in Slovenia, where the Austrian influence might be expected to have long disposed of such peasant tastes. Polenta is eaten in an amazing number of variations and it is often a substitute for bread or pasta. Making polenta has the same quasi- mystical, ritual connotations as the baking of bread and the treading of grapes.

It can either be eaten as an accompaniment to meat or cheese dishes, or on its own supplemented by a variety of toppings: cheese and soured cream, sheep's cheese, eggs, stew, etc. Here is the basic boiled polenta recipe, followed by a number of traditional elaborations. Always use coarse ground maize flour (polenta*) for the Romanian recipes and avoid the finely ground Italian variety. Romanian polenta dishes should be too thick to stir and have a strong, almost crunchy texture.

---

8 oz./250 gr. coarse maize
  (polenta*)
1 pt./600 ml. water
1 tsp. salt
1 tsp. pepper
5 fluid oz./150 ml. soured cream
  (optional)

Bring the salted water to the boil in a large saucepan. (Polenta will stick to the bottom of the saucepan, so use a non-stick saucepan and soak it in cold water as soon as you have tipped the polenta out. In Romania, a special saucepan (ceaun) will be used exclusively for the daily ritual of polenta cooking, in deference both to the importance of the dish and to the difficulty in cleaning the utensils afterwards. But if you soak the saucepan for a couple of hours the crust on the bottom will peel off without any trouble.)

When the water begins to bubble, sprinkle 2 tblsp. of the maize flour over the surface of the water. Allow the water to boil furiously and pour the rest of the maize flour in a steady trickle stirring all the time with a wooden spoon in a clockwise circular motion; do not change the direction of the stirring. Lower the heat to moderate and allow the porridge to boil for 25-30 minutes, uncovered. Polenta will bring air bubbles to the surface and might splash very hot particles of maize, so take care when you stir it. Stir from time to time to make sure there are no lumps. If lumps have formed, eliminate them by pressing them with the back of the spoon against the walls of the saucepan.

Tradition says that polenta should be thick enough for a spoon placed in the middle to remain upright. When ready, dip the spoon in cold water and fold the polenta from the walls of the saucepan inwards, turning the saucepan as you go along. Pick the saucepan by its edges with a damp cloth, shake it several times sideways and tip polenta in one go over a wooden board. Cut it into slices with a string (like a cheese cutter) and serve immediately with soured cream and pepper on top, or as the accompaniment to many of the meat, fish and cheese dishes in this book. If polenta does not come away with ease from the bottom of the saucepan, simply scoop it out with the wooden spoon: it will be none the worse, but it will not slice as neatly. If you find polenta is still too thin after 30 minutes, reduce heat to the minimum and allow water to evaporate until required thickness has been achieved.

POLENTA CAKES
SERVES 6-8

I find this the most acceptable way of serving polenta for the Western eye and palate. Polenta cakes are suitable as a decorative accompaniment to dishes where potatoes might have been used otherwise, or as the basis for an unusual starter like 'WILD MUSHROOMS AND POLENTA CAKES'. They have a tasty and satisfying texture, crunchy on the outside where a crust has formed and soft and buttery on the inside. You can be imaginative as to their shape: in my childhood rectangles and romboids were usual, but I was recently given round, thin ones in a posh Soho restaurant where they even came, as they should, with a rabbit dish.

Make a thick porridge as shown at POLENTA (MAMALIGA) but using ½ water and ½ milk for the boiling liquid. Spread the polenta on a wooden board in a 1″/3 cm. thick layer and smooth the surface with a knife or spatula. Cut out cakes about 2-3″/6-9 cm. in diameter, by pressing a glass down on the layer of polenta. Pierce a hole with the tip of a knife in the

8 oz./250 gr. coarse maize flour (polenta*)
4 oz./125 gr. butter
10 fluid oz./300 ml. milk
1 tsp. salt

middle of each cake (to eliminate the air trapped behind it inside the glass) and remove gently on to a plate.
Melt butter in a large frying pan and fry the polenta cakes for 5 minutes on each side, until a crunchy but thin crust has formed and the butter has been absorbed into the polenta. Serve very hot with a variety of meat dishes or with warm salads. Polenta cakes go especially well with rabbit dishes (see BRAISED RABBIT IN SOURED CREAM) or with a cold fish like CARP IN A GARLIC VINAIGRETTE.

POLENTA 'BEAR'
SERVES 8

Make a fairly thick POLENTA (MAMALIGA) as shown above. Grate the cheese. Take about 2 tblsps. of the porridge at a time and shape into balls the size of a medium apple. Scoop out a hole in each polenta ball, large enough to take 2 tsps. of grated smoked cheese. Replace the polenta plug you have scooped out and smooth the balls by rolling

A traditional Moldavian recipe, combining polenta with the region's famous crumbly sheep's cheese, kept in large leather pouches and smoked. You can use cheddar or an Austrian or Swiss smoked cheese as substitutes.

Fairly thick polenta made with
8 oz./250 gr. polenta* maize
flour (see POLENTA)
4 oz./125 gr. smoked cheese
4 oz./125 gr. butter

them in between your palms. Ideally you should wrap 'Bears' in foil and bake them in hot charcoal on a barbecue or in the stove, but you will get equally satisfactory results by melting the butter and frying each ball for 10-15 minutes until it has formed a golden brown crust all round and the cheese inside has melted.

MOLDAVIAN CHEESE PIE (ALIVANCA)

SERVES 6

Preheat the oven to G5/ 190C/380F.

Place the cheese in a bowl and mix it with a wooden spoon until it turns creamy and starts foaming a little. Add first the eggs, then maize meal, flour, 3 fluid oz./90 ml. soured cream, and butter. Mix well in between each ingredient. Add salt. Butter an ovenproof dish

A specific, traditional Romanian dish, blending two of the region's greatest loves: maize meal (polenta*) and curd or cream cheese.

1 lb./500 gr. curd or cream cheese
4 eggs
5 tblsp. maize meal (polenta*)
3 flat tblsp. flour
8 fluid oz./240 ml. soured cream
2 oz./60 gr. butter
1 tsp. salt

and pour the mixture in. Place it in the preheated oven and bake for 45 minutes or until the top has browned nicely and a knife plunged in the middle comes out clean.

Cut into squares while hot and serve immediately with the rest of the soured cream on the side.

POLENTA AND CHEESE PIE

SERVES 6-8

Preheat the oven to G6/ 200C/400F.

Make a softer porridge than the one shown at POLENTA (MAMALIGA), using 1 pt./600 ml. milk.

Do not allow polenta to thicken too much – you will need to spread it in thin layers.

Butter well an ovenproof dish or a casserole and cover the bottom with a thin layer of polenta (dip a wooden tablespoon in a little melted butter and use it to spread the polenta).

Grate the cheddar or smoked cheese. Spread a layer of grated cheese over the first polenta layer, dot with butter and cover with a

8 oz./250 gr. coarse maize flour (polenta*)
1 pt. 3 fl. oz./700 ml. milk
1 tsp. salt
4 oz./125 gr. mature cheddar or Austrian smoked cheese
4 oz./125 gr. cottage cheese or ¾ curd cheese mixed with ¼ soured cream/creme fraiche
4 oz./125 gr. butter
2 eggs
1 tsp. freshly ground pepper

second layer of polenta. Now spread a layer of cottage cheese well sprinkled with pepper, cover again with polenta and repeat the procedure (dotting the grated cheese layers with butter) until you have

exhausted the ingredients or your casserole is full to the top. Finish with a layer of polenta.

Beat the eggs with the remaining milk and a little salt. Pour the mixture over the polenta pie, sprinkle with grated cheese and bake in the preheated oven for 30-45 minutes or until brown on top and the cheese has melted inside. Serve immediately, in the baking dish. You can cut it in slices like a cake and serve it with MUSHROOMS IN SOURED CREAM or simply with a little salad and some soured cream on the side.

BALKAN NOODLES

SERVES 6

Preheat the oven to G5/190C/380F.
In a large saucepan bring plenty of salted water to the boil and boil the noodles in it for about 15-20 minutes or until soft but still al dente. Drain, rinse well under running hot water and drain again. In the meantime, chop finely the onion, crush the garlic and grate the walnuts to pin-head size.

8 oz./250 gr. egg noodles
6 oz./180 gr. curd cheese or
    white fresh sheep's cheese
½ onion
10 fluid oz./300 ml. soured cream
1 clove garlic
2 tsp. hot paprika
2 tblsp. grated walnuts
    (optional)
½ tsp. salt
1 tblsp. fresh mint leaves

Mix cheese, soured cream, onion, garlic, salt and paprika. Fold the mixture gently into the noodles without reducing them to an unsightly mush. Butter well an ovenproof dish. Place the mixture in it, sprinkle with grated walnuts if you wish, decorate with a few mint leaves and bake in the preheated oven for ½ hour. Serve very hot.

TRANSYLVANIAN 'GALUSHKA' DUMPLINGS

SERVES 6

Mix the flour, egg and salt well to make a thick dough. Take about ½ a tsp. of the mixture at a time and drop it in slightly bubbling stock or water. Boil for 4-5 minutes

These small, bite-sized flour dumplings are extremely popular in Transylvania, where they are eaten mainly as an accompaniment to all the 'paprika' type dishes, especially to tokana (meat stews) and to chicken or rabbit paprika: see TRANSYLVANIAN CHICKEN PAPRIKA WITH DUMPLINGS and SAXON TOKANA.

3 tblsp. flour
1 large egg
⅛ tsp. salt
1 pt./600 ml. chicken stock or
    water

until dumplings are firm and have expanded in volume. Serve hot, sprinkled with chopped parsley or in stews and soups.

SEMOLINA DUMPLINGS
SERVES 6-8 (about 8 medium-sized dumplings)

Mix the egg and butter well with a fork until the butter creams up.

Sprinkle semolina and salt over the creamed butter, little by little, mixing constantly. The end result should be like a thick yoghurt. Bring the chicken stock to the boil in a large saucepan. Take about 1 dessert spoon of the mixture at a time and drop it into the bubbling broth, making

4 oz./125 gr. semolina
2 oz./60 gr. butter
1 egg
¼ tsp. salt
2 pt./1 l. chicken stock

sure the dumplings do not touch each other and crumble.

Cover and simmer for 20 minutes over a low flame. Remove dumplings with a slotted spoon (they should

have increased markedly in volume) and place in a tureen. Pour over them a well flavoured clear broth, like SPRING CHICKEN BROTH and serve hot.

They can also be used as a lighter alternative to flour or potato paste dumplings in soups like SPRING LAMB BROTH WITH DUMPLINGS or CAULIFLOWER SOUP WITH SMETANA.

ROMANIAN 'GALUSHKA' DUMPLINGS
SERVES 6-8

Preheat the oven to G5/190C/380F.

Melt ⅔ of the butter in the stock or water and add a pinch of salt.

Bring to the boil and when liquid is bubbling, tip flour into it in one go. Mix well until flour has absorbed all the liquid and the mixture is coming away from the walls of the saucepan. Remove from the heat, continue mixing for 3-4 minutes until mixture is cooler, and then add the eggs, one by one, making sure mixture does not become too soft. Add pepper and ½ the grated cheese and mix well.

In a large saucepan, bring to

Unlike their Transylvanian counterparts (see TRANSYLVANIAN 'GALUSHKA' DUMPLINGS), these richer dumplings from southern Romania are not necessarily meant to be eaten with a 'paprika' stew. They are used, of course, as accompaniments to meat dishes and soups, but as this recipe shows, they can also be eaten on their own with cheese and a tomato sauce.

5 oz./150 gr. flour
3 oz./90 gr. butter
8 fluid oz./240 ml. chicken stock
  or water
3-4 eggs
3 tblsp. grated mature cheddar
  or Swiss cheese
1 tsp. salt
¼ tsp. black pepper
1 tblsp. tomato paste
½ tsp. caraway or fennel seeds

the boil 2 pts./1 l. salted water. Take about ½ tsp. of the mixture at a time and drop it into the barely bubbling liquid. Simmer on a low flame for 15-20 minutes.

In the meantime, dilute tomato paste in 4 fluid oz./120 ml. warm water and add ½ tsp. butter and caraway or fennel seeds. When dumplings are firm, drain well, place in a buttered ovenproof dish, pour tomato sauce on top, sprinkle with the remaining cheese and place in the middle of preheated oven for 30 minutes. Serve immediately.

CAKES
AND
DESSERTS

YEAST CAKE (COZONAC)

The Balkanic sweet tooth is legendary: in Bucharest or in Zagreb there are cake shops or tea rooms at every street corner, like pubs in an Irish village. Yeast cakes, filled with walnuts, poppy seed, tarragon or even turkish delight are great favourites, especially for breakfast and at tea time. Below is the master recipe for what is probably the type of cake most often eaten at home in the Balkans, while Austro-Hungarian cream cakes and tarts are sold in the shops. The bread-like, light consistency of the yeast cake makes it ideally suited for filling with both dry and wet mixtures. Do not skimp on the dough rising or working times: with yeast cakes — lightness is all.

Preheat the oven to G5/190C/380F.

Warm 3 tblsp. milk slightly and pour it over the yeast in a bowl.

Be careful, if the milk is too hot the yeast will 'die' and the dough will not rise. Add 1 tsp. sugar.

Boil a little more milk (about 4 fluid oz./120 ml.) and mix well with 3 tblsp. flour, making sure there are no lumps. Wait until the mixture has cooled enough for you to touch it without discomfort and mix it with the yeast, beating it well with a fork or wire whisk until mixture starts bringing up large air bubbles.

Sprinkle 1 tblsp. flour on top, cover the bowl with a cloth and set aside in a warm place to rise (on top of the cooker if your oven is on, by the radiator, etc.).

In the meantime, mix the egg yolks with the salt. They will begin to darken. Add caster sugar, a tblsp. at a time, until mixture is smooth and frothy.

Place the remaining flour in a large, deep bowl. Keep the bowl in a warm place until needed. When the yeast

---

2 lb./1 kg. plain flour

1½ oz./45 gr. yeast (the moist and pressed type)

9 egg yolks

4 egg whites

10 oz./300 gr. caster sugar

8 oz./250 gr. butter

2 tblsp. oil

1 pt./600 ml. milk

2 tblsp. dark rum

6 drops vanilla essence

8 oz./250 gr. plump sultanas

4 oz./125 gr. chopped walnuts

2 oz./60 gr. ordinary sugar

1 flat tsp. salt

---

mixture has risen (about 15 minutes) add it to the flour in the bowl. Mix well, add 7 egg yolks and another 6 fluid oz./180 ml. warm milk. (Again, take care not to have the milk too hot). Beat the egg whites to a froth and fold them into the dough. Work the dough forcefully for at least 30 minutes: fold it from the edges inwards towards the centre, knead it, spread it and repeat the procedure. After 30 minutes, melt the butter in a little milk and add it little by little to the dough, together with the oil, rum and vanilla essence,

working them into the dough one by one. If the dough is still too thick, add a little more warm milk.

Add 6 oz./180 gr. sultanas. Put the dough back into the large, deep bowl and set aside in a warm place, covered with a cloth and away from draughts, for 3 hours.

Butter 2 large cake tins. Grease your hand with a little butter and scoop out large chunks of the dough. Fill each cake tin to no more than ½ its height. Allow to rise a little longer.

Beat the remaining egg yolks and brush each cake loaf with egg. Sprinkle with ordinary sugar and with the nuts and remaining sultanas. Place in preheated oven and bake for 1 hour or until a knife plunged in the middle comes out dry. Allow to cool away from the cold or from draughts and remove from tins. Serve sliced into very thin slices, with tea or coffee or buttered, if you wish. In Romania yeast cake is sometimes eaten spread with a tangy preserve like morello cherry or quince.

WALNUT YEAST CAKE

Preheat the oven to G5/190C/380F.

Make the dough as shown at YEAST CAKE or follow this slightly quicker method: Dissolve the yeast in 2 fluid oz./60 ml. milk. Pour into a large bowl and mix in 2 tblsp. of the flour and 1 tsp. sugar. Allow to rise for 10 minutes. In the meantime, melt butter in remaining milk. Add them and remaining flour, egg yolks, remaining sugar, salt and the lemon rind and mix well with a wooden spoon. When the dough is smooth, start working it with your hands until it starts peeling off your hands and off the walls of the bowl and it starts making air bubbles on the surface. Cover the bowl with a linen towel and allow dough to rise at room temperature for 1 hour. Prepare a well floured board and tip risen dough onto it. Divide it into three loaves and roll each loaf into a

For the dough:
1 lb./500 gr. plain flour
5 oz./150 gr. butter
4 egg yolks
1 egg
3 oz./90 gr. caster sugar
1 oz./30 gr. yeast
⅛ tsp. salt
2 tsp. grated lemon rind

For the filling:
1 lb. 8 oz./750 gr. walnuts
1 lb./500 gr. caster sugar
2 oz./60 gr. butter
2 tblsp. rum
7 fluid oz./200 ml. milk

sheet the size of your baking tray (about 12"/30 cm. × 10"/25 cm.).
Making the filling:
Grate walnuts on the fine teeth of a grater or in a food processor to pinhead size. Heat milk to boiling point. Cream butter with a fork until it is soft and foamy and add to it sugar, rum, grated walnuts and hot milk. Mix well until you get a

homogeneous cream and the sugar is entirely dissolved. Divide filling into three equal parts.
Lay one sheet of dough on the board and spread ⅓ of the filling on it in an even, thin layer. Cover with the second sheet and repeat procedure, finishing with a layer of walnut mixture. Roll sheets tightly to form a cylinder the length of the baking tray. Butter the tray well and place roll in it. Do not allow it to rise any more once it has been filled and rolled – you risk getting gaps between filling and dough. Brush the cake with a beaten whole egg and place in preheated oven until a dark brown crust has formed on top and a knife plunged in the middle comes out clean (about 1 hour). Place on a rack to cool and slice into round slices when cold.

YEAST CAKE
WITH POPPY SEED

Preheat the oven to G5/ 190C/380F. Butter a baking tray well.

Make a yeast cake dough either as shown at YEAST CAKE or the slightly simplified method shown at WALNUT YEAST CAKE. While dough is rising, make the filling:

Wash the poppy seed in cold water and place in a saucepan. Bring 2 pt./1 l. water to the boil in another saucepan and pour it over the poppy seed.

Set them aside to soak for 2-3 hours.

Drain well and grind them in a mortar or food processor, taking about ½ tblsp. at a time. Replace it in the saucepan, add milk, sugar, vanilla essence and breadcrumbs and bring to the boil. Stir continuously until you get a fairly thick paste. Add butter, mix until

---

1 lb./500 gr. yeast cake dough (see **YEAST CAKE**) or:

1 lb./500 gr. flour
5 oz./150 gr. butter
4 egg yolks
1 egg
3 oz./90 gr. icing sugar
1 oz./30 gr. yeast
⅛ tsp. salt
2 tsps. grated lemon rind

For the filling:
8 oz./250 gr. poppy seed
8 oz./250 gr. sugar
3 oz./90 gr. butter
2 tblsp. fine white breadcrumbs
3 drops vanilla essence
1 oz./30 gr. sultanas
2 tblsp. rum

---

it is fully melted and set aside to cool. Soak the sultanas in 2 tblsp. rum and add them to the cooled poppy seed paste. Mix and divide the filling into 3 equal parts.

Divide the dough into three loaves. Roll each loaf into a sheet cca. ⅓"/1 cm. thick. Lay one sheet of dough flat and spread ⅓ of the mixture on it in a thin, even layer. Cover with the second sheet of dough and repeat the procedure, finishing with a layer of mixture. Roll the sheets tightly to form a thick sausage the length of the baking tray. Beat 1 whole egg and brush cake well with it. Place in the preheated oven for 1 hour or until a dark crust has formed on top and dough is light and firm. The mixture, however, should retain a little moisture. Do not allow the cake to rise once it has been filled and rolled – you will get gaps between filling and dough. Place cake on a rack to cool and serve sliced in ½"/1.5 cm. thick round slices.

TARRAGON YEAST CAKE

Preheat the oven to G5/190C/380F. Grease a cake tin.
Make the dough as shown at YEAST CAKE. Divide loaf into three ⅓"/1 cm. thick sheets.
Make the filling:
Melt the butter in a saucepan. Sprinkle fine biscuit crumbs into the foaming butter and brown them for 2-3 minutes. Remove from the flame and cool. Mix in soured cream, egg yolks, sugar and lemon peel, in this order. Mix until filling is smooth. Chop tarragon leaves very finely. Lay one sheet of dough flat on a floured board and spread ⅓ of the filling on it in a thin even layer. Sprinkle with ⅓ of the chopped tarragon leaves and cover

Whereas Romanian tastes require a strict separation of the sweet and the savoury, the filling in this Yugoslav 'potica' (yeast cake) is a mixture of biscuit crumbs flavoured with fresh tarragon leaves. The light, bread-like texture of yeast cake is extremely well served by this unusual filling.

---

1 lb./500 gr. yeast cake dough
  (see YEAST CAKE) made with:
1 lb./500 gr. plain flour
1 oz./30 gr. yeast
4 egg yolks
2 egg whites
4 oz./125 gr. butter
3 oz./90 gr. caster sugar
1 tblsp. oil
10 fluid oz./300 ml. milk
3 drops vanilla essence
2 tblsp. dark rum
⅓ tsp. salt

For the filling:
2 good bunches of fresh
  tarragon
2 oz./60 gr. digestive biscuit
  crumbs
3 oz./90 gr. butter
3 oz./90 gr. sugar
6 fluid oz./180 ml. thin soured
  cream or smetana
3 egg yolks
1 tsp. lemon peel

To finish:
1 egg
1 tblsp. icing sugar
1 tsp. cinnamon powder

---

with the second sheet of dough. Repeat the procedure, finishing with a layer of filling. Roll cake into a tight cylinder.
Beat the remaining egg and brush roll with it. Place roll in the baking tin and put it straight into the preheated oven. (If you allow roll to rise once it has been filled you risk getting gaps between filling and dough). Bake for 1 hour, until a dark brown crust has formed on top of the roll and a knife plunged in the middle comes out clean. Cool cake in the tin, remove and sprinkle with icing sugar mixed with cinnamon. Slice into thin, ⅓"/1 cm. round slices and serve with hot chocolate and WILD STRAWBERRY PRESERVE.

EASTER CAKE
WITH SOURED CREAM

SERVES 6-8

This is a variation on the yeast cake theme, traditionally served at the Easter Night supper. Orthodox tradition prescribes that the congregation should walk around the church seven times, carrying lit candles in their hands, following the midnight service on the eve of Easter Sunday. Back home, in the middle of the night, a collation is, of course, called for, especially by the children for whom this is the one time of the year when they are allowed to stay up late. Two rituals are central to this light meal: Hard boiled eggs, whose shells have been dyed in vivid colours and sometimes decorated with considerable artistry during Lent are now knocked against each other and eaten when cracked. The second delight of the night is provided by the 'breaking' of the Easter Cake (Pasca), a round sweet yeast cake filled with either soured cream or curd cheese (see EASTER CAKE WITH CHEESE below).

Preheat the oven to G5/190C/380F. Butter a large round flan or soufflé dish. Reserve ⅛th of the dough and roll out the rest with a rolling pin into a sheet of dough about ¹/₆"/0.5 cm. thick. Line the flan dish with it. Shape the reserved dough into 2 thin, long ropes. Pleat them and stick them all around the edge of the flan dish to increase its height a little.
Allow the dough to rise a little more in the dish.
In the meantime, prepare the filling:
Mix 5 egg yolks with the salt until they start to

1 lb./500 gr. yeast cake dough (see YEAST CAKE)
2 oz./60 gr. butter

For the filling:
1¼ pt./750 ml. thick set soured cream
4 oz./125 gr. flour
6 egg yolks
3 egg whites
5 oz./150 gr. sugar
6 drops vanilla essence
rind of 1 lemon
2 oz./60 gr. plump sultanas
½ tsp. salt

darken. Add sugar and mix well to get a frothy cream-like texture. Add the flour, soured cream, vanilla essence, grated lemon rind and the egg whites beaten into a froth. Pour mixture over the dough taking care it does not rech the edges formed by the pleated dough. Beat the remaining egg yolk and brush dough edges with it. Sprinkle the sultanas on top of the mixture and bake in the preheated oven for 1 hour. The dough should be plump and the filling nicely set and with a slight golden crust. Allow cake to cool before removing it from the dish.

EASTER CAKE WITH CHEESE

Preheat the oven to G5/ 190C/380F. Butter a large, round flan dish. Roll dough and line flan dish (bottom and edges) as shown at EASTER CAKE WITH SOURED CREAM.
Make the filling:
Mix cheese well with the butter and sugar. Add salt, then whole eggs, one by one.
Add flour. Mix well. If you have used a particularly thick cream cheese, you can

1 lb./500 gr. yeast cake dough (see YEAST CAKE)
1 oz./30 gr. butter
2 egg yolks

For the filling:
1 lb./500 gr. cream cheese, curd cheese or unsalted cottage cheese
4 oz./125 gr. sugar
3 eggs
1½ tblsp. flour
2 oz./60 gr. butter
6 drops vanilla essence
rind of 1 lemon
2 oz./60 gr. plump sultanas
½ tsp. salt

thin it out with 1 tblsp. single cream. Add the lemon rind, vanilla essence and sultanas. Mix well until filling is smooth. Pour it into the flan dish and smooth the top with a flat knife.
Beat the 2 egg yolks and brush filling and dough edges with them.
Bake in the preheated oven for 1 hour. Cool in the dish before removing it.

TURKISH DELIGHT CAKE

Preheat the oven to G5/ 190C/380F.
Butter and flour well a cake tin. Mix the eggs and sugar until they begin to froth and to increase in volume. Add the milk little by little, mixing all the time. Add the oil in the same way. Sprinkle bicarbonate of soda over mixture, add flour and mix well. Chop walnuts and mix with the sultanas. Add them to the mixture. Soften the turkish delight pieces slightly by rolling them under your palms on a flat

8 oz./250 gr. flour
6 oz./180 gr. sugar
2 eggs
5 fluid oz./150 ml. oil
5 fluid oz./150 ml. milk
4 oz./125 gr. turkish delight (lemon and raspberry flavours)
1 oz./30 gr. walnuts
1 oz./30 gr. sultanas
½ tsp. bicarbonate of soda
1 oz./30 gr. mixed cut lemon and orange peel

board. Cut them to form small, thin rolls.

Pour half the cake mixture into the prepared cake tin. Place the turkish delight pieces at equal intervals over the mixture and cover with the rest of the mixture. Smooth top with a flat knife, sprinkle with orange and lemon peel and bake in the preheated oven for 1 hour or until a knife plunged in the middle of the cake comes out dry. Cool the cake before removing from the tin and serve sliced into very thin slices.

CHEESE STRUDEL 'CAPSHA'

SERVES 6-8

'Capsha's' Restaurant and Cafe have been for over a hundred years the centre of Bucharest gastronomic life, as well as a meeting point for politicians, writers, artists and journalists. Situated at the corner of Calea Victoriei – the main artery in Bucharest, named after the victory over the Turks which brought Romania's independence in 1877 – and the smaller Edgar Quinet street, "Capsha's" could not fail to become the centre of social life in inter-war Bucharest as it was placed in the middle of a fashionable quadrangle which included the University, the Military Club, the newsrooms in Sarindar, (the Fleet Street of Bucharest) and the old National Theatre, destroyed in an American air raid in 1944. The luxurious restaurant was the province of Romanian nabobs, grown rich on the exploitation of Carpathian oil, while the cafe saw an endless stream of well dressed ladies and young men of dubious profession carting away in large wooden boxes the famous "Capsha" chocolates, while trying to avoid staring too much at the tables noisily occupied by gesticulating writers and journalists. Its windows facing Calea Victoriei were downright intimidating in their oppulent displays of expensive chocolates, while at the tables, both inside and on the pavement, the flower of Bucharest youth spent whole days gossiping over pistacho ice creams and long colourful cocktails. The cheese strudel below was one of the more Balkanic delicacies to be found at 'Capsha's' well into the sixties, alongside superb chocolate cakes like 'Timish', 'Indienne' and the CHOCOLATE INGOT described below.

Preheat the oven to G5/ 190C/380F.
Make the filling first:
Mix the cheeses well with the butter to obtain a smooth paste. Add the eggs, milk, flour, sugar, salt, vanilla essence, cinnamon, lemon rind and sultanas at the end. Mix well with a wooden spoon until ingredients are thoroughly blended.
Cover a table or other large flat surface with a clean table cloth and place 2 sheets of filo* pastry flat on it. Dot with butter.
Place the cheese mixture onto the pastry sheets and spread it with a spatula in a

---

2 large sheets of filo* pastry (cca. 10 oz./300 gr.)
3 oz./90 gr. butter
2 oz./60 gr. icing sugar
5 fluid oz./150 ml. soured cream

For the filling
4 oz./125 gr. sheep's cheese or other crumbly white cheese
4 oz./125 gr. curd or cream cheese
2 eggs
⅛ tsp. salt
3 oz./90 gr. sugar
6 drops vanilla essence
1 oz./30 gr. plump sultanas
3 oz./90 gr. unsalted butter
1 tblsp. milk
1 tsp. flour
rind of 1 lemon
½ tsp. ground cinnamon

---

thick even layer. Dot well with butter. Fold the edges of the pastry sheets on top to cover mixture completely. Now roll the table cloth inwards, starting at the narrow end of the table, to obtain a thick strudel roll. Cut the roll into 3 equal pieces and place in a buttered baking tray large enough to take them in one row. Dot all over with butter and bake in the preheated oven for 30-45 minutes, or until the pastry is golden brown and crispy. Sprinkle with icing sugar and serve hot with dollops of soured cream on the side.

PLUM DUMPLINGS

SERVES 6-8 (about 20 dumplings)

Dumplings of all sorts are a Transylvanian favourite, no doubt under Hungarian influence. Plum dumplings are probably the best known variety and can be eaten on their own, as belly-stretching 'afters' or as part of a meat dish from the stew family (see SAXON TOKANA and SERBIAN MUTTON TOKANA). In Hungary and in Austria savoury dumplings are usually made of bread, but in Transylvania fruit dumplings, based on a potato paste, are more usual. They should never be heavy – on the contrary, they are supposed to give the cook scope to display lightness of touch and powers of invention. As the basic paste is almost always the same, once you have mastered the basic dumpling dough, experiment with other fresh fruit, jams and combinations of fillings.

Boil the potatoes in plenty of water and peel them afterwards. Pass them through a sieve, through the fine holes of a mincer or blend in a food processor. Add 3 oz./90 gr. flour, egg yolk, salt and ¼ tsp. sugar. Work lightly with your fingers and add gradually more flour until you get a smooth, soft but not sticky dough. Roll into a long cylinder about 1"/3 cm. thick. Leave to stand for 1 hour at room temperature. In the meantime, open plums into halves, but only as much as you need in order to remove the stones (try to use very ripe plums). The plums should stay attached at the end opposite the stalk.

Put a pinch of cinnamon and ¼ tsp. sugar inside each

---

13 oz./400 gr. potatoes
(preferably floury ones)
4-5 oz./125 gr. flour
⅛ tsp. salt
2 oz./60 gr. sugar
1 egg yolk
2 oz./60 gr. fine white
breadcrumbs
2 oz./60 gr. butter
½ tsp. ground cinnamon
about 20 ripe plums

---

plum.

Cut round slices off the dough roll, about ⅓"/1 cm. thick. Flatten them by hand to get a square of dough large enough to roll around your plums. Place a plum in the middle of a dough square, fold dough all around it and roll it in between your palms to make a smooth ball. Bring water to the boil in a large saucepan. Add a little salt, reduce heat until water is only simmering but bubbles are still rising and drop dumplings one by one into the water. Cover and poach for about 20 minutes or until dough has firmed and plums are soft.

Melt the butter in a frying pan and brown the breadcrumbs lightly in it. Remove the dumplings with a slotted spoon, drain well and roll each dumpling into the buttered breadcrumbs, in the frying pan, until they have sweated away most of the water (cca. 5-10 minutes over a low flame).

Sprinkle dumplings with sugar if you are serving them for pudding, or serve them as they are with a TOKANY, PAPRIKASH or RABBIT WITH OLIVES.

CURD CHEESE DUMPLINGS

SERVES 4 - 6

Mix the cheese, egg, semolina and salt with a wooden spoon. Mix well to obtain a firm consistency. Add the lemon rind and mix again.

Dip your hands in flour and make round dumplings by rolling 1 tblsp. of the mixture at a time between your palms. Flatten dumplings a little by pressing in between your palms and make a dimple in the middle of each dumpling with your forefinger.

Bring a large saucepan of water to the boil and drop the dumplings in it one by one, making sure water does not bubble too strongly. Poach the dumplings until they have all risen to the

This is a different type of dumpling, called 'Papanashi', based on a lot of fresh white cheese thickened with a little semolina and flavoured with lemon rind. A childhood treat in Romania, they are extremely easy to prepare and make an ideal light supper pudding.

---

8 oz./250 gr. curd or cream
   cheese
1 large egg
3 tblsp. semolina
1 tblsp. flour
2 oz./60 gr. butter
1 tblsp. fine white breadcrumbs
¼ tsp. salt
rind of 1 lemon
2 tblsp. sugar
¼ tsp. cinnamon
¼ tsp. nutmeg
pinch of ground cloves
5 fluid oz./150 ml. soured cream

---

surface. Lower heat to the bare minimum and leave dumplings in the hot water for another 10 minutes (at no time should the dumplings boil in fiercely bubbling water – they will turn mushy).

In the meantime, melt the butter and lightly fry breadcrumbs in it. Drain the dumplings well, add to the frying pan over a low flame, roll them in the buttered breadcrumbs and sweat all the water out of them. Mix the sugar with spices and sprinkle on both sides of the papanashi.

Serve very hot with a large dollop of soured cream on top.

FRIED CHEESE CAKES (PAPANASHI)

SERVES 4-6

Separate the eggs. In a bowl, mix cheese, yolks, flour, salt and lemon rind to obtain a soft mixture, barely holding together. Beat the egg whites until stiff and fold them gently into the mixture.

Take a tblsp. at a time and shape soft, oval dumplings, dipping your hands in a

Yet another variation on the CURD CHEESE DUMPLINGS above, this time using flour instead of semolina and frying the mixture instead of poaching it, which creates a lovely contrast between the crunchy crust and the soft, creamy middle.

10 oz./300 gr. curd or cream cheese
2 eggs
3 tblsp. flour (or 2 tblsp. flour and 1 tblsp. semolina)
2 oz./60 gr. butter
2 oz./60 gr. sugar
$\frac{1}{4}$ tsp. cinnamon
$\frac{1}{4}$ tsp. nutmeg
pinch of ground cloves
5 fluid oz./150 ml. soured cream
$\frac{1}{4}$ tsp. salt
rind of 1 lemon

little flour to prevent sticking.

Heat the butter in a frying pan and fry the dumplings until they turn golden brown on both sides, and the crust is very crunchy. Mix the sugar with spices and sprinkle on both sides. Serve immediately, with soured cream on the side.

APPLE AND CINNAMON BALLS

SERVES 6-8

Mix the eggs and flour until you get a thick batter. Thin it out with the milk, but only to the consistency of mashed potatoes.

Peel the apples and remove cores and pips. Grate the apples finely and eliminate as much of the juice as you can by squeezing gently with the palm of your hand against a flat board.

3 eggs
5 sweet apples
1 tsp. cinnamon
3 oz./90 gr. flour
2 fluid oz./60 ml. milk
1 tblsp. icing sugar
3 fluid oz./90 ml. oil or mixed oil and butter

Add the grated apples to the batter. Add the cinnamon and mix well. Take 2 tsp. of the mixture at a time and make balls the size of a large walnut by rolling mixture in between your palms.

Heat the oil or butter in a frying pan and fry apple balls until gold all over. Roll them in icing sugar while still hot and serve warm.

SIGNOR FELIX'S
MORELLO CHERRY TART
SERVES 6-8

'Signor Felix' was a patissier from Piedmont who has entered Romanian cooking history as the first person to convert the natives to the 'literature of sugar'. He was also famous in the Iassi of the 1840s for another innovation: not content with selling ice creams and boiled sweets, he divided his single-room shop in two and opened a high fashion milliner's shop alongside his cakes. As M. Kogalniceanu remembers, Signor Felix's ice creams where necessary to cool the fiery looks thrown by the dandies of the day towards the milliner's girls who could be seen through the partition glass working at their hats and bonnets. 'Signor Felix had therefore his ways for cooling the stomachs and at the same time setting fire to the hearts: ice cream and milliners'.

Preheat the oven to G3/ 170C/335F. Butter an ovenproof flan dish and sprinkle with flour.
Wash the cherries, discard their stalks and remove stones. Place them in a colander to drain while you are making the tart base. Separate the eggs. Mix the yolks with the sugar until they start foaming and rising. Add bicarbonate of soda. Beat the whites to a froth and add them to the

---

1 lb./500 gr. morello cherries, fresh or tinned (unsweetened)*
1 oz./30 gr. fresh white breadcrumbs
1 oz./30 gr. flour
1½ oz./45 gr. grated walnuts
½ tsp. bicarbonate of soda
5 oz./150 gr. sugar
5 eggs
1 tblsp. icing sugar

---

mixture. Add fine breadcrumbs, flour and finely grated walnuts. At the end, add the drained morello cherries.
Pour mixture into the buttered flan dish and bake in the preheated oven for ½ hour, or until a knife plunged in the middle comes out clean. Allow the tart to cool, remove from flan dish and cut into squares. Serve lightly sprinkled with icing sugar.

CHEESE PIES 'CREANGA'

Ion Creanga was a famous Moldavian writer and story teller of the late nineteenth century. He made these cheese pies famous through repeated mentions in his folkloric legends and especially in his memoires of an idyllic childhood, spent in a remote village in the heart of the Moldavian countryside.
He was also a legendary eater. Having abandoned country priesthood for a career as a writer, he left his native village and settled at Iassi, the capital and a town of some sophistication, with western aspirations. Confronted with the 'delicate' manners of the 'townies', Creanga 'doesn't bother to pick, with his thick fingers, the crayfish tails one by one. He draws the entire cauldron to his side of the table, plunges a hairy hand in it, pulls out a fistful of crayfish and proceeds to munch his way through the whole lot, spitting the shells out like a thresher spraying out the chuff. He ate once ten eggs, a basin of plums, a cauldron full of corn on the cob, and this only for starters. Weakened by having fasted on doctor's orders, he calls for a whole loaf of bread, a chicken boiled with garlic, a saucepan of stuffed cabbage leaves, eight of his favourite pies folded with their 'skirts up' and a vat of wine. By the age of forty, however, the slim country deacon of salad days had started to swell. This modern Gargantua now waddles down the streets of Iassi, knotted stick in hand, but still as upright as ever ... (G. Calinescu – *Istoria Literaturii Romane*, 1941).

Preheat the oven to G5/ 190C/380F.
Crumble the yeast and place it in a bowl with 2 tblsp. slightly warm water. Add 2 tblsp. flour over it, little by little, mixing all the time to make a paste the consistency of mayonnaise. Sprinkle a little more flour on top, and place yeast mixture in a warm place (on top of the heated oven, or similar) to rise for ½ hour.
In the meantime, beat the eggs well. Melt the butter in a little saucepan.
Place remaining flour in a large bowl, make a hole in the middle and pour in beaten eggs, pinch of salt, melted butter and oil. Add the risen batter and work dough strongly with your hands until it comes away from the walls of the bowl and off your hands. Add a little warm milk at a time, as

---

1 lb./500 gr. flour
½ oz./10 gr. yeast
2 eggs
1 tblsp. butter
1 tblsp. oil
5 fluid oz./150 ml. milk
1 tsp. sugar
pinch salt

For the filling:
5 oz./150 gr. curd or cream cheese (or unsalted sheep's cheese if you can get it)
1 oz./30 gr. butter
2 eggs
1 tsp. flour
2 tblsp. milk
1 tsp. sugar
2 tsp. grated rind of lemon
pinch salt

To finish:
1 tblsp. icing sugar
10 fluid oz./300 ml. soured cream

---

you work the dough, until mixture is medium soft.
Make the filling:

Mix well the cheese and butter in a bowl. Add 1 egg, flour, milk, salt, sugar and lemon rind. Mix well.
On a floured table, roll the dough into fairly thin sheets. Cut into squares of about 3"/9 cm. and place a little cheese mixture in each. Fold each corner of the square inwards, towards the centre, like folding an envelope (hence the popular name of these pies: 'skirts up'). Fold the newly formed corners of these envelopes in their turn, to secure the cheese 'letters' inside. Beat 1 egg and brush pies with it. Place on a buttered baking sheet and bake in preheated oven for 30-45 minutes or until risen and gold on top. Serve warm, with soured cream on the side and sprinkled with icing sugar.

GRAPE-PICKER'S PUMPKIN PIE
SERVES 6

Preheat the oven to G5/190C/380F.

Remove pumpkin skin and seeds. Grate its flesh on the medium teeth of your grater or in a food processor.

Melt 2 oz./60 gr. butter in a saucepan, add grated pumpkin, ½ the sugar and ½ the milk. Bring to the boil and simmer until pumpkin is soft, adding the rest of the milk until liquid is totally absorbed. Remove from flame and allow to cool. Separate the eggs and mix well egg yolks with 2 oz./60 gr. butter and remaining

---

8 oz./250 gr. filo pastry
1 lb./500 gr. pumpkin
6 oz./180 gr. caster sugar
6 oz./180 gr. butter
5-6 drops vanilla essence
5 fluid oz./150 ml. milk
3 eggs
1 tblsp. icing sugar
6 fluid oz./180 ml. soured cream

---

sugar. Beat the whites until stiff and fold gently into the pumpkin mixture. Add vanilla drops.

Butter a baking tray well and line it with two sheets of filo pastry. Spread a little mixture over them in a thin, even layer and repeat procedure until you have exhausted mixture and pastry, finishing with a layer of pastry. Prick the top layer with a fork, sprinkle with a little milk, dot with butter and place in the preheated oven for 45 minutes-1 hour or until a knife plunged in the middle comes out clean. Sprinkle with icing sugar and cut into squares while still warm. Serve with soured cream on the side.

PEAR BUCKWHEAT SPONGE
SERVES 4-6

Separate the eggs. Beat the egg yolks and caster sugar until creamy. Beat the egg whites and salt until stiff. Fold alternate tblsp. of buckwheat flour and egg white into the yolk mixture. Pour into a well greased, 8"/20 cm. cake tin (preferably the type with a removable bottom). Bake in preheated oven for 20-30 minutes or until a knife plunged into the middle of the cake comes out clean. Remove from tin and cool on a cooling rack.

In the meantime, make the syrup:

Peel the pears. Place all the syrup ingredients into a saucepan and bring to the

---

An unusual light Yugoslav pudding, with a spicy wine sauce and using buckwheat instead of flour, probably under a (long forgotten) Russian influence.

---

3 oz./90 gr. buckwheat flour
3 eggs
2 oz./60 ml. caster sugar
pinch of salt
grated rind of 1 lemon
1 oz./30 ml. butter for greasing cake tin

For the syrup:
2 large ripe pears
12 fluid oz./360 ml. dry white wine
4 oz./125 ml. brown or demerrara sugar
1 cinnamon stick
1 vanilla pod or 6 drops of vanilla essence
1 clove

---

boil. Plunge the peeled, whole pears into the boiling syrup, reduce heat, cover and simmer for 15 minutes or until pears are almost soft. Remove pears from syrup with a slotted spoon and slice quickly into thin oval slices with a sharp knife.

Remove the syrup from the heat, allow to cool until bubbling has subsided and pour over the sponge. Allow sponge to absorb the syrup (it should only take a few seconds), decorate with the sliced pears and serve immediately, while still warm. Serve with cream if you wish.

BREADCRUMB SAVARIN
SERVES 4-6

Preheat the oven to G5/190C/380F.

Separate the eggs. Beat the whites and reserve. Mix yolks with sugar and vanilla essence until they turn white and foam up. Add the breadcrumbs, flour and fold whites into the mixture. Butter a 9"/22 cm. (outer diameter) savarin mould, sprinkle with a little flour and pour mixture in.

Bake in preheated oven for 15 minutes.

In the meantime make the

4 eggs
4 tblsp. sugar
4 tblsp. fine white breadcrumbs
3 drops vanilla essence
¾ level tblsp. flour
1 oz./30 gr. butter
10 fluid oz./300 ml. whipping cream
1 tblsp. apricot or strawberry jam
4 oz./125 gr. raspberries or wild strawberries (optional)

For the syrup:
5 fluid oz./150 ml. water
6 oz./180 gr. sugar
2-3 tblsp. rum.

syrup:

Melt sugar in the water until fairly thick and allow to cool for 3 minutes. Add rum. Take the savarin out of the mould and sprinkle with syrup 2-3 times until the pastry is well soaked. Replace in oven for another 5 minutes. Allow to cool, spread a thin layer of jam on top. Fill the hole in the middle with fresh raspberries or other fruit and cover it with whipped cream.

PLUMS IN BULGARIAN BRANDY
SERVES 4-6

Preheat the oven to G2/155C/310F.

Cut the plums in two and remove stones. Place them in a casserole and sprinkle sugar over them. Add the cinnamon stick and lemon peel. Pour wine over the plums, cover and stew for 45-60 minutes or until plums are soft.

2 lb./1 kg. ripe plums
4 oz./125 gr. brown sugar
1 stick cinnamon
rind of 1 lemon
4 fluid oz./120 ml. sweet Tokay*, Madeira or Marsala wine
2 fluid oz./60 ml. Bulgarian plum brandy or Romanian tzuika* or similar
2 oz./60 gr. plump sultanas

In the meantime, soak the sultanas in the plum brandy. When the plums are ready, remove some of the cooking juice if you have too much, add the soaked sultanas and the plum brandy they have been soaked in, and serve immediately, with thin slices of TARRAGON YEAST CAKE if you wish.

179

BUCHAREST BAKED QUINCES
SERVES 4

'Bucharest always had for me something of ancient Bagdad's appeal and I imagined it as a miniature city of the 'Arabian Nights'. Travellers who had visited it came back with tales of Oriental luxury and brilliance that eclipsed Paris, the city of light. How could it help being a dazzling city when it combined the rich colours of the Turk with the classical elegance of the Greek? In the folk-lore of the Romanian villages the fairy city is always Bucharest, and in my wanderings among the peasantry and Gypsies they would draw for me fantastic pictures of unbridled luxury and exotic vices that recalled Imperial Rome.' (W. Starkie – *Raggle-taggle*, 1929).

Preheat the oven to G5/ 190C/380F.
Wash the quinces well and pat them dry. With a grapefruit knife or a very sharp small knife, scoop out the hard cores and the seed boxes.
Put a little sugar or (incomparably better) a fruit flavoured SHERBET like the one described at BITTER CHERRY SHERBET below, inside each quince. Add a pinch of cinnamon.

---

4 medium quinces
4-6 oz./125-180 gr. sugar or
   BITTER CHERRY SHERBET
2 oz./60 gr. sultanas
2 fluid oz./60 ml. pear brandy*
   or light rum
1 tsp. ground cinnamon

Place the quinces in a casserole and pour 3 fluid oz./90 ml. water around them. Bake in the preheated oven for 1 hour or until quinces are almost entirely soft. The sugar inside the quinces will melt half way through – replenish it with remaining sugar and cinnamon. Soak the sultanas in the alcohol and add them to the quinces when the second lot of sugar has melted.
Allow to cool a little and serve in their juice, topped with a tsp. of morello cherry or ROSE PETAL PRESERVE each.

LJUBLIANA PRETZELS
SERVES 6 (12 fingers or 8 figures of eight)

Preheat the oven to G7/ 220C/450F.
Mix all the ingredients (not the granulated sugar) with a wooden spoon in a bowl or using a food processor. The mixture should achieve dough consistency. Wrap the mixture in clingfilm and place in fridge for ½ hour. Taking about a dessert spoon at a time, shape the mixture into fingers cca.2"/6 cm. long (they will spread further while baking) or into figures of 8 (for the latter take cca. 1 tblsp. at a time). Roll the pretzels in the granulated sugar and place on a greased baking tray. Bake them in the preheated oven for 20 minutes or until crisp on the outside. Cool on a cooling rack and serve on their own or as an accompaniment to stewed fruit or Turkish coffee.

---

7 oz./210 gr. plain flour
3 oz./90 gr. caster sugar
1 oz./30 gr. cocoa powder
2 oz./60 gr. grated walnuts
2 oz./60 gr. butter
3 drops vanilla essence
grated rind of 1 lemon
½ tsp. ground cinnamon
pinch baking powder
1 egg
½ tblsp. single cream
2 tblsp. milk
1 oz./30 gr. granulated sugar
   (for decoration)
1 oz./30 gr. butter (for greasing
   baking tray)

BOSNIAN BISCUITS

Preheat the oven to G6/ 200C/400F.
Grease a baking tray well. Soak the raisins in rum or brandy. Beat together the eggs and sugar. Slowly mix in the flour, grated chocolate and raisins. The mixture will come out coffee-coloured.

2 eggs
2 oz./60 gr. sugar
3 ½ oz./100 gr. plain flour
1 oz./30 gr. chopped walnuts
1 oz./30 gr. cooking chocolate
1 oz./30 gr. sultanas
1 tsp. rum or brandy

Pour mixture on to a baking tray in a thin (⅓"/1 cm.) layer and bake at the top of the oven for 1 hour.
Cut into squares while still hot. Allow to cool and serve with Turkish coffee or hot chocolate.

ALMOND BRITTLE

Preheat the oven to G4/ 180C/355F.
Grease a baking sheet well. Put the butter, honey, sugar, vanilla essence, cream, into a saucepan. Bring to the boil, stirring continuously with a wooden spoon. Boil for at least 5-6 minutes, until the mixture turns dark brown and has the consistency of porridge. Add the chopped figs and whole almonds and

A very sweet, crunchy accompaniment to coffee, showing how oriental Balkanic tastes can sometimes be. It makes a change from after dinner mints, however.

2 oz./60 gr. butter
2 oz./60 gr. honey
5 ½ oz./165 gr. sugar
2 drops vanilla essence
3 fluid oz./90 ml. double cream
2 oz./60 gr. dried figs, finely chopped
5 oz./150 gr. whole almonds
1 oz./30 gr. cooking chocolate (optional)

continue stirring for another 2-3 minutes. Pour the mixture on the baking sheet in a flat, thin layer. Bake for 4 minutes at the top of the oven. Remove and place on a cooling rack. When cool, brush with melted chocolate if you like (the brittle is already very sweet). Cut into squares and serve with Turkish coffee at the end of the meal.

HAZELNUT MOUSSE
SERVES 4

Separate the eggs. Whip the whites with 3 oz./90 gr. of the sugar until stiff. Whip the yolks with remaining sugar and vanilla essence. Grind the hazelnuts very finely and mix with the egg yolks. Whip double cream until stiff. Mix the egg yolk and nut mixture with the

4 oz./125 gr. hazelnuts
6 oz./180 gr. caster sugar
2 drops vanilla essence
1 tsp. cherry brandy/pear brandy*/plum brandy*
5 fl. oz./150 ml. double cream

cream. Fold the egg whites in. Place in glasses or in a

rectangular metal form and place in the freezer for 4 hours until set. Allow to stand at room temperature for 5 minutes before serving. You can also pour the mousse without freezing as a rich sauce over stewed prunes or figs or over WALNUT YEAST CAKE.

CHOCOLATE INGOT
SERVES 4

Break the chocolate into small squares, and place them in a saucepan on top of boiling water (bain-marie). Stir until it is completely melted. Add the rum, sugar and chopped walnuts. Mix until smooth. Remove from the fire and dip saucepan in a larger saucepan filled with cold

An unusual chocolate biscuit which does not require baking.

4 oz./125 gr. cooking chocolate
4 oz./125 gr. caster sugar
1 oz. chopped walnuts
1 egg
1 tsp. rum
1 oz./30 gr. icing sugar

water. Add egg. Mix well. Mixture should be very thick but not too dry. Turn onto a wooden board sprinkled with icing sugar. Make a low, rectangular shape like an ingot. Allow to dry at room temperature for 24 hours. Slice and serve (with whipped cream if you wish).

WALNUT TRUFFLES
MAKES 20 TRUFFLES

Grate the chocolate. Chop the walnuts to pinhead size. Mix the chocolate and icing sugar, then add walnuts. Add rum or plum or apricot brandy. Mix well with a wooden spoon for about 5 minutes.
Sprinkle granulated sugar on a plate and on your hands.

An incredibly easy way of making truffles, without any cooking.

4 oz./125 gr. plain cooking chocolate
4 oz./125 gr. icing sugar
4 oz./125 gr. walnuts
1½ tblsp. dark rum or plum brandy* or apricot brandy*
2 tblsp. granulated sugar

Take a teaspoonful of mixture at a time, cover in granulated sugar and roll in between your palms to make a small ball. Leave the truffles to dry for 12 hours at room temperature. Ideally served with Turkish coffee at the end of a meal.

PRESERVES
AND
SHERBETS

ROSE PETAL PRESERVE

FILLS a 2 lb./1 kg. JAR

Perhaps the greatest sign of 'latin indulgence' to be found in the Balkans, is the way in which Romanians eat fruit preserves. Enter a Romanian household at any time of the day and you will be presented at once with a tray loaded with the three ritual elements of Balkanic hospitality: a glass of ice-cold water, a diminutive, steaming cup of Turkish coffee and – the 'piece de resistance' – a saucer full of delicious home-made preserves. You will be expected to eat these as they come, with a teaspoon, without spoiling this ultimate luxury by spreading them on anything as prosaic as bread or toast. The cold water and the bitter coffee are there – if truth were known – only as foils to the preserves and above all as incentives to ask for, and be given, second and third helpings. Walter Starkie recalls being invited to an official visit to the palace of the Grand Metropolitan of Transylvania, where preserves were 'brought by a footman, in place of afternoon tea, and served on little glass plates with a spoon ... after you had eaten your portion you drank a glass of water.' The gallery of Romanian preserves is infinite and ranges from those familiar to the Western palate, like peach or raspberry, to the truly exotic like the ones made of rose petals or of green, black or 'rotted' walnuts. Other, less exotic but still unusual Romanian preserves are: quince, water melon, honeydew melon, Morello cherry.

Choose red scented roses. Pick the petals one by one, tear off the white bits near the stalks, shake them individually to shake off any yellow polen and stamens. Place petals in a colander and shake again, until no stamens are left.
Pick 5 oz./150 gr. of the cleanest, freshest petals, rejecting ruthlessly any stained, brown or dead ones. Reserve the latter to make the rose flavoured syrup.
Mix the citric acid into the chosen, clean petals, stirring gently with your hand. The petals will soften, redden and curl up into little crinkly balls. Take care not to stir too vigorously and tear the petals. Reserve in the fridge while you deal with the other ingredients.
Boil the remaining petals, including those you rejected as brown or dead, in 2 pt./1 l. water for 5 minutes. Place a thin mousseline over a

8 oz./250 gr. rose petals*
2 lb./1 kg. sugar
½ tsp. citric acid
1 tsp. lemon juice

bowl and strain the rose water through it. Measure out 3 glasses of this liquid (cca. 18 fluid oz./550 ml.) into a jam-making pan or similar and add the sugar. Heat syrup gently until sugar has dissolved fully. Add the reserved rose petals from the fridge and increase flame. Boil on a lively flame until jam begins to thicken. Add lemon juice, skim and test to see if the jam is set enough: remove pan from the fire, and drip a few drops of syrup onto a saucer. Allow syrup to cool – if it is thick enough when cool, remove pan from the fire. If not, replace pan on the hot flame, stir gently and try again every 5 minutes until you have achieved the desired consistency.
When ready, pour hot jam into a spotlessly clean bowl from which any remnant of grease has been removed. Cover with a clean cloth and cool jam completely before pouring it into clean jars, wiped with a clean cloth and dried in a warm oven. Tie jars with greaseproof paper and keep in a cool, dry place.
Not many people in this country will want to indulge their sweet tooth in the way Romanians do. Rose petal preserve, however, has an extraordinary, pungent, exotic aroma and can be used in small quantities as an addition to worthy but perhaps slightly bland dishes, like CHEESE DUMPLINGS or one of the YEAST CAKES. In small quantities this preserve also goes well with venison (see HAUNCH OF VENISON IN SOURED CREAM).

YOUNG WALNUT PRESERVE

FILLS two 2 lb./1 kg. JAR

This is a good example of a preserve which is clearly meant for eating on its own and not for spreading (see ROSE PETAL PRESERVES). There are three types of walnut preserves: White — in which the unripened walnut is removed from its shell before cooking; Black — in which the walnuts are cooked in their shells; and 'Rotted' — in which the walnuts are softened and ripened in water prior to their cooking in the jam syrup. The differences may be too subtle for the untrained Western jam guzzler, but all three preserves aim for the same effect: a slightly crunchy, slightly nutty core preserved in a rich sweet syrup. The nature of these preserves makes them suitable for usage in 'nouvelle cuisine' type dishes — they are as decorative as they are fragrant.

Using a very sharp knife, peel green skin off the walnut centres. You may wish to use gloves, as the unripened walnuts shed a dark 'ink' which is hard to wash off. Throw centres into a bowl of cold water as soon as you have peeled them. Bring plenty of water to the boil, drain the cold water in the bowl and pour the boiling water over the walnuts. Leave them to soak for cca. 10 minutes. In the meantime, boil a second kettle of water and repeat the procedure 5 times, using fresh boiling water every time. Drain the last lot of hot water and rinse walnuts in cold water. Soak again for 10 minutes and go on draining, rinsing and soaking another 5 times, this time with cold water.
In the jam-making pan, bring 1 pt./600 ml. water to the boil. Pour sugar in and

100 young walnuts (picked before the hard shell has formed — in England this is usually towards the end of July — and while the green outer skin is still on. They are the types of walnuts used in this country for pickling)
1 lb./500 gr. sugar
juice from ½ a lemon
1 vanilla pod or 6 drops vanilla essence

simmer over a low flame until sugar is fully dissolved. Increase flame and boil rapidly, skimming scum off the top. When syrup starts to thicken, drain walnuts well and add to the jam pan. Add vanilla pod or essence. Continue to boil briskly until jam has thickened (see testing procedure at ROSE PETAL JAM). Add lemon juice towards the end of the boiling process. Cool in a clean bowl and bottle in large jam jars.

To make BLACK WALNUT preserve proceed as above, but instead of peeling and soaking walnuts, boil them over a high flame in plenty of water for about 1 hour or until green skin splits and peels off easily. Drain, remove skins and the thin black 'veins' in the middle. Boil again, changing the water 5 times as above and proceed with the syrup as shown.

To make ROTTED WALNUT preserve put whole green walnuts in a large jar and cover with water. Keep them in a cool place for 10 days to rot the green skins. Change the water every day. Drain, peel the rotted skins off, wash in running cold water and drain again. Make the sugar syrup and add walnuts directly, without further soaking or boiling.

WILD STRAWBERRY PRESERVE

FILLS a 2 lb./1 kg. JAR

Pick nice, slightly under-ripe wild strawberries and discard their little stalks.

It is much better if you do not need to wash them, but if it cannot be avoided, lay them on a clean towel afterwards and pat them gently dry.

In a copper jam pan, bring the sugar mixed with 18 fluid oz./540 ml. water to the boil over a low flame until sugar has totally dissolved. When sugar has dissolved, increase flame and boil quickly until syrup has thickened enough. (Test it by dripping 2-3 drops of syrup into a glass of cold water: if syrup crystalizes into clear drops you can

The Balkans have a great tradition of using wild fruit and herbs and wild strawberries are picked widely both in Romania (in the fir and pine woods of the Carpathian mountains) and in Yugoslavia, in the Slovenian hills at the bottom of the Alps. They make superb preserves, of course, because of their slightly bitter taste and 'heir small size, which enables them to keep a 'crunch' even when boiled in the sugar syrup.

1 lb./500 gr. wild strawberries*
2 lb./1 kg. sugar
juice of 1 lemon

pick with your fingers, it is ready; but if it dissolves immediately in the water,

continue boiling). Skim the scum off the syrup.

When syrup has thickened add wild strawberries and allow syrup to bubble up once or twice. Remove pot from the flame and cool for 15 minutes. The wild strawberries will release their juice into the sugar syrup. Replace pot on a lively flame and bring back to the boil. Skim any scum rising to the surface. Test jam consistency as shown at ROSE PETAL JAM and add lemon juice towards the end of the boiling process. Cool preserve in a very clean bowl and pour into the jar.

BITTER CHERRY SHERBET

FILLS a 2 lb./1 kg. JAR

If you thought eating preserves by the spoonful was a pinacle of tooth-rotting indulgence, here is something to top it all: the Romanian and Bulgarian versions of sherbet have very little to do with the fizzy powder you buy at the corner shop in this country. Even in Turkey, where the notion and the name have come from, sherbet is primarily a sweet syrup used for cold drinks or for pouring over puddings. But in the northern Balkans sherbet has evolved into a thick, trickle-like sugar paste, flavoured with a variety of pungent aromas (fruit juice, vanilla, chocolate, etc.) and eaten on its own, by the spoonful. It is a great favourite of the scorching Romanian summers, when a teaspoon full of sherbet is dipped into a glass of iced water, thus achieving the double effect of slightly flavouring the water and giving the sherbet a crispy 'bite'. You can flavour sherbet with any fruit that will produce a glassful of juice and you can add to it almonds or hazelnuts. Although I have long weaned myself off eating sherbet by the spoonful, I still find it delightful in small quantities as a flavouring to fruit stewed in wine or with sharp, tangy desserts such as BAKED QUINCES. I have chosen bitter cherries for this master recipe because their bittersweet taste contrasts beautifully with the sugary syrup, but you can use ordinary black cherries, strawberries, blackberries, apricots, lemons, vanilla, coffee, chocolate or almost anything else you care to experiment with. See below for WATER LILY and other FLOWER SHERBETS.

Wash the cherries and remove stalks. Boil the cherries in a saucepan with 4 fluid oz./120 ml. water for about 5 minutes. Allow them to cool in their juice and strain through a thick mousseline. Allow the liquid to rest until clear and any residue has settled at the bottom.

Measure out 10 fluid oz./300 ml. of the liquid.

Place the sugar in a jam copper pot and pour cherry liquid over it. Bring it to the boil over a very low flame until the sugar is fully dissolved.

Increase to a lively flame and skim any scum rising to the top. Wipe the sides of the pot with a wet cloth to remove any shred of scum. Test the consistency of the syrup by dripping a few drops of syrup into a glass of cold water. If the sugar does not dissolve immediately, but first crystalizes into drops you can pick out with your fingers, the sherbet is ready. If sugar dissolves immediately, replace copper pot on the flame and continue boiling fast. When the sherbet has thickened sufficiently,

---

2 lb./1 kg. bitter cooking cherries (in this country, the May-duke variety is the nearest to the half white, half red, bittersweet cherries found on the continent towards the end of June)
2 lb./1 kg. sugar
1 tsp. lemon juice
6 drops vanilla essence

---

remove from the flame, cover with a wet cloth and allow to cool until you can touch it by hand without discomfort.

Wedge the pot solidly into another saucepan or in between the upturned legs of a stool and mix sherbet vigorously with a wooden rolling pin or similar, turning in one direction only. When sherbet starts changing its colour add the lemon juice and continue stirring for another 5 minutes. Scoop sherbet out of the pot and into a jar by hand or with a wooden spoon. Tie the mouth of the jar with greaseproof paper as well as covering it with a lid and store in a dry cool place, but not in the fridge.

WATER LILY SHERBET

FILLS a 2 lb.-1 kg. JAR

Sherbets scented with essence of flowers are as subtle as they are romantic. While you could probably buy most fruit sherbets in the shops in Romania, flower ones are strictly home made and can make stunning flavourings for pancakes, fruit or 'nouvelle cuisine' type dishes. This master recipe uses water lilies (you will obviously have to gather your own) but I have used the same method to make sherbets with linden flowers, camomile and rose petals which you can buy in the shops here*.

Pick only the nicest, cleanest lily petals. Retain only the yellow ones and shake each one to remove any stamens or polen. Bring 2 pt./1 l. water to the boil and pour it over the flowers placed in a bowl. Cover bowl to avoid losing any of the aroma and set aside to rest until cold. Strain liquid through a thick

---

**1 lb./500 gr. water lily flowers
2 lb./1 kg. sugar
1 tsp. lemon juice**

---

muslin and measure out 18 fluid oz./540 ml. Pour this quantity of liquid over the sugar in a jam copper pot and then proceed as shown at BITTER CHERRY SHERBET.

The flower sherbet consistency should be slightly thicker than the fruit one. Allow to cool until you can touch it by hand without discomfort and mix with a wooden rolling pin or similar. Add lemon juice towards the end. The flavour will be extremely delicate.

188

WHERE
TO GET
BALKAN
FOODS

Do not let some of the ingredients in this book put you off because you think they may be unobtainable in your area. You will be surprised how much a good local grocer can get for you simply by passing your order on to the right wholesaler. But if your local suppliers fail, try the addresses below (for each ingredient marked with a * in the recipes there is a supplier's name; the addresses are at the end of this index).

Bran (raw/natural)	Culpepper's or Holland & Barrett
Cabanos Sausages	Roma Delica
Calf's brains	Drury Swindon
Cashcaval cheese	Atalanta U.K.
Chanterelles	Covent Garden New Market
Crayfish	C. J. Newnes
Fetta cheese (Romanian Telemea)	Atalanta U.K.
Filo Pastry	J. Sainsbury's & local Greek shops
Hominy (maize)	Encona brand by Enco
Langoustines	C. J. Newnes
Lovage (herb)	Culpeppers's
Morello cherries (sweetened)	Braybrooke – Hungarian Foods Ltd.
Morello cherries (sour)	Hero Brand at Fortnum & Mason, etc.
Pig's tails	Any slaughter house
Pike/pike-perch/zander	C. J. Newnes
Polenta (maize flour)	So-Ho Brand by Guy, Leonard & Co.
Raddichio	Covent Garden New Market
Rose petal jelly (French)	Fortnum & Mason's
Rose petals	Culpepper's
Sea bream	C. J. Newnes
Sterlet	C. J. Newnes
Sturgeon and smoked	C. J. Newnes and
Sturgeon (batog)	occasionally Selfridges Food Hall
Wild strawberries	Covent Garden New Market
Brandies and spirits	see Yugoslavian section of wines (Vitcovitch Brothers)

SUPPLIERS' ADDRESSES:

ATALANTA UK Ltd.

– sole importers of Romanian foods – Imperial House, Dominion Street, London EC2M SA

BRAYBROOKE – HUNGARIAN FOODS, Ltd.

– 38-40 Featherstone Street, London EC1. Tel.: 01-253-0571

THE BUCHAREST GROCERY

— 5235 Hollywood Boulevard, Los Angeles 90027. Tel.: 213-462-8407

COVENT GARDEN MARKET AUTHORITY

– New Offices, Pascal Street, London SW8. Tel.: 01-720-2211

CULPEPPER'S Ltd.

– Herbalists – Head office: 21 Burton Street, London W1. Tel.: 01-499-2406

F. DRURY AND SON,

The Abbatoir, Tockenham, Wootton Bassett, Swindon, Wilts, Tel.: Swindon 852467

ENCO PRODUCTS,

LONDON, Ltd.

– 71-75 Fortess Road, London NW5. Tel: 01-485-2217

FORTNUM & MASON Ltd.,

181 Piccadilly, London W1. Tel.: 01-734-8040

GUY, LEONARD & Co., Ltd.,

71 St. John's Street, London EC1M 4AR

HOLLAND & BARRET Ltd.,

12 Gloucester Road, London SW7. Tel.: 01-584-0372

C.J. NEWNES

– Wholesale Fish Market, Office 11, Billingsgate Fish Market, West India Dock, London E14. Tel.: 01-515-0793

ROMA DELICA

– 83-87, Scrubs Lane, London, NW10. Tel.: 01-969-6787

If none of the above can help you, this is a very helpful organization:-

DELICATESSEN AND FINE FOOD ASSOCIATION

– 6 The Broadway, Thatcham, Newbury, Berks. RG13 4JA. Tel.: 0635-69033

BALKAN
WINES &
SPIRITS

The Balkans have produced wines from times immemorial, as both soil and climate favour the growth of sturdy grape varieties. The main wines imported into this country come from Yugoslavia (mainly Slovenia) and Bulgaria. Both countries have made deliberate efforts to promote and market their cheaper wine varieties, perceived, rightly as it turned out, as foreign currency earners in Western countries where wine drinking did not have a long tradition, and where price often tended to be more important than quality. This led to the spread of relatively anonymous wines, like the Slovenian Rieslings, at the expense of more interesting local wines derived from native grapes. In recent years, however, there have been some marked improvements in the quality of the 'westernized' varieties imported to this country, notably the Bulgarian Cabernet Sauvignon, and the importers have also started to venture into the less known area of wines derived from native grape varieties. Romanian wines, however, fall very much behind, due to a lack of marketing effort on the part of the Romanian authorities, as well as to the sad state of neglect that the Romanian wine-making industry, once one of the best in Europe, now finds itself in. Yugoslav and Bulgarian wines are sold widely in supermarkets and off-license chains, but you may need to approach the main shippers for the rarer, native varieties. I have, therefore, listed the principal importers for each country.

BULGARIA

Main importers – BULGARIAN VINTNERS COMPANY Ltd., LECTOR COURT, 151 FARRINGDON ROAD, LONDON EC1R 3AD. Telephone: 01-278-8047.

The Bulgarian wine industry underwent a massive programme of expansion and rationalization after the war. It now produces almost 1,000 million kg. of grapes a year, over ¾ of which are for wine production. Bulgaria exports 85% of its wines, mainly to other Comecon countries, but increasingly to the West as well, especially to Germany. All wines are aged in oak, partly local and partly American, with the final ageing done in bottles.

Bulgarian wines are classified by law into three main categories: Standard, High and Special (for fortified and dessert wines). The High Quality wines are further subdivided into three groups, including the highest appelation – 'Controliran Region', the equivalent of the 'Appelation d'origine controle' in France.

There are five main wine producing regions in Bulgaria, each specializing in different varieties of grapes:

The Northern region produces mainly red grapes and is the largest wine making region in the country. The best grape varieties are the imported Cabernet Sauvignon and Merlot and the native Gamza and the best wines are made in the Suhindol district, where both soil and climate are similar to those in Bordeaux.

The Southern region also grows imported grape varieties, including Merlot and Pinot Noir, but here the hotter climate is best suited to the sturdiest native grapes: Pavid, which makes a rough but full table red, and Mavrud. The legend has it that in the reign of Khan Krum the population of his capital, Pliska, was terrorized by a lion. A local hero, called Mavrud, fought and killed the lion, sustaining himself during the battle by drinking a wine made of a particular local grape. That grape was then named Mavrud in his honour. The Mavrud reds are extremely full bodied, with a good nose and they age well. The best come from the slopes of Mount Rhodope, at Asenovgrad near the city of Plovdiv. They are by far the most popular wines drunk by the Bulgarians themselves, overshadowing the varieties better known in the west.

The Balkan region produces wines in the valleys under the Balkan Mountains, especially the Sungurlare valley and the Rose Valley (so named after another great traditional Bulgarian industry – the making of rose essence and rose water). Western grape varieties here are Muscat Ottonel and Riesling, while the native wines are made of Misket grapes.

The Eastern region bordering on the Black Sea grows mainly white wine grapes and produces mainly wines of lesser quality. Main varieties of grapes are: Riesling, Chardonnay, Sauvignon and the Eastern European Rkatzitelli. The main producing area is Choumen in the North-East, where most Bulgarian whites imported to this country come from.

The South-Western region is a small strip of land alongside the Yugoslav border under the Rila mountains. Here the warm Mediterranean climate can be felt and there is wide-scale cultivation of the red Melnik grape. Second only to Mavrud in popularity inside Bulgaria itself, the Melnik wines are heavy, with a good nose and they say in Bulgaria they are: 'so thick you can carry them in a handkerchief'.

The main varieties of wine imported to Britain and distributed mainly through the Thresher's off-licence chain, are:

White Wines

(mostly light table wines, cheap but without distinction)
Mehana Dry White: fresh, fruity but rather thin.
Mehana Medium White: not one of my favourites. Thin and too sweet.
Bulgarian Sauvignon Blanc: a recent growth in Bulgaria. A decent dry white, with a fresh taste but not enough fruit.
Bulgarian Chardonnay: dry, with a strong nose and decent fruit, but not enough body.
Novi Pazar Chardonnay: a much better Chardonnay wine, made with some care in the controlled Novi Pazar area in the Northern Region. A "Controliran Region" wine, aged in oak casks and in the bottle.

Red Wines

Bulgarian Cabernet Sauvignon 1981/1983: made from vines brought from Bordeaux, the wine made around the town of Suhindol is aged in oak for at least 3 years. The Cabernet grapes produce a ruby wine, with a good oaky nose and a decent blackcurrant taste. The best known Bulgarian wine here, it is good value, if still a little rough.

Svichtov Cabernet Sauvignon: a 'Controliran' wine. Made in Northern Bulgaria on the shores of the Danube, it is aged in oak and has good body and flavour.

Suhindol: a 'Controliran' wine made from the native Gamza grapes. Good fresh taste with a sometimes overpowering nose.

Asenovgrad Mavrud: my favourite Bulgarian wine. Rich, full bodied and well flavoured it will keep well. Mavrud wines are bottled locally at Asenovgrad.

Sakar Mountain Cabernet 1978: an improving wine coming from the Southern region of Bulgaria. Good lingering blackcurrant flavour, with a full body and some depth.

ROMANIA

Main importer – MILTON STAR Ltd. PRUDENTIAL HOUSE, WELLESLEY ROAD, CROYDON, CR9 2DQ. Telephone: 01-681 8175.

The Romanian wine making tradition goes back five thousand years, long before the Roman conquest of Dacia. The vineyards at Cotnari and Husi, in Moldavia, founded in the sixteenth century by the Moldavian Prince Stefan 'The Great', produced famous wines until well into this century. Even Robert Browning got to taste the famous Cotnari and he mentions it in one of his poems. Unfortunately, a combination of neglect and bad marketing has caused Romanian wines to be almost entirely forgotten in the West. Nevertheless, some of them are still worth exploring, even though they have declined somewhat since their days of glory. The most interesting wines are those made from indigenous grapes: Feteasca, Grasa, Crimposia and so on. Western vines are also grown, including the classic Sauvignon Blanc, Chardonay, Pinot Noir, Merlot and Cabernet Sauvignon. The reds are aged in oak casks for several years, but the best Romanian wines tend to be white. There is no regulation by law of Romanian wines, but they fall into several traditional regions:

In Moldavia the best wines are still made at Cotnari (both dry and sweet whites) and Husi in the north and at Odobesti in the south. A particularly rewarding Moldavian native grape is the Tamiioasa variety, which makes a rust-coloured wine, very aromatic, with a distinctive scent of flowers. The Cotnari Grasa variety is the best, producing an unusual white wine high in sugar content which can reach up to 14 degrees strength after three years of ageing. The Cotnari wine has the distinctive quality of changing its colour with age from yellow into an unusual shade of green. Cotnari wines are similar to Tokay, but they tend to be drier and have more body. Cotnari also produces a sweet wine similar to Beaumes-de-Venise.

In Transylvania the main vineyards are at Tirnave, with a particularly good dry Pinot Gris near Alba Iulia. In Dobrudja by the Black Sea there are good reds made at Murfatlar. Some decent Muscat Ottonel, reputed to 'last' up to 4 minutes in the mouth, as well as the fruitier, fresher Austrian Neuburger are grown at Babadag, by the Danube.

In the south, near Bucharest, are the extensive vineyards of Dealu Mare where Cabernet Sauvignon has supplanted the older native 'Crimposia' grapes of Valea Calugareasca which made a full bodied, oily wine, full of flavour. Finally, a sharp, acidy yellow 'wine drinker's wine' is made at *Dragasani,* on the Olt Valley in south West Romania. Unfortunately these native wines have not yet penetrated the Western conscience and they are not, on the whole, imported here.

The main Romanian wines available in this country are:

White Wines

Sauvignon Blanc 1982/4: crisp, dry but rather tasteless, from the Tirnave and the Murfatlar vineyards.

Blanc Murfatlar Riesling 1983: Dry and palatable, closer to the Alsatian style than to the German or Yugoslav Rieslings.

Feteasca 1982: the only native wine so far imported to Britain. A medium dry wine with a distinctive flavour.

Chardonay 1975: less acid than in most Chardonay wines, but too sweet for my taste.

Muscat Ottonel 1970: a dessert wine, but from the lesser vineyards at Murfatlar, not from Cotnari.

Red Wines

Cabernet Sauvignon 1983: full bodied but nowhere near the better-made Bulgarian variety.

Pinot Noir 1983: a robust wine with a good nose. Slightly sweeter than usual, as the grapes are 'late picked'. No subtlety, but good value as a table wine.

Merlot 1980/81: fruity flavour and decent body, but again, not as well made as the French or even the Bulgarian equivalents.

Main importers: TELTSCHER BROTHERS LTD., LUTOMER HOUSE, WEST INDIA DOCK, PRESTONS ROAD, LONDON E14 9SB. Telephone: 01-987-5020 (they import mainly Lutomer Laski, i.e. Slovenian wines).

VITCOVITCH BROTHERS, LITTLE MOSTAR, VIRGIL STREET, LONDON SE1 7EF. Telephone: 01-261-1770 (a wider range of wines from Serbia, Herzegovina and Dalmatia, more representative of the Yugoslav wine industry as a whole).

Because of some aggressive and skilled marketing, Yugoslav wines tend to be thought of mainly as the Lutomer Laski Rieslings of Slovenia. These have achieved the title of the most popular light white wines in Britain, a reflection more of their low price than of their high quality. I am no great admirer of these light wines and much prefer the fuller bodied native wines from Serbia and Herzegovina. As Yugoslav wines are extensively featured and reviewed in this country, I will try to concentrate more on the lesser known types.

Wine is made in most of the Yugoslav Republics, but most of it is drunk internally. Only the Slovenian wines known under the generic name of Lutomer Laski Riesling are primarily grown for export. Lutomer Laski comes from a delimited area of Slovenia, which is divided into three main areas: Primorski in the west, Posavski in the south and Podravski in the east. The best Rieslings, benefitting from a favourable micro-climate at the foothills of the Alps come from the Lutomer-Ormoz subdivision of the Podravski region. In my estimation these sub-German wines are less interesting than the wines made in the Mostar region of Herzegovina as well as the full bodied table reds from Montenegro.

Besides the Riesling grapes, Yugoslav vineyards grow the classical Cabernet Sauvignon, the Gewurtztraminner, the Sauvignon Blanc and the Merlot grapes. Interesting native types of grapes include the Plavac grape grown mainly on the island of Hvar in the Adriatic, the Vranac grape of Montenegro (both producing full reds) and the Zilavka of Herzegovina which gives a dry, respectable white. Yugoslav wines are regulated by law and the mark to look for is the appelation 'Kvalitetno vino', the equivalent of the French 'Appelation d'origine controles'.

The main Yugoslav wines sold in this country are:

White Wines

Lutomer Laski Riesling: Britain's brand leading medium dry white.

Lutomer Pinot Blanc: drier, crisp wine with the delicate nose of the Pinot grape but without much body.

Lutomer Gewurtztraminner: fruity, medium dry with very little acid. If you like cheaper German whites you will like this one. I don't. There is also a Serbian equivalent called Milion Gewurtztraminner, made at Dobanovci, near Belgrade from grapes grown in Vojvodina, by the Danube. Somewhat better than its Slovenian partner.

Laski Riesling Slamnak: bottled at source, this is a pale yellow wine with good fruit. Limited quantities as it comes from a single vineyard.

Zilavka Mostar: a dry, characteristic country wine from Mostar in Herzegovina. Similar to some extent to Provence wines, it is much more interesting than its fruity but characterless brothers from the north. It is widely drunk in Yugoslavia itself, expressing the dry, rocky terrain and the dry, sometimes harsh climate around the ancient town of Mostar.

Red Wines

Slovin Cabernet Sauvignon: made in Istria, a decent, full, soft wine.

Milion Cabernet Sauvignon: a Serbian brother, from the Royal Serbian caves at Oplenac. Full bodied table wine, rougher than the Istrian.

Merlot: bottled in Yugoslavia, a drinkable soft ruby wine. Passable bouquet and quite fruity. Grown either in Istria or in Serbia, at Vranje (the latter is marketed under the name Milion Merlot).

Vranac: smooth red wine made from a native type of grape. Made in Montenegro, it has power as well as some subtlety. Worth a try.

Peljesac: a table wine, full and rough, it needs to be drunk outside in a lot of sun to come into its own.

Faros: made exclusively on the island of Hvar, from the native Plavac grape. Rich, good body, but not a lot of nose.

SPIRITS

There are several types of spirits made in the Balkans. The weak imitations of Western spirits, like Yugoslav Maraschino or Bulgarian brandy are not really worth mentioning; but the native fruit spirits are definitely worthy of attention. Unfortunately, the only Romanian spirit imported to this country, and only occasionally, is the 'tzuica' (plum brandy). Look out for the label saying 'tzuika batrina', it means 'aged tzuika' and it is the superior type. None of the brands sold commercially are even remotely close to the home made brews available in the villages: fiery, distilled up to three times and aged in oak for up to 10 years. To get them, however, you will have to travel to Romania. There are, nevertheless, some good spirits imported from Yugoslavia on sale in this country:

Romanian Tzuika (plum brandy)
Serbian Slivovica (plum brandy) up to 55% alcohol
Klekovaca (Serbian juniper brandy)
Travarica (Dalmatian herb brandy)
Vinjak (Serbian grape brandy)
Lozavaca (grape spirit from Titograd)
Orahovac (walnut liqueur)

Other Yugoslav spirits, not yet widely available:
Brinovec (Slovenian juniper brandy)
Sadjevec (made in Croatia from several fruits: apples, plums, pears)
Viljamovka (pear brandy made in a Slovenian monastery)

ACKNOWLEDGEMENTS

This book could not have come into being without the generous help of the many friends and relatives who gave their recipes and their time to the project. Many thanks and gratitude to:

My mother who dug out and put at my disposal the recipes collected over the years by her own mother and family.

My father who badgered all and sundry into writing out and sending their recipes to me.

My aunts Macu and Bianca and my friends Malica Schechter, Ruxandra Obreja, Eligia Helmer and Zora Koren in Yugoslavia who shared their recipes and old books.

Susan and Peter Tegel, Charmian Hoare and Annie Corbett for their invaluable help in trying out recipes.

Andrew Holehouse for his expert tasting.

Kevin O'Donohoe for doing the London research and compiling the indices.

Last but by no means least to Elspeth Cochrane and Roderick Brown who turned an idea laughed at over tea and biscuits into solid reality.

INDEX

INDEX BY
RECIPE TITLE